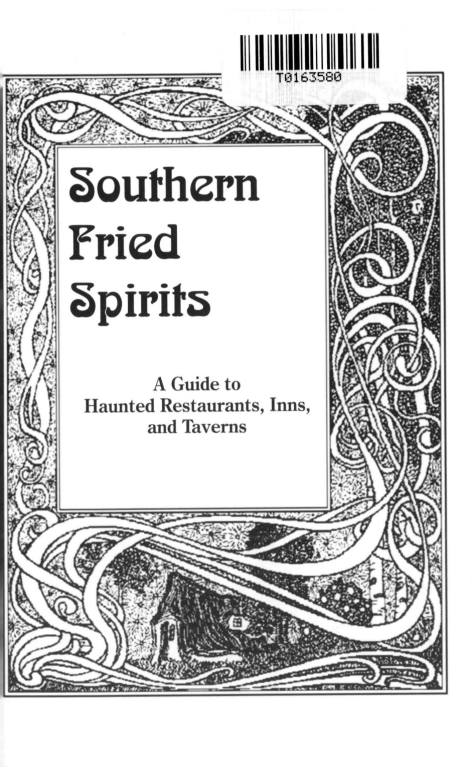

Southern Fried Spirits

A Guide to Haunted Restaurants, Inns, and Taverns

Southern Fried Spirits

A Guide to Haunted
Restaurants, Inns, and Taverns

Robert J. Wlodarski and
Anne Powell Wlodarski

Republic of Texas Press
Plano, Texas

Library of Congress Cataloging-in-Publication Data

Wlodarski, Robert James.
  Southern fried spirits: a guide to haunted restaurants, Inns, and
  taverns / by Robert J. Wlodarski and Anne Powell Wlodarski.
        p.   cm.
  Includes bibliographical references and index.
  ISBN 1-55622-776-0 (pbk.)
  1. Haunted hotels--Southern States.   2. Haunted places--Southern States.
  3. Ghosts--Southern States.   I. Wlodarski, Anne Powell.   II. Title.

  BF1474.5.W56   2000
  133.1'0975--dc21
                                            00-027025
                                            CIP

© 2000, Robert J. and Anne Powell Wlodarski
All Rights Reserved

Printed in the United States of America

Photos by author except where otherwise noted.

ISBN 1-55622-776-0
10 9 8 7 6 5 4 3 2 1
0004

All inquiries for volume purchases of this book should be addressed to
Wordware Publishing, Inc., at 2320 Los Rios Boulevard, Plano, Texas
75074. Telephone inquiries may be made by calling:
(972) 423-0090

Drink and be merry,
for our time on earth is short,
and death lasts forever

Amphis, 330 B.C.

". . . .pubs and taverns are the natural place for a family gathering, entertainment or simply a quiet drink with friends. It was Dr. Samuel Johnson who asserted that 'there is nothing which has yet been contrived by man by which so much happiness is produced as by a good tavern or inn.' And where better to enjoy the pleasure of home-like comforts than 'a good tavern or inn'—especially one that is haunted."

Andrew Green, *Haunted Inns and Taverns*
(1995), Shire Publications Ltd.

Then stand to your glasses steady
and drink to your comrade's eyes.
Here's a toast to the dead already
And hurrah to the next who dies.

Popular drinking song at the Whitechapel
Club in Chicago

Table of Contents

Table of Contents

Acknowledgments

Like any recipe, a book needs a wide assortment of ingredients and careful preparation to become a finished product. The author is like the chef, and the people who contribute their time, energy, and knowledge give the creation its substance and final form. Without even one of the ingredients, the final product may not come to fruition or achieve its full potential.

First and foremost, to the excellent staff, including our friend Ginnie Bivona at Republic of Texas Press, who believed in this concept, waded through the documentation, and helped organize the numerous ingredients into a coherent and user-friendly format—thanks from the bottom of our hearts. We are extremely pleased that this book will make an important travel companion for those in search of an other-worldly place to eat or drink. This book is not for the average traveler, but rather for the spirited adventurer in search of something unique. Travel and spirits do mix.

To our many good friends and those who we met along the way who we hope will remain in touch for their enthusiastic support and cooperation including:

Chris Woodyard—A very appreciative thanks for the numerous contacts she provided us, as well as her reinforcing feedback during the course of this project.

Richard Senate—A dear friend, well-known author and publisher of ghost books, ghost hunter extraordinaire, and supportive colleague over the years, who was generous with advice and was always there when we had a question. Be sure to browse Senate's web pages at www.phantoms.com/ghost.htm or www.ghost-stalkers.com.

Dennis Hauck—The author of the ultimate ghost hunter's guide to the United States, which was the sourcebook that inspired this adventure into the unknown. His e-mails and suggestions were most valuable.

Acknowledgments

Martin Leal—Our ghost hunting friend in San Antonio and member of the International Ghost Hunters Society, who went out of his way to help us obtain photographs of a number of establishments. When you are in San Antonio, be sure you take his inspiring Hauntings History of San Antonio ghost tours, which are offered every day of the year (210-436-5417).

Arthur Myers—For his wonderful trilogy: *Gazetteer, Register,* and *Ghost Hunter's Guide*, and his help in locating various listings around the United States.

Dr. Larry Montz and **Daena Smoller** of The International Society for Paranormal Research (ISPR), P.O. Box 291159, Los Angeles, California 90027 - (323) 644-8866 - (800) 829-GHOST - E-mail: ghost@hauntings.com for all their help in obtaining stories and photographs for most of our New Orleans listings.

The **Houghton Mifflin Company**, who graciously provided complimentary copies of their Best Places to Travel Series, which in turn, opened up additional research channels for obtaining additional listings. They are a wonderful series of books that fuel the desire to find the most unique accommodations available.

To **Docia Schultz Williams**, a fellow Republic of Texas Press author, for her interesting and well-researched works dealing with Texas haunts, which helped us in our research endeavors. (*Spirits of San Antonio and South Texas*, co-authored with Reneta Byrne; *Ghosts Along the Texas Coast*; *Phantoms of the Plains: Tales of West Texas Ghosts*; *When Darkness Falls: Tales of San Antonio Ghosts and Hauntings*; and *Best Tales of Texas Ghosts*).

To Matthew and Henrietta Wlodarski, and David and Emma Lou Powell who raised us with open minds, instilled in us a desire to learn, encouraged us to take the less-traveled path through life in exploring the world, and encouraged us to seek answers to what lies beyond this plane of existence. They gave us the seen and unseen world as a laboratory, with all its wondrous mysteries to explore, and in turn, fostered a responsibility in us to leave something for the next generation to ponder and enjoy. Hopefully we have done this and will continue to do so by writing these books.

And last but not least, to the gracious and helpful owners, managers, innkeepers, and the hosts of the restaurants, taverns, hotels, inns, and bed and breakfasts across haunted America listed herein. They believed in this book enough to provide the facts, history, list of paranormal events, and photographs that gave life to this book. We thank them profusely and hope when they read the book, they will be pleased with the job we did.

To **Shane A. Gage**, for permission to use his painting of Evans Pelican Inn. Gage, a preservationist of the Pelican Inn, painted this picture for Hope Evans as a Christmas present in 1997.

To those who published the books referenced in each story, as well as those listed in the back of the book—a profound thanks. Without this reference data, we would never have undertaken this project. Keep writing those great bits of folklore, history, and legend that contribute to who we are—the creative in all of us is enhanced by the magic of your storytelling. These books educate as well as enthrall children and adults and keep us all coming back for more.

To the children who love to read ghost stories, for they are the next generation of storytellers who will continue the legacy of making spirits a part of our heritage and legacy.

To all would-be writers, never give up on your dream. If you have an idea for a good, spirited book, go for it with all the passion and perseverance you are able to muster. You may be one of the yet-to-be-published writers out there who is able to fill in the gaps that still exist in states, counties, or cities without their own ghost stories.

Introduction

Though terrified, curiously I was never afraid. It must have been a child's delight in terror. And to the degree that we remain child-like, the supernatural not only continues to intrigue but very much seems a real possibility. And so to this day, I remember the stories. Such lasting power must make them true. And those voices, although the same that spoke of Santa Claus, they would never lie. I believed.

Walter Nicklin, Editor & Publisher—Foreword in
Virginia's Ghosts by L.B. Taylor

Have you ever dined, imbibed, or spent the night somewhere and had that uneasy felling of being watched—no, not by an anxious waiter or waitress desiring to take your order or your money, by a fellow patron who is just browsing, or a smiling staff person eager to please—but by an unseen presence? Have you ever sworn that you caught a brief glimpse of "something" pass by you, out of the corner or your eye, yet when you glanced over, there was nothing there? Have you ever felt a cold rush of air blow by you, or through you, leaving a hint of perfume or a chill running down your spine? Perhaps it was a ghost.

Have you ever sworn on a stack of Bibles that you experienced something unexplainable—a ghost—but your friends try to explain it away as just your imagination or perhaps the extra glass of beer or wine pulsing through your bloodstream. However, you continue to claim that you saw what you saw, when you saw it, believe it or not. But what was it? If not caused by an overactive imagination or "one too many," what did you see or feel? Perhaps it was a brush with the paranormal, an encounter with the unknown, a brief visit by a ghost or spirit. It's cause for celebration, not evaluation.

Ghosts are part of a magical universe embraced by children and adults in every culture. It is part of our myth and folklore. Storytelling helps educate and keep us in touch with our past. Telling ghost stories is part of a tradition of communicating ideas, fears, and history since the beginning of mankind. Although the stories are often frightening, without a good scare, a good laugh is greatly diminished. Ghosts can also instill a healthy fear of the unknown as well as help overcome it by providing possible answers to what lurks in the shadows. Whether they can be scientifically explained or not, ghosts remain an integral part of our belief system. References to ghosts and spirits can be found in every society and culture, a testament to the fact that man cannot control everything or know everything. Most of us like a good mystery, and ghosts still represent one of the biggest unsolved mysteries in our universe.

This book was written for the spirited and adventuresome person who is looking for something different while dining and drinking. If you're tired of returning to the same old uneventful dining establishment, tavern, or bar, you now have a choice. For a hauntingly unforgettable evening, you can visit one of the establishments listed in this book. Most of the places have been around for quite awhile, some dating back to the eighteenth century. Some establishments are even historic landmarks. These places all have one thing in common—they are haunted.

The answer to why so many restaurants and taverns are haunted may lie in the fact that where people have gathered repeatedly over a long period of time and where emotions, both good and bad, have been released, there is apt to be a psychic imprint left behind, or a haunting. These were places where murders, suicides, illness, battles, domestic and personal disputes, as well as parties, love, romance, laughter, gala events, and personal triumphs occurred. Many times the answer as to why a particular place is haunted lies in the history of the place or the land it occupies. Also, the energy that remains does not necessarily have a direct association with its present function—time and space do not seem to apply to ghosts; they continue to manifest when and where they choose without concern for existing physical law impediments.

Another interesting observation we made after gathering this data is that paranormal activity almost always began or increased after a given place was renovated or remodeled—perhaps the ghosts were content with their old surroundings, but when tampered with, decided to let the intruders know how they feel about the changes.

The listings in this book were researched in order to provide prospective guests with only those establishments that have a benign history of hauntings. Essentially, a haunting represents someone who has passed away yet sometimes returns to the physical reality for various reasons. Some spirits led normal, happy lives, while others died tragically or violently. For whatever reason, they choose or are forced to remain where they are.

A majority of the stories seem to reflect spirits who choose to remain behind to watch over the place they helped build or take care of when they were alive. Therefore, they have the best interests of the guest at heart—almost like guardian angels. They do like to play and throw occasional tantrums; however, in many of those cases they just want to be noticed. Most of the time, talking to them, assuring them, or just saying you don't want them around at a particular time will do the trick. Certainly some people who have a paranormal experience with the supernatural are frightened—after all it's the unknown. However, if the lucky person manages to calm himself and enjoy the moment, he is usually the first one who wants to see more. In fact, he often becomes a future ghost hunter, craving additional paranormal experiences. Therefore, we suggest you come in with an open mind and try to find exhilaration, not fear, in an encounter with the unknown.

The basic objective of this paranormal travel book is to introduce humans to spirits in a friendly environment and provide the selective traveler with the unique opportunity for encountering something out of the ordinary. Most of the people we interviewed took pride in the fact that their establishments have someone "watching over them" and have often given the ghosts affectionate names and welcomed them into the family. They enjoy the otherworldly companionship. We hope you will too. We don't guarantee you will see a ghost or have something extraordinary happen to you, but we do feel that at the very least, you will be able to dine or drink in a haunted establishment and take home with you a memory you will treasure for a lifetime and perhaps beyond.

When you travel to a location in this book, we recommend you have a good map with you and that you look in the reference section of the establishment you are going to visit and do a bit of additional reading. Contact the establishment and talk to the owner or manager about the hauntings. They may have a new story to tell. Most of the establishments are on the Internet, so we recommend that you check out their web sites. The better prepared you are, the more enjoyable your visit.

We attempted to be as accurate as possible with the history, ghost stories, facts, and references; however, we are human. If there are problems or discrepancies, we kindly ask you to notify us in order that we may make the corrections for future editions. If you come across a haunted restaurant or tavern that we don't have listed, please send us the name, phone number, address, and if you can, obtain a postcard, brochure, or business card, and we will follow up on the lead. Your name will also be included in updates as a contributor to a new listing.

Ultimately, we hope you have a good time with this book.

Keep your wits about you, and while lifting a glass in toast, you might take a moment to salute those who have gone before you but have chosen to remain behind—in spirit. *Southern Fried Spirits* welcomes you into a world where you may not need food or drink to see a spirit, but it may help.

HAPPY HAUNTING!

Arkansas

Van Buren

Old Van Buren Inn and Bed and Breakfast

The city of Van Buren, Arkansas, was incorporated in 1845. It has a current population of fewer than 19,000 people. Historic downtown Main Street Van Buren is a five-block area that has been restored to look as it once did in the late 1800s. It features seventy restored turn-of-the-century buildings, all listed on the National Register of Historic Places. The Old Van Buren Inn is a local landmark situated in the heart of the historic district. The fixtures in the building include Tennessee Valley marble, a variety of hardwood from around the world, and ornate tinwork. The former bank that occupied this building managed to survive a number of attempted hold-ups and robberies, but it was finally closed during the Great Depression.

In 1840 President Van Buren granted the corner lot of what is now Seventh and Main to a private individual. A building was constructed on the lot shortly thereafter, and sometime before 1882 it burned down. In 1882 the construction of a bank building was begun. It was seven years in the making and was hailed as one of the most advanced architectural buildings of its time. The Crawford County Bank opened in 1890 and functioned as a bank

1

until 1930. The bank finally closed its doors when it merged with another bank in town. After that time, the building housed a gas office until the mid-1950s, followed by an antique store, coin shop, flower shop, and shirt shop. Jackie Henningsen purchased the building in 1988 and restored it from top to bottom. Shortly after the completion of the restoration process, the spirits of the Old Van Buren became restless. Henningsen, who prefers to call the spirits "energies" or her "others," provided the following litany of events:

In 1989 Henningsen began work on the remodeling process. At the time, the building was empty and stripped, since it had been abandoned for over a year. While awaiting approval to begin remodeling, Henningsen had to walk the halls with flashlights, because the inspector would not allow the electricity to be turned on due to the deteriorated state of the old cloth wiring. Therefore, most of the work was performed during daylight hours.

Even during daytime, no one was really enthusiastic about walking to the second floor alone. Without exception, every time people walked along the second floor hallway, the hair would stand up on the back of their neck. Henningsen said, "There was a constant feeling that someone was walking beside you or brushing up next to you." When a person walked down the stairway to reach the ground floor, he would always have to hold on to the handrail because it felt like someone was trying to gently push him or needed room to pass. Over the years, individuals who rented the building have come into the restaurant and told Henningsen that they were either gently pushed while descending the stairs, that their hair was standing on end, or that they passed through cold spots while walking down the hallway.

In 1990 a female merchant, whose store lies across the street from the Inn, was on her way to work when she pulled up to the stop sign on the corner of Seventh and Main. As she was about to go, the woman happened to glance up at the Van Buren Inn, and she saw a woman standing in front of a second-floor window, looking down on the street. The fact that a woman was watching from the window was not unusual. What was, however, was the fact that within seconds the mysterious figure simply vanished while the

woman looked on. Instead of driving away, she decided to park the car and enter Henningsen's restaurant a few minutes later. Obviously very shaken and extremely nervous, the woman tentatively approached Henningsen. After hearing the woman's story, Henningsen thought she was joking and didn't take her seriously at first. That's when the woman became angry and agitated. She swore that she had witnessed a woman staring down at her from a second-floor window, then disappear. The whole episode frightened her so badly that the woman stayed for several cups of coffee to quiet her nerves. The woman proceeded to describe the phantom lady as having dark hair, pulled up on her head, and wearing a dark skirt with a white blouse. Henningsen said there was no such person in the building now, nor had there ever been a person fitting that description living in the building that she could recall. With that, the woman quickly gulped down her coffee, paid her bill, and ran out of the inn.

During February 1990, at around 10:00 P.M., Henningsen and her male companion were lying in bed, reading, while Henningsen's three-year-old grandchild rested between them. The large room was on the top floor of the old bank building. Additionally, there were two dogs situated at the foot of the bed. As Henningsen was waiting for her daughter to come and pick up her child after work, strange sounds began coming from the stairwell just outside the room. The dogs immediately jumped up from their positions by the bed and ran to the front door, sniffing and growling the entire way. Slowly getting up out of bed, Henningsen could clearly hear a woman crying, and the perturbed woman was slowly climbing the thirteen steps to reach her door. The dogs continued growling and whining at the sounds coming from the hallway.

Henningsen thought one of the tenants, a woman who worked in the restaurant, and her boyfriend had a fight, and that she was going to have to hear the whole story in a few minutes. Waiting outside her door for a knock that never came, Henningsen waited near the door for a few more seconds before opening it. The dogs immediately bolted out of the room but never made another sound. They just stood at the top of the landing and looked down into the darkened stairwell. Henningsen followed her dogs to the top of the landing and waited for the woman to come into view. No one came up the stairs, which frightened Henningsen, who finally yelled to her friend that she thought someone had broken into the building. Her companion grabbed a gun, and they both searched the building from top to bottom, but they could not find the cause of the footsteps or the crying. The woman she thought might have been the cause of the crying was not in—nor was her boyfriend.

Another event happened to Henningsen's sister, who came to visit from California to help her renovate the building. While her sister was working in the hall on the second floor of the building, she saw a young woman fitting the description others had given of a ghostly guest, even though Henningsen's sister had no knowledge of the prior events that had taken place in the old building. On this occasion, her sister happened to glance up to see a woman walk into one of the upstairs rooms. Knowing she was alone, Henningsen's sister thought someone had inadvertently come upstairs and was lost. She followed the woman into the room and was about to ask her what she was doing there or if the woman needed help, when the woman abruptly turned, stared at Henningsen's sister, then slowly vanished.

One day Henningsen came home from a date and found muddy footprints in the hall on the second floor. The prints began in the middle of the floor and ended in the main room where most of the sightings occur. The wet footprints just appeared and disappeared without going in any particular direction.

Another time she was cleaning the B & B and was locked up for the evening. As she was singing to herself and finishing dusting off a table, Henningsen chanced to look into the mirror hanging on the wall in front of her. Standing in the mirror alongside her was another spirit, which made the front page of the Fort Smith paper, in color.

During lunch one cold and rainy day, there were only a few guests in the place, including a woman and her husband who had pulled off the freeway to find somewhere to have lunch. The couple read the back of her menu and noticed that the place was haunted. Their curiosity piqued, the couple asked if they both could go upstairs and have a look around. Granted permission to look around, the couple left on their little journey. About ten minutes later, the woman came running down the stairs and told Henningsen that a man who limps from an injury suffered during the Civil War and a very unhappy young woman who cries a lot were both upstairs. The couple had never been to the inn before, and the information on the menu was too general for them to have known about the phantom woman and man. However, the visiting couple had accurately picked up on two of the Old Van Buren spirits.

On another occasion, three people came to the Inn from out of town. They had never visited the place before. While taking a tour of the Green Room (the name of the room where most of the sightings occur), the man in the group, who said very little during the entire tour, suddenly blurted out that the bank president and his wife, who were standing in the corner of the room (only he could see them), were very unhappy and confused because things keep changing around them. He continued, saying that the two spirits don't know what's happening to their familiar surroundings (ask Henningsen for the strange twist to the story).

One day a woman who was going to rent a shop on Main Street came in for lunch. Having come from another state, the woman had only lived in the area a couple of weeks before dropping in to visit. She loved the restaurant and wanted to bring her daughter back on Sunday. Henningsen said she would not be there, but the woman was welcome to come back with her daughter and look around anyway. Apparently, the woman and her daughter visited the inn, and while they were standing in front of the building, the girl looked up to see a woman in the second-floor window looking down at her. The girl began hearing voices telling her things about the building, things no one but Henningsen knew, such as where to find things hidden in the floor and who the woman is. Thinking her child was possessed, the woman called her preacher to exorcise the spirit (Henningsen has more about this one, too).

Most children and dogs don't like to enter the building, because they see things that adults cannot or won't see. Henningsen has actually watched her grandchild's eyes follow something down the hall after which she refuses to be put down on the floor. Between 1990 and 1992 an odd assortment of guest complaints included: the hot water heater being turned off by unseen hands; doors being opened after they were securely shut; someone taking a bath when there was no one in the building; and, lights turning themselves on and off without human assistance. Henningsen's final note to us read, "Tons and tons of this stuff happens, but I know you can't use it all." You'll have to visit the Old Van Buren Inn to see what the other tales are.

Address:	633 Main Street, Van Buren, Arkansas 72957
Phone:	501-474-4202
Fax:	501-474-8992
Proprietors:	Jacquline Kay Henningsen
Accommodations:	Three guestrooms decorated in handpicked Victorian antique furniture are located on the second floor.
Payment:	Visa, MasterCard, Discover, American Express, Diners Club, Carte Blanche
Helpful Information:	Van Buren Chamber of Commerce, 813 Main St., Van Buren, AR 72956 - (501) 474-2761 or 1-800-332-5889

References:　　　Personal communication, Old Van Buren Inn;
Robin Mead, *Haunted Hotels: A Guide to American
and Canadian Inns and their Ghosts*; *Press
Argus-Courier,*"Landmark building noted for
ghostly past" by Dennis MaCaslin, February 18,
1998

Florida

The Biltmore Hotel

Talk about a great location, the Biltmore Hotel is situated less than fifteen minutes away from the Miami International Airport and provides easy access to beautiful beaches and excellent shopping. Downtown Miami is within a ten-minute ride on Metrorail, a transit system lying only a few minutes from the Biltmore. The remarkable Biltmore Hotel has been multifunctional since its construction, having served as a hotel, hospital, and a school before being abandoned for ten years. After extensive renovation, it now stands as one of the most luxurious hotels in the world and is listed on the National Register of Historic Places. Celebrities such as President Calvin Coolidge, the Roosevelts, Vanderbilts, Eddie Rickenbacker, Douglas Fairbanks, the Duke and Duchess of Windsor, Ginger Rogers, Judy Garland, Bing Crosby, Al Capone, former First Lady Barbara Bush, President Clinton, President Menem of Argentina, Robert Redford, Lauren Bacall, and Gloria Vanderbilt have all stayed at this grand hotel.

Land developer George E. Merrick, founder of the University of Miami, created Coral Gables. In 1924 Merrick joined forces with hotel magnate John McEntee Bowman to build a hotel that would serve tourists, sportsman, and the fashion conscious. Ten months

and $10 million later, the Biltmore debuted with an inaugural cere-
mony that was remembered as the evening of a lifetime. Fashion
shows, gala balls, grand pool parties and weddings, world-class
golf tournaments, and big bands entertained wealthy, well-trav-
eled visitors. The Biltmore made it through the Depression by
hosting aquatic galas that featured young Jackie Ott, the boy wonder who would dive from an eighty-five-foot platform, and Johnny
Weissmuller. During World War II, the War Department converted
the Biltmore to a hospital. The hotel was also the early site of The
University of Miami's School of Medicine. The Biltmore remained
a VA hospital until 1968. It was unoccupied from 1973 until 1983,
when the city began restoration to make the Biltmore once again
one of the finest hotels in the world. Almost four years and $55
million later, the Biltmore opened on December 31, 1987, as a
first-class hotel and resort.

With restoration, the Biltmore was reborn. However, with the
rebirth of the building came the resurrection of the past in the
form of spirits. One of the hotel's spirits may be that of Thomas
"Fatty" Walsh, a petty gangster who left New York in 1928 with a
friend to avoid the police and begin a new life in Florida. Soon he
was befriended by another gangster who rented the thirteenth and
fourteenth floors of the Biltmore and ran a club that catered to the
Miami in-crowd. Essentially, it was a legitimized speakeasy,
allowed to operate because the law seemed content to look the
other way. As Walsh and his partner Arthur Clark were living high
on the hog, money rolling in at every throw of the dice, their rela-
tionship soured. When two gangsters didn't get along, there was
rarely a peaceful resolution. Something had to give. In this case,
Arthur Clark got the best of Thomas "Fatty" Walsh, shooting him
in one of the tower rooms while a hundred or so guests stood by.
Walsh subsequently died from his wounds, and Clark was forced to
flee to Havana. There were rumors that the police, on the take
from Clark, engineered his safe passage to Cuba. Both gangsters
passed unceremoniously into history—or at least Clark did. Some
say that Walsh never left, his presence still haunting the Biltmore
Hotel.

During 1978 parapsychologists, psychics, and guests entered the deserted Biltmore Hotel for a seance prior to its transformation into the grand hotel it is today. None of the participants were told of the circumstances surrounding their visit or what they might expect to find while touring portions of the structure. During the walk-through, some individuals immediately pinpointed several paranormal hotspots within the building. There was residual energy recorded in the elevators and within certain areas on the thirteenth floor. To a person, there was an overwhelming feeling that something traumatic had taken place on this floor, a fact that was later confirmed during the subsequent seance.

Comments from the group included residue feelings of strong emotions, parties, drinking, gambling, and a tragic accident that is replaying itself within the walls of the old Biltmore. Furthermore, the participants felt there was a direct association to the elevators with regard to all the partying and emotion. One psychic was able to pick up on a short, elderly man with a cane watching the group closely. The consensus was that a tragedy took place that affected the thirteenth and fourteenth floors. Additionally, they concurred that the misfortune involved many people who somehow participated directly or indirectly in the event, including men with badges—the police.

After the seance was completed, a distinct tapping noise could be heard when the tape was replayed. In fact, the tapping noise drowned out most of the conversations. A consensus after the seance suggested that hundreds of entities were present on the thirteenth and fourteenth floors, and a strong psychic energy was present in the elevators. When everyone who participated in the walk-through and seance was gathered together, a retired chief of the Coral Gables Police Department confirmed that the psychic investigation corroborated information that had never been published in the newspapers, such as the elevators frequently not working and the fact that a man had been murdered in front of a large gathering during a party. As it turned out, the retired law enforcement official was one of those who had investigated the penthouse shootings in 1929.

The following year, in 1979, a group of Science Fiction Club members decided to perform a kind of psychic evaluation and investigation of their own. They performed their own walk-through of the still-vacant Biltmore Hotel. For several hours the group carried their tape recorders from floor to floor and room to room, without apparent results. When they finished their psychic tour, they replayed their tapes. They were sure that the walk-through was a bust in terms of picking up on psychic phenomena. However, after listening to the tapes, they were stunned to hear not only sounds associated with their investigation, but strange noises and voices that the group did not hear when they were passing through the various floors and rooms. The unexplained noises definitely did not belong to any member of the group.

A number of unexplained events have been blamed on Walsh, although other energy forces may also have caused the events. Doors have been opened for waitresses who pass through the kitchen to the dining area with serving trays in their hands; lampshades have been reported missing on a number of occasions; cryptic messages have been found etched on bathroom mirrors; strange shadows pass along the hallway walls; and phantom lights, haunting voices, and the feeling of being watched pervades portions of the hotel to this day. The hauntings have always been described as benign and not harmful, although the spirits have thrown a scare or two into an unsuspecting staff person or guest.

Mobsters used the hotel for gambling and other illegal activities, and at least one man died violently in 1929. The hotel was used as a hospital and a place where wealthy socialites spent many a pleasant night. Is it any wonder then that the hotel is haunted? Where good times and bad were so plentiful, so is the potential for remnant energy of those bygone days. Come see for yourself, but make sure you keep an eye out for the spirits of the Biltmore Hotel, where past and present sometimes collide in a quiet hallway, room, or elevator.

Address:	1200 Anastasia Avenue, Coral Gables, Florida 33134
Phone:	(305) 445-8066
Fax:	(305) 913-3159

Toll Free Number:	1-800-727-1926
Amenities:	European feather beds, artwork, and plants in all guestrooms; safes, valets, and minibars; heated pool; golf course; magnificent views
Accommodations:	280 guestrooms and suites
Payment:	Most major credit cards
References:	Joyce Elson Moore, *Haunt Hunter's Guide to Florida*; Richard Winer and Nancy Osborn, *Haunted Houses*; *Miami Herald* (Craig Matsuda, "They Seek Phantom of the Biltmore," October 28, 1979); *Miami Herald* (Donna Gehrke, "Biltmore Hotel Offers Some Ghostly Delights," October 30, 1994); *Floridian* (Ginger Simpson Curry, "Keeping Spirits Up," February 14, 1982).

Don CeSar Beach Resort

The Don CeSar is the only historic resort on the Gulf of Mexico. The hotel opened its doors in the late 1920s as a playground for the rich and famous including F. Scott Fitzgerald, Lou Gehrig, Clarence Darrow, and Al Capone. The famous hotel struggled to remain open through the Depression and World War II. Beginning in 1942 the Don served as convalescent center and Veterans Administration headquarters until finally closing down in 1963. Preservationists had a hand in saving and revamping the old hotel.

The resort was the dream of an Irishman and real estate tycoon named Thomas Rowe, who built the hotel in 1928 to resemble the Royal Hawaiian on Waikiki Beach. The cost of his dream was roughly $1.2 million. The Depression, World War II, and Rowe's death had immense impacts on the functioning of the hotel. When Rowe died without signing a will, his estranged wife of thirty years became the reluctant heir. In less than three years under her ownership, the resort lost its prominent standing among major resorts. In 1942 the U.S. Army purchased the Don for an "assessed value" of only $450,000 and quickly converted the structure into a convalescent center for World War II airmen. After the war the Veterans Administration stripped it and moved out in 1967, after they were unable to afford necessary repairs.

Fortunately, as with a number of historic buildings, a local preservation group stepped in to save the Don from demolition. The group rescued the resort hotel by locating a buyer who shared Thomas Rowe's vision of grandeur and elegance. After a complete restoration, the Don once again opened its doors in 1973 as a first-class luxury resort on Florida's Gulf Coast. It became popularly known as the Pink Castle. From September 1985 until January 1989, extensive renovations transformed the ornate Spanish interiors with light woods and fabrics, creating a pastel Continental look. In 1994 a multimillion-dollar revitalization included the addition of a 4,000-square-foot, full-service Beach Club and Spa, prompting the change of the resort name to Don CeSar Beach Resort & Spa.

Although the hotel changed ownership and uses, one thing remained constant: the spirit or spirits on the property. It has been rumored for years that one of the ghosts who remained true to the hotel was none other than its original owner, Thomas Rowe. Local legend has it that Rowe built the pink castle-like resort for Spanish opera star Lucinda. Although their love was strong, some say an eternal love, Lucinda's parents forbade the romance and moved their daughter as far away from Rowe as possible. Never forgetting his one and only love, Rowe wrote to Lucinda often, but always his letters were returned unopened. It was a cruel romantic tragedy, right out of a Shakespearean play.

One day Rowe, while living in New York, received a newspaper clipping announcing the untimely death of Lucinda. With the clipping came his only response from the woman he loved so deeply, a letter from her asking him to forgive her parents. In closing, Lucinda said that she and Rowe would find each other once again—for time and love are eternal. Lucinda told Rowe that she would wait for him by their fountain to share their timeless love. The letter was addressed to her beloved Don CeSar, a lead character in a light opera, and signed Maritana, a part she had sung in a London opera. Following the news of Lucinda's death, Rowe's failing heath caused him to move to Florida, where he built a palace for him and Lucinda and designed a courtyard where both lovers could meet again one day. Rowe, known for his pink suits and a Panama hat, died of a heart attack in the hotel lobby in 1940.

Construction workers spotted Rowe's ghost a number of times, wearing his trademark Panama hat and pink suit, strolling through the lobby and the corridors on the fifth floor where Rowe had once lived. It wasn't long before the resort staff was also reporting his luminous figure floating around other parts of the refurbished resort. In a bizarre twist, the new owner, fearing that ghosts would be bad for business, supposedly made a deal with Rowe's restless spirit during a man-to-ghost confrontation in the resort's kitchen. The new owner politely asked Rowe to leave, and the spirit adamantly refused. After all, Rowe built the place for his immortal love, so why should he leave.

The owner then offered a compromise. He promised that he would dedicate four rooms of the hotel to Rowe and would decorate them in 1920s decor to fit the period Rowe was familiar with in life. All he asked for in return was that Rowe not harass the guests. Apparently the deal was an ectoplasmic success, because from that day on, the spirit of Rowe and that of his phantom bride Lucinda have maintained a very low profile. Occasionally the two spirited lovers have been sighted walking hand in hand, Rowe in his light-colored suit and Lucinda in a Spanish gown—but they have not disturbed the resort guests. A deal is a deal, whether it is consummated in this life or the afterlife.

Although the ghostly couple, whose love conquered time, still roams through the Pink Castle and the adjoining grounds, they keep pretty much to Rowe's earthly bargain by confining most of their haunting to the rooms that were allocated for his afterlife pleasure. Even if the story is mostly folklore and legend, it's a good one that has stood the test of time, because tragic love stories are the stuff that dreams and legends are made of. A good love story never dies, nor does it fade away.

Address:	3400 Gulf Boulevard, St. Petersburg, Florida 78373
Phone:	813-360-1881
Fax:	813-367-3609
Toll Free Number:	1-800-282-1116
Contact:	Brenda Cannon, office manager
Amenities:	Restaurant; bar; air conditioning, phone, minibar, cable television in the room; pool; sauna; fitness room; conference rooms
Accommodations:	232 rooms and 43 suites
Payment:	Visa, Diners, American Express, MasterCard, Japanese Credit Bureau
References:	Personal communication, Don CeSar Resort; Robin Mead, *Haunted Hotels: A Guide to American and Canadian Inns and Their Ghosts*

Ḧomestead Restaurant

The city of Jacksonville, with a population of almost 700,00, is located along the nation's longest north-flowing river, the St. Johns. The city is home to the NFL franchise Jacksonville Jaguars and the Homestead Restaurant. The Homestead is situated on a Spanish land grant of Castro y Ferrer, which was conceded by Spanish governor Enrique White to Don Juan McQueen in 1792.

Originally from South Carolina, McQueen came to Florida in the 1780s and quickly acquired extensive land holdings, while serving as militia captain of the St. Johns River District. Among his land holdings was a 2,000-acre grant on Pablo Creek near the mouth of the St. Johns River. McQueen died of typhus in 1807, but Eugenia Price immortalized him in the historical novel *Don Juan McQueen*.

The Homestead Restaurant property passed through a number of owners, until Mrs. Alpha O. Paynter, one of Jacksonville's most successful restaurateurs, purchased it. The Homestead, a two-story pine log building, was constructed in 1934 and was originally designed as a private residence and boardinghouse for Mrs. Paynter. The interior floor plan and a majority of the significant interior materials and features remain intact. The original interior features include the log walls, a massive uncoursed limerock chimney, log door joists, pine flooring, and exposed trusses at the second-story level. It currently serves as the dining area for the restaurant.

The building has been the home of the Homestead since the late 1940s, and it represents the only building that is at least fifty years old and constructed of log in Jacksonville. In 1962 Mrs. Paynter sold the restaurant to Preben Johansen, a prominent Jacksonville city commissioner. The Homestead is currently owned and managed by the Macri family.

The Homestead has yet another distinguishing characteristic that sets it apart from most other establishments: It is haunted. The ghost of former owner Alpha Paynter is said to roam the restaurant. Paynter's ghost has been sighted and heard by bartenders, employees, and guests over the years. Her apparition has appeared near the large limestone fireplace in the center of the main dining room, as well as in other parts of the restaurant. On one occasion, an exterminator refused to go back inside the establishment when he was hit by what he swore felt like a shoe. Crouching near the fireplace in a hard-to-reach area, he was rudely hit on the top of his head. Rising quickly to his feet, he turned around, but there was no one there. Realizing he was the only one in that part of the building, he panicked and quickly ran outside, leaving his equipment behind. A staff person had to retrieve his

tools and bring them outside. Refusing to finish the job, he left in a hurry, but not without recommending that management call in a different kind of exterminator—one that eliminates ghosts.

Another time, during the busy Halloween season, a skeptical busboy began taunting the Homestead spirit, claiming there was no such thing as a ghost, because if there was, the ghost would show itself to him, rather than hiding like a coward. The challenge was readily accepted by Paynter, who instantly began tossing all of the tea pitchers from a nearby shelf to the floor directly in front of the taunting staff person. The awestruck busboy later related how each pitcher appeared to be lifted off the shelf by unseen hands and thrown to the floor in front of him, as he stood there in disbelief. He made no more bold taunts, learning a valuable lesson—never tease a ghost.

Make no mistake, Alpha Paynter is still watching over her beloved restaurant, making herself known in a number of ways to those who tease or provoke her, or to unsuspecting guests, employees, or maintenance personnel who just happen to be in her path when she is passing through. Perhaps she is just curious about what's happening to the Homestead and plays pranks, materializes, talks, or moves things about when she is in a playful mood or when she feels that the decor in the restaurant need a little rearranging. She's definitely not a harmful spirit, but don't push your luck by provoking her. The home sweet Homestead is still her choice of local haunts, and it doesn't seem to matter to those working there that Paynter orders from an otherworldly menu.

Address:	1712 Beach Boulevard, Jacksonville Beach, Florida 32250
Phone:	904-249-5240
Fax:	904-241-8811
Proprietors:	Steve Macri, owner; Patty Lee, manager
Business Information:	Open every day for lunch from 11:00 A.M. to 4:00 P.M.; and dinner from 4:00 P.M. to 10:00 P.M.
Payment:	All major credit cards
References:	Personal communication, The Homestead Restaurant; Dennis William Hauck, *The National Directory: Haunted Places A Guidebook to Ghostly Abodes, Sacred Sites, UFO Landings, and Other Supernatural Locations*

Ḩarry's Seafood, Bar, Grill

St. Augustine is the oldest city in the United States, with a history that predates Juan Ponce de Leon's arrival on April 3, 1513. The first permanent European settlement was established 1565 by Pedro Menendez de Aviles.

The structure that later became Harry's Seafood, Bar, Grill was built in the 1740s as the original bayfront home for Juana Navarro, a native of St. Augustine. Juana had just turned sixteen when she wed Salvador de Porras in 1745. In time, their family grew to include nine children. One of their daughters, born in 1753, was beautiful Catalina. Unfortunately for the de Porras family, in 1763 Florida became a British Colony, and they were forced to leave their home and flee to Cuba. In 1784 St. Augustine once again came under Spanish rule, and Catalina returned, this time with her new husband, Xavier Ponce de Leon, to reclaim their land and home. A bitter ten-year custody battle for the land ended in victory for Catalina and Xavier.

During the early 1800s the home was sold to Joseph LoRente and his wife. LoRente died tragically in 1813 when a hurricane sunk his ship, the *Dos Hermanos*. Eight years later the widowed Mrs. LoRente sold the home for $2,400 to Charles W. Bulow, a wealthy plantation owner. In the 1840s the property was bought by Burroughs E. Carr. In 1884 a fire destroyed the home and other properties, except for the south wall, which still remains. The home was painstakingly rebuilt to exacting Spanish colonial specifications, and for most of the 1900s it remained private. However in 1976 the home was converted into a popular restaurant. The establishment was first called Catalina's, after the original owner's daughter, then the Charthouse. Finally it was named Harry's Seafood, Bar, Grill, a name it retains today.

Harry's, a popular restaurant for humans, is also a local haunt for spirits. This paranormal location is frequented by strange and unexplainable events that continue to this day. Although the emphasis has always been on the great food, the topic of spirits is never far behind in the conversation. A former manager, while performing his nightly rounds, was making his way down the back stairs at around 1:45 A.M., when he began to smell a strong scent of perfume. The fact that there was no one else around at the time caused the manager to be a little apprehensive. As he concluded his inspection, he noted that the scent slowly disappeared. Although he never saw anyone else, living or otherwise, and never heard any mysterious voices, he still could not explain the scent of perfume that seemed to materialize out of nowhere.

On another occasion, a young child was visiting the restaurant with his mother. After situating themselves comfortably at a table and while they were waiting for a waiter, the child suddenly began pointing to a nearby table and blurted out to his mother that there was a ghost at the table. A frantic mother was quickly joined by a nearby staffperson, who looked over at the table where the child was excitedly pointing. Of course, neither the mother nor the waiter could see anyone human sitting at the table. However the staff had been around long enough to know that Harry's had a reputation for being haunted, and they believed that the child had seen the friendly spirit of the restaurant. The mother felt that since the ghost didn't bother her child and because the staff was so nice in taking the time to explain the history of the hauntings, she would stay for a delicious lunch.

The bar, which was constructed in 1907, has been witness to a number of unexplainable events. Glasses have flown off the counter, landing on the floor, sometimes unbroken; a basket of freshly laundered uniforms once exploded into flames for no apparent reason. (The fire department could find no logical explanation for the spontaneous combustion.) A number of staff members have watched in stunned silence as wispy shadows have moved through the restaurant or floated along the walls when they were cleaning up after hours. Many individuals have felt cold drafts in areas where there were no windows or doors open, no fans operating, no air-conditioning vents around or other possible physical causes for the gusts of air and sudden cold spots. The saloon-style doors in the bar area have opened and closed by themselves as a bartender was closing up for the night. The door to the men's room has been known to open and close by itself in front of startled guests and staff, who upon further inspection find no one inside. Unexplained footsteps have been heard at various times throughout the building, and the scent of lilacs oftentimes manifests out of nowhere.

The ghost of Harry's has been called Bridgett. The young woman supposedly died in an 1884 fire that consumed the building. She continues to make her presence known in various parts of the restaurant. Her apparent love for lilacs will oftentimes materialize as a strong scent, which wafts through the bar area, dining area, as well as other rooms in the building. Bridgett has been known to leave items on the floor, show herself to unsuspecting staff and guests, and announce her arrival as cold spots, drafts, perfume, and as a soft, whispering voice. A visit to this local haunt may produce more than just a casual afternoon and evening of good dining and drinking—you may see Bridgett, the spirit of the restaurant.

Address:	46 Avenida Menendez, St. Augustine, Florida 32084
Phone:	904-824-7765
Fax:	904-824-7899
Contact:	Billy Fernandez
Business Information:	Daily happy hour; lunch is served until 4:00 P.M.; dinner is served from 4:00 P.M. until closing.
Payment:	Most major credit cards are accepted
References:	Personal communication, Harry's Seafood, Bar, Grill; Dennis William Hauck, *The National Directory: Haunted Places*; Joyce Elson Moore, *Haunt Hunter's Guide to Florida*; *The Compass* (Karen Harvey, "Phenomena," June 21, 1990); Cherie Navidi-O'Riordan, "Site History of 46 Avenida Menendez," St. Augustine Historical Society; Suzy Cain and Dianne Thompson Jacoby, *A Ghostly Experience: Tales of Saint Augustine Florida*

Island Hotel

Cedar Key is located on a small barrier reef on the Gulf side off the Florida coastline, north of St. Petersburg. Cedar Key occupied a critical location during the Civil War, where blockade runners exported cotton and lumber and imported food and other supplies to the Confederacy. A hurricane all but destroyed the small city in 1896.

The Island Hotel is one of Florida's most famous bed and breakfasts and is listed on the National Register of Historic Places. Constructed in 1859, the establishment at Cedar Key is constructed from seashell tabby with oak supports. The walls have withstood hurricanes for almost one hundred fifty years, and its sloping wooden floors have survived the passage of time—and several feet of water. Originally built as a general store and post office, the building has changed little through time. The bar was painted in 1945 with murals of Cedar Key, Florida, and King Neptune, after whom the bar is named.

After Major John Parsons built the structure, which became Parsons and Hale's General Store, Cedar Key began to expand. During the war, Union soldiers burned down almost every building in Cedar Key except the general store. Some historians believe that Union forces, after taking over Cedar Key, used the building as troop quarters and as a warehouse. After the war, the general store reopened, serving as a customshouse and headquarters for the Cedar Key post office. John Muir noted the general store in his journal while trekking from Kentucky to Cedar Key. Sometime in the 1880s the place functioned as a restaurant and boardinghouse, with President Grover Cleveland once spending the night at Parsons and Hale's.

During 1896 a major hurricane severely damaged the island city and the store. Francis Hale, one of the original owners, died in 1910. In 1914 Langdon Parsons, son of John Adams, sold the building to Simon Feinberg, who turned the building into the Bay Hotel. As part of the renovations, a second-floor balcony was added

around the southern and western sides of the hotel. The hotel was managed by the Markhams until 1918. Feinberg died in the hotel on May 11, 1919, under questionable circumstances. As one story has it, Feinberg's manager had a still in the attic, which was against Feinberg's religious upbringing. One night the manager prepared a grand dinner for Feinberg, who dined and went to bed; he never woke up. A number of people concluded that he was poisoned by the manager—that is, everyone except the police.

Over the years the hotel changed owners: J.B. Pauline Witt and later, George Lewis. It was called the Cedar Key Hotel, then the Fowlers Wood. A man named Critteenden managed the hotel in the 1930s. During the Depression, the hotel was almost burned to the ground several times; each time the place was spared by a quick response from the local fire department. A Mr. Ray Andrews acquired the hotel in the late 1930s, and his brother-in-law and sister, Forest and Nettie Andrews, ran it during the war years. The hotel became run down, and it took Bessie and Loyal Gibbs, who arrived in 1946, to make the place livable. They restored the place and renamed it the Island Hotel, which has remained. The hotel and bar became a notable hangout for locals and celebrities like Pearl Buck, Vaughan Monroe, Tennessee Ernie Ford, Frances Langford, Myrna Loy, and Richard Boone.

Hurricane Easy hit Cedar Key in 1950, blowing the roof off the hotel. It was subsequently remodeled. Gibbs died in 1962, and his ashes were scattered in front of the hotel so he could be near the place he loved so much in life. In 1973 Bessie Gibbs sold the hotel to Charles and Shirley English. Two years later Bessie Gibbs died, and her ashes were scattered in the Gulf waters. The English family operated the hotel until 1978, when it was sold to Harold Nabors, who remodeled the bar. It was sold once again to Marcia Rogers in 1980. Jimmy Buffet visited the bar many times over the years, giving impromptu concerts in the Neptune Bar. The restaurant became nationally famous, and in 1984 the Island Hotel was listed on the National Register of Historic Places. During the late 1980s the Neptune Bar changed to a coffee and juice bar, much to the consternation of the locals who had made the bar a nightly stop-off point. In 1992 Rogers sold the hotel to Tom and Allison Sanders. Once again the Neptune Bar reopened. In 1996 Dawn Fisher and Tony Cousins bought the hotel, and they upgraded and renovated the hotel to its present state.

According to former and present owners, staff, and locals, the Island Hotel is definitely haunted. A number of bona fide spirits are said to still use the hotel. In fact, the friendly spirits may be former owners and guests who enjoyed the hotel so much while they were alive that some chose to remain behind in familiar surroundings. Considering that it has been in operation since 1859, it is no wonder that strange things continue to be reported.

Several of the ghosts have been tentatively identified based on those who have sighted otherworldly apparitions and have been able to match their descriptions with photographs, likenesses, or depiction's of the dearly departed who once walked through the building in the flesh. One spirit seems to be none other than Simon Feinberg, who some believe was poisoned by his former manager. Another spirited guest appears to be that of Bessie Gibbs, who arrived with her husband, Loyal, in 1946 to take over and restore the property.

Over the years the spirits of the Island Hotel, whether they are Simon, Bessie, both of them, or other unidentified entities, have played assorted tricks on management and staff. They have repeatedly locked doors to various rooms, forcing them to enter by other means. Often a door left open only minutes before by a staff person has been found locked from the inside when the person returns. After access is made, there is never anyone else in the room, and there is no way for a person to have left the room without being observed.

Other times housekeeping or staff would be standing near a door when it would open and then close as if someone had either entered or left—no one in the flesh is ever spotted when this happens. Additionally, guests have reported seeing a lady dressed in white walk into their rooms right through the entrance door, come sit on the bed next to them, then vanish as they stare in amazement. Other times, the phantom lady in white will be spotted walking across a guestroom and disappear through the wall.

A seance was one held in the hotel, apparently aimed at conjuring up a spirit that the participants believed belonged to Bessie Gibbs. The results, though unscientific, concluded that Gibbs's former upstairs room is definitely haunted—but Bessie is not alone. Psychic investigation confirmed the presence of several other spirits in addition to that of Bessie Gibbs, although her spirit seems to be the most dominant.

Other spirits have been known to frequent not only Bessie's old room, which has been likened to a gateway to another dimension, but also the front portion of the hotel. Here, strange and unexplainable noises have been frequently heard; lights will flicker on and off without a known cause; doors have been known to open and shut by themselves; there are countless reports of cold spots, breezes, and drafts without a known source; and some report pervasive feelings of being watched or followed.

Address:	P.O. Box 460 Cedar Key, Florida USA 32625
Phone:	352-543-5111
Fax:	352-543-6949
Toll Free Number:	800-432-4640
E-mail:	hotel@islandhotel-cedarkey.com
Proprietors:	Dawn and Tony Cousins

Amenities:	No televisions and no telephones in the rooms; not wheelchair accessible; the restaurant serves a distinctively Cedar Key menu.
Accommodations:	13 guestrooms;11 have private baths, and all have air conditioning; some have old-fashioned claw-foot tubs, and all have the original hand cut wooden walls and floors; the room rate includes a full waitress-served breakfast in our dining room
Business Information:	Open all year round; bar and restaurant open every day. The restaurant 6:00 P.M.-9:00 P.M./Bar 5:00 P.M.-11:00 P.M.
Payment:	Visa, MasterCard, Discover
References:	Personal communication, The Island Hotel; Joyce Elson Moore, *Haunt Hunter's Guide to Florida*; Tom Sanders, "A Brief History of the Island Hotel," Island Hotel, Cedar Key, Florida

Ashley's Restaurant

The town of Rockledge is situated on the east central Florida coast, twelve miles north of Melbourne. When Ashley's Restaurant opened in 1933, it was called Jack's Tavern, an establishment that catered to a very upscale crowd. In 1943 the owner was drafted and had to sell the restaurant. It was resold three years later and renamed Cooney's Tavern. Clayton Korecky's son inherited it and later sold the establishment to Willie Schuhmacher, who renamed it the Mad Duchess. Three years later it was sold again and the name once again changed, this time to The Caboose. Later a man named Scott Faucher bought it, then sold it to the present owner, Greg Parker. With Parker came the present name, Ashley's Restaurant and Lounge.

The large Tudor-style building is constructed of wood and heavy beam, with a quiet lounge area set off by the dark wood walls, reminiscent of an English pub. Upstairs at Ashely's tables are placed around the railing, affording a view of the downstairs area. Although the owners of the establishment have frequently changed, one thing has remained constant—Ashley's is one of the most haunted restaurants in America. Not convinced, all you have to do is ask any number of psychics, paranormal investigators, former owners, the current owner, or any number of employees and guests who have frequented the place. Most people have come away with the same feeling—that an ever-present psychic energy envelops the restaurant.

As an example, a former manager, while working late at night, felt a gust of wind blow right past him, even though all the doors and windows were closed and the air conditioning wasn't functioning in the area he was standing. On a number of occasions the police had to be summoned after closing time, when lights were reported on and there was movement observed inside. Upon investigation, no intruder was every found lurking inside, and nothing was ever taken. It wasn't vandals who were triggering alarms, turning on the electricity, or moving around inside; it was the spirits of Ashley's.

Pictures, five at a time, have been known to fall off the wall sometime during the night. In the morning, however, they are always found lying neatly face up and with no broken glass anywhere to be found. Hurricane lamps are sometimes found lit with no explanation, even though they have all been put out while closing up. Management and employees call their spirit Sarah, although psychics sense more than one spirit present.

During an investigation by the Rockledge Police Department in 1980, they found the manager's office in complete disarray. Papers and books were strewn everywhere, and the safe holding cash had been opened. The baffling thing was, nothing was taken. The final police report deemed the incident "suspicious" but that's all.

Employees have learned over the years to avoid entering the storage rooms by themselves. One waitress, upon entering one of the rooms alone, encountered a woman sitting at a desk. As the stunned waitress held her breath, the figure vanished. Another staff person, while stretching to reach some glasses on a high shelf, felt her leg accidentally kick someone. She immediately apologized and turned to see whom she had kicked. There was no one else in the room with her.

The kitchen has also had its share of strange phenomena. A cook opened the restaurant one morning to find breadbaskets scattered around the kitchen. He was the same person who had neatly stacked them the night before and then locked up, and no one had come in between the time he closed and reopened the restaurant. Another cook stood in amazement as a jar flew off the counter, barely missing him, hit the floor—and didn't break. Several times exhaust fans, which have to be turned on manually, have suddenly started up by themselves.

The ladies restroom is also a hotbed for paranormal events. One time a woman came out of the bathroom screaming after a toilet seat exploded while she was standing nearby. Another time, while a female patron was alone in the bathroom, the bathroom door suddenly opened and shut. Also, when she tried to leave the bathroom, she couldn't get out. The door wasn't locked, but she couldn't budge it. Then, all at once, the door swung open by itself. When the woman finally rushed out, there was no one anywhere near the door.

The bar area is also known to have spirited activity. Bartenders have heard their names called out or whispered but they have always failed to find the source. Employees who work late often report crazy things happening near the bar, like the time a piece of lemon flew out of the sink and landed across the room. Glasses have been known to shatter, begin moving on their own, or slide unassisted across the bar.

Psychics usually need no more than a few minutes inside to reach the same conclusion—Ashley's is an extremely haunted restaurant. One psychic actually witnessed two uniformed men dragging a man down the stairs, followed by a young girl who was begging them to stop. The scene abruptly ended when all the phantom participants vanished. Another time a psychic saw a woman, who was bleeding profusely, run downstairs. The psychic followed the frantic woman only to see her disappear before reaching the end of a hallway.

A newspaper article may provide a clue as to the identity of the often-sighted spectral lady. In 1934 the body of nineteen-year-old Ethel Allen, a frequent guest at Jack's Tavern, was found on the shores of Indian River near Eau Gallie. The body was badly mutilated, and it was only identified because of a tattoo located on the right thigh just above the knee. Reports say that she was last seen at Jack's tavern with a well-dressed, nice-looking man. The murder was never solved.

Malcolm Denemark, a photographer, captured a strange image while photographing an outside portion for a newspaper article in 1982. When he took the photograph in the patio of the restaurant, there was no one in the area. After developing the film, he saw an image of a man entering the lobby. There was no shadow cast by the person, who looked like a waiter, although other items in the picture had shadows. The *National Enquirer* ended up buying the picture, and they ran an article about the restaurant.

Photo by Malcolm Denemark showing mysterious image in patio that was not present at the time the photograph was taken.

Loyd Auerbach wrote in his *FATE Magazine* column "Psychic Frontiers" in July 1994 about Ashley's Restaurant, and he said that the place has had a number of ghostly sightings, odd phenomena, and even odder witness reactions. In June of 1993, as Martin Caidin and gifted psychic Sybil Leek walked through the place, Leek felt a presence and followed a coldness that settled in the dining room. Sybil turned and pointed to the spot where she saw an entity. As Caidin and a television crew watched, a chair rose slowly, rotated, moved to almost the center of the room, then came to rest back on the floor. This happened to Leek on several visits to the restaurant, although on one occasion, instead of a gentle display of force, the chair flew across the room and smashed against the wall.

Auerbach participated in a pilot for a television series entitled *Haunted America*. As part of the show, Auerbach interviewed the owner, current and ex-employees, and locals. The stories were fantastic. Lights, kitchen appliances, and power tools would come on after closing with no one there. Glasses would fly all over the place; fire extinguishers went off by themselves; a high-pitched scream could be heard on more than one occasion. Cool breezes would engulf people; the front door to the bar would swing open and no one would be there; a woman in the ladies dressing room had a window continually open on her, even after she shut and locked it. A cleaning person watched as a roll of toilet paper was spinning on the floor when no one else was in the room; two female bikers went to use the ladies room and left screaming. They were immediately followed by two burly gentlemen, who went in to check the situation out. Within a few minutes they also came running out. The group left without saying what had frightened them.

Over the years, the most often reported apparition is that of a woman dressed in 1920s attire, who appears in the bathroom toilet stalls and in the mirror.

For Auerbach and the investigative team, their walk-through of the place witnessed fully charged batteries drain in less than five minutes, and the batteries heated up and burned out for no apparent reason. Infrared thermographic video equipment was then used. A red light went on, and it began recording what looked like a head-shaped spot of darkness on a monitor. Another monitor in the ladies bathroom picked up what looked like a cylindrical object floating in midair. The object maneuvered around a person's hand, then looked like it was melting into the wall.

Arthur Myers, in his book *The Ghostly Register: Haunted Dwellings, Active Spirits, a Journey to America's Strangest Landmarks,* described the ghost of Ashley's as Ethel Allen, who came to grief one night about fifty years ago. Her death took place in an area where the storage room is now. The place is now a dead end, a service area, but it used to be where the front door of the building was. She was running from someone and trying to get out. A man caught up to her, put both hands on her shoulders, shoved her to the floor, and finished the murder there. Another entity is a little girl, about six years old, who was killed in an automobile accident on U.S. Highway 1 just outside the restaurant. She died on the road, but her spirit apparently wandered into the restaurant where it remains. Then there is an elderly waiter who likes to take customers' orders and then disappear without bringing their food. Try visiting Ashley's for some dinner, a drink, and some real spirits.

Address:	1609 South U.S. Highway 1, Rockledge, Florida 32955
Phone:	407-636-6430
Proprietors:	Greg and Sue Parker
Business Information:	Monday-Thursday: 11:00 A.M.-12:00 P.M./ Friday and Saturday: 11:00 A.M.-2:00 A.M./ Sunday: 12:00 noon-12:00 midnight
Payment:	Visa, MasterCard, American Express
References:	Personal communication, Ashley's Restaurant; Dennis William Hauck, *The National Directory: Haunted Places: A Guidebook to Ghostly Abodes, Sacred Sites, UFO Landings, and Other Supernatural Locations*; Arthur Myers, *The Ghostly Register: Haunted Dwellings, Active Spirits, a Journey to America's Strangest Landmarks*, Chicago; *Reader's Digest*, "Quest for the Unknown"; *FATE Magazine* ("Psychic Frontiers" by Loyd Auerbach, July 1994); Joyce Elson Moore, *Haunt Hunter's Guide to Florida*; *Cocoa Tribune* ("Brutally Murdered Body

of Cocoa Girl Is Found Yesterday," November 22, 1934); Billy Cox, *Florida Today* ("Lingering Guests," July 4-8, 1982; Jeff Klinkenberg, *St. Petersburg Times* ("Spirits in the Night," September 10, 1986)

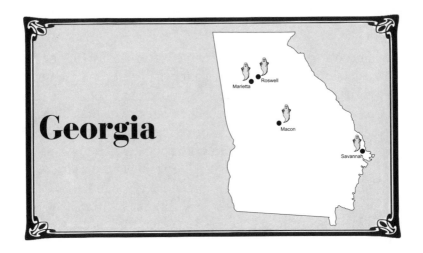

Georgia

The 1848 House

This National Register building is an authentic plantation home situated on thirteen acres of land in Marietta, Georgia, a city of over 44,000 inhabitants, located north of Atlanta. This famous restaurant has received numerous awards including AAA's "Four Diamond Award," Wine Spectator's "Award of Excellence," Distinguished Restaurants of North America Award, and *Atlanta Magazine*'s "Best Southern Cuisine."

Marietta was still a pioneer community in 1832 when the first settlers arrived, and shortly thereafter the Cherokee Indians were forced to leave. The seventeen-room plantation home was completed in 1848 by Marietta's first mayor, John H. Glover, and was named Bushy Park two years before the first railroad was completed through town. A man named Glover sold the plantation to Francis H. McLeod in 1851, and after his death, his daughter, Sarah Elizabeth, and her husband, William King, lived in the home. King was the son of Georgia's founder, Roswell King.

During the Civil War, most of the King family relocated to Savannah for safety. But not Mr. King, who stayed behind in his beloved mansion with all the servants and kept a diary describing the "Battle of Bushy Park." A bullet is still embedded in the wooden doorframe—a reminder of the battle. Bushy Park served as a hospital for the Union forces after the battle, and the northwest corner bedroom was used as an operating room. Because William King had been a personal friend of General Sherman before the war, the mansion was spared from Sherman's fiery rampage. When the Federal army left the mansion after the war, the soldiers stripped the plantation of all furnishings and valuables.

When William B. Dunaway acquired the restaurant in 1992, he became the twenty-third owner of Bushy Park. After extensive renovations, he restored the house to its 1850 greatness and renamed it 1848 House. The ante-bellum 1848 House in Marietta is family owned and operated. The restoration of the 1848 House to its antebellum heritage has included the grounds, which have been returned to former grandeur with plants that would have been around during the 1850s.

Almost everyone in Marietta knows about the ghost of the 1848 House. In fact, their web site reads, "The Ghosts of 1848 House—Do you believe?" Based on various accounts, a number of management and staff have experienced the paranormal while working in the restaurant. Most of the reported paranormal events consist of rocking chairs that move back and forth by themselves; a red light that moves across the floor and walls, yet has not produced a logical source to date; noises coming from the upstairs closets when no one is up there; doors that have a mind of their own, preventing staff from opening them one minute, then a short time later magically becoming unlocked; chandeliers that suddenly begin swinging back and forth as if someone is pushing them; and clocks that begin running backward.

With all the strange occurrences that have occurred over the years, there has been only one reported sighting of a ghost, although many guests have felt a "presence" in certain rooms within the beautiful restaurant. The general consensus is that the establishment actually has two resident spirits—a man and a woman. One ghost likes to inhabit the first floor of the building, while the second spirits seems to enjoy entertaining on the second. To further complicate matters and no doubt add to the spirited

instability within the building is the fact that the two ghosts don't seem to like each other.

No one seems to know who the ghosts might be; however, that didn't prevent them from obtaining names—George and Lillian. These are not bad or harmful ghosts, just playful, pesky, and mischievous ones. According to the owner, the staff finds the ghosts to be perfect alibis, and the spirits are blamed for just about anything that goes awry.

An article entitled "Mysterious Spirit Continues to Roam Freely at 1848 House" in the *Marietta Daily* was provided courtesy of the 1848 House. Excerpting from the reprint: Late one evening after a long shift at the 1848 House Restaurant in Marietta, general manager Don Couvillion was ready to call it a night. Couvillion and two of the employees were turning off the lights, locking doors, and sweeping up after dinner guests at about 12:30 A.M.—but that's not what the clock said. The electric Coca-Cola clock read 11:00 P.M., with the second hand speeding wildly counterclockwise. As a chill shot up Couvillion's spine and the hairs on the back of his neck stood at attention, he witnessed what others said was a typical visit to the plantation home on South Cobb Drive by their mischievous friend "George," a harmless apparition. Couvillion, a business-minded manager, who never believed in ghosts before, had no explanation for the backward spinning clock.

Several employees, including longtime Marietta resident and 1848 House proprietor Bill Dunaway, say the wandering spirit of the restaurant occasionally stirs up trouble and taunts the staff. Former employee Alice Upright was relaxing with a cup of coffee after her shift was concluded, when a chandelier in one of the dining rooms started to swing back and forth. The shocked employee could only watch in stunned silence. After a bartender investigated and found no logical explanation for the event, both concluded that George, the resident ghost, was probably performing for her like a trapeze artist.

An employee named Barbara was present when George began playing with the light fixtures. Three times the restaurant lights blinked before she got up the courage and ordered the pesky ghost to cease playing with the electricity. The obedient George abruptly stopped.

The owner thinks George may be the ghost of a Civil War soldier who decided not to leave one of Marietta's oldest homes. During the war, the Union army used the home as a hospital for federal soldiers. The former operating room was on the second floor of the restaurant, in an area now occupied by a dining room. As the Confederate army retreated from the battle of Kennesaw Mountain, a number of Southern soldiers were killed or wounded near the 1848 House, then called Bushy Park. Perhaps George was one of those soldiers. Dunaway says he's not sure who or what is causing the supernatural occurrences in the restaurant, but he's sure about something—he's not going to stay here late at night by himself and find out.

Add to the other events the fact that a scent of sweet perfume is occasionally experienced; furniture is often moved from one location to another; glassware is sometimes rearranged by unseen hands and even broken. Glasses have been known to fly off the shelf for no apparent reason; lights have flickered off and on in various parts of the restaurant; a black cane-bottomed rocking chair, situated on the verandah, has begun rocking all by itself. The shadow of a person has been seen walking up the stairs and then vanishing down the hall or floating into one of the rooms. During Christmas, while one of the owners was arranging a table display using fruit and evergreens, the fruit suddenly disappeared, and a flower arrangement on a table was pulled right out from under a man while he was dining.

The restored 1848 House Restaurant is endowed with fabulous food, atmosphere, and spirits—the kind you can drink and some you can occasionally see through. It's well worth the visit, even if nothing unusual happens.

Address:	780 South Cobb Drive, Marietta, Georgia 30060-3115
Phone:	770-428-1848
Fax:	770-427-5886
Proprietors:	William B. Dunaway
Business Information:	Open for general dining Tuesday through Sunday nights, Sunday for Jazz Brunch, and anytime for private functions
Accommodations:	Eleven different authentically furnished rooms, eight with fireplaces
Payment:	Most major credit cards are accepted
References:	Personal communication, The 1848 House; Barbara Duffey, *Angels and Apparitions: True Ghost Stories from the South*; Nancy Roberts, *Georgia Ghosts*

The Pirates' House

The Pirates' House is located in Savannah, Georgia, and is situated where the first experimental garden in America once stood. When General Ogelthorpe and his colonists arrived from England in 1733, they camped near the present city hall, roughly seven blocks west of The Pirates' House. Ogelthorpe and his colonists founded Savannah. The experimental garden was modeled after the Chelsea Botanical Garden in London. Botanists were sent from England to procure plants from around the world for the experimental garden: vine cuttings, fruit trees, flax, hemp, spices, cotton, indigo, olives, and medicinal herbs. From this garden were distributed the peach trees, which have since given Georgia and South Carolina a major commercial crop, along with the upland cotton, which later comprised the greater part of the world's cotton commerce.

The small building adjoining the Pirates' House was erected in 1734 and is said to be the oldest house in the state of Georgia. The building originally housed the gardener of Trustee's Garden. His office and tool room were in the front section, his stable occupied the back room, and his hayloft was upstairs. The bricks used in the construction of this old Herb House, as it is called today, were manufactured a block away under the bluff by the Savannah River, where brickmaking was begun by the colonists as early as 1733.

Around 1753, when Georgia had become firmly established and the need for an experimental garden no longer existed, the site was developed as a residential section. Since Savannah had become a thriving seaport town, one of the first buildings constructed on the former garden site was naturally an inn for visiting seamen. Situated a scant block from the Savannah River, the inn became a rendezvous of pirates and sailors. Here, seamen drank heavily while discussing their adventures. This very same building was converted into one of America's most unique restaurants—The Pirates' House.

Even though every modern restaurant facility has been installed, the very atmosphere reflecting the days of wooden ships and iron men has been carefully preserved. In the chamber known as the Captain's Room, negotiations were made by shorthanded ship's masters to Shanghai unwary seamen to complete their crews. Stories still persist of a tunnel extending from the old rum cellar beneath the Captain's Room to the river through which these men were carried, drugged and unconscious, to ships waiting in the harbor. Many a sailor drinking at the Pirates' House awoke to find himself at sea on a strange ship bound for a port half a world away.

A Savannah policeman, as legend has it, stopped by the Pirates' House for a friendly drink and awoke on a four-masted schooner sailing to China from where it took him two years to make his way back to Savannah. Hanging on the walls in the Captain's Room and the Treasure Room are frames containing pages from a rare, early edition of the book *Treasure Island*. Savannah is mentioned numerous times in this classic by Robert Louis Stevenson. In fact, some of the action is supposed to have taken place in the Pirates' House. Legend has it that Captain Flint, who originally buried the famous treasure on Treasure Island, died upstairs in the Pirates' House.

The Pirates' House has been recognized by the American Museum Society, which lists the historic tavern as a house museum. The property was acquired by the Savannah Gas Company in 1948. Mrs. Hansell Hillyer, wife of the president of the company, took a great interest in restoring the building and ultimately transformed the place into a restaurant. Today it is a famous hangout for locals and tourists, who come to enjoy delicious Southern specialties served in fifteen dining rooms. There is also the Window Shop, Hannah's East, the piano and jazz club, and ghosts!

The feisty spirit of pirate Captain Flint is said to haunt the Pirates' House. According to legend, as Flint was near death, he asked for one more sip of rum. Today, staff and guests have heard Flint's cries echo throughout the restaurant. Additionally, his scar-faced apparition has been sighted in the enormous basement tunnel that was discovered during renovations to the structure. The cavernous tunnel leads to the river where the pirates probably made their escape as well as brought in their booty. For the most part, however, the Captain's Room seems to be Flint's favorite place to hang out—he is said to have taken his last breath in the room. Sometimes the spirit raises such a racket that waiters will not venture into the room. The phantom has been known to make loud noises, cast shadows, rattle dishes, and is even said to be responsible for somber music that drifts through the place.

The long tradition of strange noises, unexplained footsteps, and lights emanating from the top floor of the building continues today. Employees and managers rarely enter that portion of the building at night alone. A solitary venture into Captain Flint's domain seems to scare the heck out of everyone who tries. A psychic once visited the restaurant and immediately upon entering, had a strong reaction, which consisted of goose bumps, sadness, and apprehension. As she walked into the area of the cellar stairway, she smelled blood and felt a negative energy nearby. The psychic was convinced that the spirits of many young men, taken against their will by pirates, were still trapped in the basement area. Her overwhelming, negative feelings also yielded a prediction that a fire would soon occur in the place. A short time later, a fire did break out over the den area but was fortunately extinguished before major damage was incurred.

A private room known as Hideaway No. 4, a wait station for servers, is known for intense paranormal encounters. Servers have felt an invisible hand wrap around their ankles and have witnessed a picture on the wall, which continues to fly off its support, landing near the startled spectators. Then there are the occasional cold spots and uneasy feelings of being watched or followed that seem to pervade the area.

The attic door is another area where "strange things" happen. A busboy has spotted a ghostly apparition, and others have seen shadows and heard eerie voices come from the confining space. A group of intrepid explorers, including a psychic, spent some time in the place when it was closed to the public. After a protective invocation, the paranormal party began. Strange letters like "aticc," and "hous out." emerged from the pens of some of the individuals as they tried their luck at automatic writing. A flashlight, pointed at an area where sightings frequently occurred, suddenly went dead. Near the stairs, everyone felt an intense presence, and in the attic they all saw large blocks of darkness that shifted around and moved forward. The group was extremely apprehensive at this point, and they quickly took photographs and left the building.

And so, as the unexplained laughs, whispers, cursing, guttural commands, shadows, cold spots, and apparitions continue, the Pirates' House remains one of the most haunted restaurants in Savannah, if not the United States—beware of Captain Flint, eh mate!

Address:	20 East Broad Street, Savannah, Georgia 31401
Phone:	912-232-5757
Fax:	912-232-5757 x 130
Contact:	Sandy Hollander/Linda Lane
Business Information:	Open daily: lunch from 11:30 A.M.-2:30 P.M./dinner (Monday-Saturday) from 5:30 P.M.-9:45 P.M. daily/

	Sunday brunch from 11:00 A.M.-3:00 P.M. 5:00 P.M.; private luncheons available; there is a bar; not wheelchair accessible; there is a nonsmoking area
Payment:	Most major credit cards accepted
References:	Personal communication, Pirate's House; Dennis William Hauck, *The National Directory: Haunted Places: A Guidebook to Ghostly Abodes, Sacred Sites, UFO Landings, and Other Supernatural Locations*; Nancy Rhyne, *Coastal Ghosts: Haunted Places From Wilmington, North Carolina to Savannah, Georgia*; Margaret Wayt De Bolt, *Savannah Spectres and Other Strange Tales*; Nancy Roberts, *Haunted Houses: Chilling Tales from Nineteen American Homes*; Nancy Roberts, *Georgia Ghosts*; John Ryan (*Georgian Guardian*: "Shiver Me Timbers: The Pirates' House is Haunted").

The Public House Restaurant

The Public House is situated on Historic Roswell Square in Roswell, Georgia. Located north of Atlanta, Roswell, a small city of around 50,000 people, was founded in 1839 by businessman Roswell King, who was the leading supplier of cotton and woolen goods to the Confederacy. The building originally served as a commissary for the Roswell Mill but in 1976 was converted into a restaurant.

As an integral part of nineteenth-century Roswell, the Public House has enjoyed a great deal of activity since its beginning as a mill store. The main area of the present-day restaurant was the third and final structure built for the local mill workers, providing a general store in which the workers could purchase every necessity for private and business life. The smaller area of the restaurant, partitioned by brick columns, was originally the Dunwoody Shoe Shop, which was built around 1920.

The mill, located directly behind The Public House, manufactured thread cotton and woolen goods. The Roswell Manufacturing Company is said to have monopolized the trade in all general supplies. However times became very difficult during the Civil War. Clothes and food were in short supply. The people had useless currency, and almost everything purchased had to be paid for with edible goods such as chickens, eggs, meat, and flour, etc. Desperate families gathered early at the mill store in hopes of purchasing some of the small amounts of thread the company would sell for cash. Long lines formed, creating a mass of angry people outside the doors of the Public House.

The Public House looks out over the Roswell Park. In 1905 a gazebo was built there for President Teddy Roosevelt when he visited the birthplace of his mother, Minnie Bulloch. Roosevelt's mother was the daughter of the wealthy James Bulloch, and she and Teddy Sr. were married in the historic Bulloch Hall near The Public House. The fascinating history of the structure takes on added interest as it is reported to be haunted.

The restaurant management provided some information, prepared by Suzanne Stephens, which discusses the spirits as follows: Legend has it that The Public House is haunted by the spirits of Michael, a seventeen-year-old Union soldier, and

Katherine, his young love. Both are said to be quite active in the restaurant. Michael and Katherine have been known to dance through the loft, sit in the high-back chairs looking out over Roswell Square, and play mischievous jokes on the Public House staff. The loft area, which serves as a piano bar, was once the Roswell Funeral Home. There is a large opening over the dining room where coffins were lowered to the ground—an appropriate and comfortable home for Michael and Katherine.

According to management, curtains have been found hanging in positions not the way they were intended. Many unexplained noises come from inside when lone employees are working late. Miscellaneous items such as keys are often moved or hidden by some force to extremely out-of-the-way places in the restaurant. Pictures on the walls have been found turned toward the wall when people arrive for work, and there are times when the manager has opened the restaurant and found pots and pans strewn across the floor of the restaurant.

On several occasions the waitresses have inspected the tables, arranged for the next day, with napkins, silverware, and glassware properly in place. When the waitresses arrived first thing the next morning, they found one table in the corner in disarray. The napkins had been opened, silverware moved, and wineglasses relocated to a different spot, just as if someone had been eating there. Perhaps the two spirits of the Public House Restaurant wanted to spend some quality afterlife time alone by candlelight, listening to their favorite ethereal music, and reminiscing about their past life.

Three visitors once spotted the apparition of a young girl floating across the dining room, while other waiters and waitresses have sensed her presence at the top of the stairs. One guest actually saw Katherine's ghost standing at the top of the stairs for a few seconds before she vanished. The manager has noticed that the two wing-back chairs in the second floor loft have oftentimes been moved to face the window, as if two people were sitting down and watching the activity in the square below. Other staff members have witnessed chairs move by themselves. This phenomenon has occurred so many times that the activity is considered commonplace—it's no big deal. Sometimes the manager arrives at work in the morning and all the shades in the place are up, even though they had been drawn down the night before.

The spirited Public House has more to offer than just superb cuisine and a cozy setting. It also offers a tale of romance that transcends time and seems to be re-enacted within the walls of the spirited establishment on a regular basis.

Address:	605 South Atlanta Street, Roswell, Georgia 30075
Phone:	770-992-4646
Fax:	770-992-8320
Contact:	Mike Behan, general manager
Business Information:	lunch: Monday-Friday: 11:30 A.M.-2:30 P.M.; Saturday and Sunday 11:30 A.M.-3:00 P.M./dinner: Monday-Thursday 5:30-10:00 P.M.; Friday and Saturday 5:30-11:00 P.M.; and Sunday 5:30-9:00 P.M.
Payment:	Most major credit cards are accepted
References:	Personal communication, The Public House Restaurant; Barbara Duffey, *Angels and Apparitions: True Ghost Stories from the South*; Nancy Roberts, *Georgia Ghosts*; *Newcomer's Guide*, "Spirits Linger in Legend and Sighting," (July 22, 1990), Marietta, Georgia

17 ℏundred 90

Located in Savannah, Georgia, this Federal-style structure was built over the foundations of older buildings that date back to the 1790s—where the restaurant obtained its name. The restaurant walls are fashioned from very old brick, with the interior containing original wide beams and flagstone flooring. The garden dining area and kitchen are situated within a structure built around 1820 for Steele White, a prominent Savannah merchant, shortly after his marriage to Anna Matthewes Guerard.

The inn, restaurant, and lounge were refurbished in antiques and reproductions of the period. Chris Jurgenson came to Savannah in 1976 and bought the building where the restaurant is located. The present restaurant was born from a burned-out shell of a building. The building is listed on the National Register of Historic Places and is also listed as being very haunted.

The building is said to contain three spirits. The first is Anna Powell, who according to local lore was to have been married to a German sailor who went to war and never returned for her. Sad and despondent over her lost love, Anna committed suicide by jumping from the top of the house to her death. She has been felt throughout the inn by guests who mentioned returning to their room to find their clothes had been laid out for them in a meticulous fashion. There are also reports in the room of cold spots, mysterious footsteps, and lights that seem to have a mind of their own.

A second spirit is said to be that of an indentured servant who worked for the original owners in the original kitchen area, which is now the main dining room. When the restaurant/bed and breakfast opened for business in 1976 as the first full-service bed and breakfast in the historic district, it was reported that anytime a female waitress entered what used to be the servants' kitchen, knives and other utensils would relocate from the tables to the floor. This strong female presence may be that of a black cook—a large, aggressive woman who was in charge of the house in the 1850s. She has been sighted wearing several bracelets, and she does not want another woman in her kitchen.

A third ghost seems to be that of a merchant marine who lived above the carriage house while visiting Savannah. His apparition has been seen walking through the wall in the garden room (once a courtyard). A bartender once noticed a pale image going into the kitchen before disappearing through a wall.

On one occasion, several ladies came to the 17 Hundred 90 looking for a room. When they entered the upstairs bedroom, one of them leaned her head against a wall and, after a few seconds of silence, said there was a ghost in the room. The woman, who had psychic abilities, said the spirit was named Anna and that the

female phantom was very friendly. Anna, it seems, is responsible for unoccupied chairs that suddenly begin rocking back and forth, startling staff and customers. She has also been blamed for opening and closing windows in various parts of the building, making the old stairs creak when she decides to take a late night stroll, flushing toilets in some of the rooms while stunned guests look on, and for her strong persona, which follows people around the building.

But why blame everything on Anna? Sensations of cold that mysteriously pass through the corridors and rooms, chilling people to the bone, all the doors and windows that open and shut on their own, the gentle shoves that suggest one should get out of the way, the gentle whisperings from out of thin air, and other myriad unexplainable events that take place most certainly can be attributed to the ghostly triad, rather than a single spirit. Strange things continue to occur at the 17 Hundred 90 Inn, especially late at night and on Sundays. Oftentimes the telephone rings in what was once Anna's room, and there is no one there. Even the telephone company can't find the cause of the problem, and they say it's impossible for a phone to ring up there without going through the switchboard.

So the next time you visit this historic house, be prepared for some haunt cuisine, a rocking chair claimed by an otherworldly guest, an occasional toilet flushing on its own, a phantom phone call, and other strange events. If you are caught unprepared, you have only yourself to blame, not the spirits of the 17 Hundred 90 who await your visit.

Address:	307 East President Street, Savannah, Georgia 31401
Phone:	912-236-7122
Fax:	912-236-7123
Toll Free Number:	800-487-1790
Innkeeper:	Rita Dow
Accommodations:	14 beautifully appointed guestrooms
Amenities:	A complimentary bottle of wine; continental breakfast; the 17 Hundred 90 restaurant, and the Garden Room
Business Information:	lunch: (weekdays only): 11:30 A.M.-2:00 P.M./lounge: 12:00 noon-midnight/ cocktail hour: 4:30-8:00 P.M./ dinner nightly including Sunday from 6:00-10:00 P.M.
Payment:	Visa, MasterCard, American Express
References:	Personal communication, the 17 Hundred 90; Dennis William Hauck, *The National Directory: Haunted Places: A Guidebook to Ghostly Abodes, Sacred Sites, UFO Landings, and Other Supernatural Locations*; Nancy Rhyne, *Coastal Ghosts: Haunted Places From Wilmington, North Carolina to Savannah, Georgia*; Margaret Wayt De Bolt, *Savannah Spectres and Other Strange Tales*; Nancy Roberts, *Georgia Ghosts*

The Olde Pink House Restaurant and Planters Tavern

Today, the Pink House is a beloved local treasure, a widely recognized restaurant, and a national historic landmark. It is also the only remaining eighteenth-century mansion in Savannah. One of its many rooms was set aside as a conference room where secret meetings were held that eventually helped secure American independence. The Olde Pink House was one of the few buildings that survived the 1796 fire that destroyed over two hundred Savannah homes. Toward the end of the Civil War, it was headquarters for Union general Zebulon York.

The structure was built on land granted by the Spanish Crown in 1771. It was not only the talk of Savannah; its reputation reached the European continent. Originally the building was the home of James Habersham, a famous trader and governor of Georgia before independence. By 1811 the soft native brick began to bleed through the plastered walls and mysteriously changed the color of Habersham House from white to Jamaican pink, and that is where it obtained its name, the Pink House.

In 1811 the Habersham House became Georgia's first bank, the Planters Bank, containing the savings of all the colonists in the vicinity. The enormous cast-iron vaults with dungeon-like doors are used today as the wine cellars for the restaurant. In 1865 during Sherman's march to the sea, the halls of Habersham were opened to military generals, and General York set up headquarters. After the Civil War the property changed hands many times and was used as an office building, bookstore, and colonial tearoom—it also housed ghosts!

It is widely believed that the spirit of the original owner, James Habersham, haunts his former home, making his presence known primarily from October to March (probably because he chose not to live in the house during the hot and humid summer months when he was alive). Most of the former as well as current restaurant staff recalled stories about the ghostly phenomena, including the ghost's apparent love of lighting candles when the place was closed for the evening. On other occasions, passers-by have noticed candles lit after hours and not a soul stirring inside. A concerned report to the local authorities or owner always produced the same result—no one inside and nothing stolen.

Habersham's spirit is constantly brushing by staff members and guests, who have felt him as a cold breath of air or something that forced a chill up their backs. The popular ghost has been sighted in the kitchen and dining areas, where he is known to stand guard over the employees—they constantly report a feeling of being watched. Sometimes, when Habersham is pleased with a particular item on the menu, a waiter or waitress will sense him nearby and turn in time to see an approving look as his spirit floats back into the kitchen.

Gas fireplace logs suddenly will light by themselves and candles will flame up even though there is no one sitting at a particular table. Once, a bartender felt a firm hand on his shoulder as he was working. Thinking it was a fellow employee, he turned around but saw no one there. Habersham seems to pick on some employees, while not bothering others. They will hear their name called or actually feel as if someone is prodding or pushing them while they are working. The owner doesn't mind if Habersham keeps the staff on their toes.

The chandeliers have been known to sway from side to side for several minutes, then abruptly cease. Some mornings, when the manager arrives early, all of the candles resting on the tables and in the windows have burned down to the candleholders, though not a candle was left lit the night before.

One guest described the time he attended a banquet at the restaurant. While he was eating dinner, he felt as if someone was watching. He quickly looked up to see a strange-looking man standing across from his table, eyeing his main course. The man was attired in an old-fashioned suit and was staring at the guest intently. He recalled that the man was wearing a wig reminiscent of the late 1700s. After a few seconds of eye-to-eye contact, the guest turned to summon the waiter, who came rushing over. When the man turned to look at the odd intruder, he had vanished. He asked the waiter who the man in the period attire was, but the waiter had no idea who he was talking about, having seen no one that night fitting the description. The curious guest spent the rest of the night searching the house for the eighteenth-century gentleman—to no avail.

On another occasion, when a group of people were celebrating in the lounge area on the ground floor after the restaurant was closed for the evening, over twenty witnesses were greeted by the sight of a hazy, vaporous apparition descending the stairs and heading toward the tavern area. The stunned group ran from the building, not wanting to find out who it was or where the spirit was heading next.

Habersham's portrait still hangs in the building's foyer, which he had remodeled to his specifications before moving in about 1779. His father noted that his son was honorable, a gentleman of gentle temperament, and proud of his home. It seems as if James Habersham is so attached to his former residence that he refuses to leave. Come to think of it, why would he, with plenty of food, spirits, and so many guests to wait on.

Address:	23 Abercom St., Savannah, Georgia 31401
Phone:	912-232-4286
Fax:	912-231-1934
Contact:	Beth Double, general manager
Amenities:	The Olde Pink House is lovingly restored and furnished with antiques and paintings, with fireplaces aglow in every room. Below these stately dining rooms, two huge hearths, velvet sofas, polished brass work, and massive dark oak ceiling beams provide a dramatic setting in the Planters Tavern, Savannah's most popular night spot.
Business Information:	Restaurant: nightly from 5:30-10:30 P.M./Planters Tavern: 5:00-11:00 P.M. Sunday-Thursday; 5:00 P.M.-midnight Fridays and Saturdays
Payment:	Most major credit cards are accepted
References:	Personal communication, The Olde Pink House; Dennis William Hauck, *The National Directory: Haunted Places: A Guidebook to Ghostly Abodes, Sacred Sites, UFO Landings, and Other Supernatural Locations*; Nancy Rhyne, *Coastal Ghosts: Haunted Places From Wilmington, North Carolina to Savannah, Georgia*; Margaret Wayt De Bolt, *Savannah Spectres and Other Strange Tales*; Nancy Roberts, *Georgia Ghosts*

Kentucky

Wilder

Lexington

Bobby Mackey's

Deep, deep in yonder valley,
where the flowers are sweet in bloom,
There sleeps my own Pearl Bryan,
'neath the cold and silent tomb

Department of Library Special Collections,
Folklife Archives, of Western Kentucky
University, Bowling Green, Kentucky

Bobby Mackey's is located in Wilder, Kentucky, which is in Kenton County, across the Ohio River from Cincinnati. Bobby Mackey's has been the focus of a number of paranormal investigations over the years. Each investigation overwhelmingly concluded that the establishment is home to several negative spirits, who continue to raise hell.

The building, constructed in the 1850s, was used as a slaughterhouse, with a deep well excavated in the basement to contain animal blood and body fluids. When the packing plant closed down in the late 1800s, occult groups used the well for ritual purposes. In 1896 two cult members beheaded Pearl Bryan and used the well for their ceremonies. According to Douglas Hensley, author of *Hell's Gate*, Pearl was five months pregnant, and there were indications that she had been murdered after her boyfriend, Scott Jackson, botched his attempt to perform an abortion on poor Pearl. Two men, Alonzo Walling and Scott Jackson, were convicted of the murder and sentenced to death. Before being hanged the two men were offered life sentences in exchange for disclosing the location of Bryan's missing head—both refused.

During Prohibition, the building became a speakeasy where several mob-related murders occurred. In the 1930s the place became a nightclub called the Primrose and later, the Latin Quarter. The owner's daughter, Johanna, apparently fell in love with one of the singers at the club and became pregnant. The furious owner had the boyfriend killed. His daughter was so distraught that she first poisoned her father, then took her own life. The bodies of the father and daughter were found in the now notorious basement. An autopsy revealed that Johanna was five months pregnant at the time of her death.

Finally, the structure became a popular bar and dance location. However, even good times could not negate the tortured history of the place—a history that included ghosts.

Over the years, since Bobby Mackey's became a famous nightspot, reports of strange events have become commonplace. Staff and guests have reported events ranging from poltergeist-like phenomena, to disembodied voices, eerie laughter, and unexplained footsteps. Several individuals have been physically assailed by the unhappy spirits. Over thirty people have signed sworn affidavits to the effect that the place is haunted. A customer who was attacked in the men's room even tried to sue the owner because he did not have the ghost removed. For more information about the history of Bobby Mackey's Music World, we recommend the book *Hell's Gate* by Douglas Hensley.

An exorcism failed to halt the paranormal activity. In September 1994 a customer was assaulted in the men's restroom by a ghost wearing a cowboy hat. People who spent the night in the place were plagued by spirits entering their dreams. A staff member, who was also a caretaker, would check all the doors, windows,

and lights each night before retiring. As an added precaution he performed a second check to find that the bar lights would be on, the front doors would be unlocked, and the jukebox would be playing "The Anniversary Waltz," even though the machine was unplugged.

One of the ghosts has been described as a dark shadowy figure that was very angry. His presence would most often be felt or seen behind the bar. Also, the figure of a woman, who came to be known as Johanna, would be frequently sighted in various parts of the building. The spiritual energy in the basement was the strongest, most likely because it was the area where satanic practices occurred. It was the place where Pearl Bryan was murdered and the area where the blood from dead animals was poured—it became known simply as "Hell's Gate." Holy water sprinkled in the basement only seemed to rile the spirits. A cloud was seen rising up from the well, releasing something terribly evil during one of the frequent encounters between the living and the spirit world.

Of all the spirits residing at Bobby Mackey's, Johanna is said to be the most persistent. She always announces herself by leaving a scent of rose perfume. No one else ever wore that brand, and yet it would permeate the club for extended periods of time. Some psychics believe that when Joanna leaves her calling card, a tragedy will follow shortly. Former owner Buck Brady, who was told by the Mafia to sell or die, sold but swore vengeance on the gang. He is said to be yet another in the long list of ghosts who frequent the establishment.

The owner's wife even felt the evil force and smelled the rose perfume. When she was five months pregnant, she was in the basement when the scent of roses filled the air. Within seconds an unseen force swirled around her and something grabbed her around the waist, as if it was trying to get her child. It picked her up and threw her down. She finally got away, but not before hearing something vehemently yelling at her to get out of the place.

On one occasion, a man performing odd jobs at the club was removing old light fixtures from the dance floor. As a staff person approached, he noticed small handprints on the back of the worker, as if someone had been hugging him. There was no one else in the club at the time. Many witnesses have reported seeing the spectral image of a headless woman moving through the nightclub and a man standing behind the door. People have been pushed, shoved, touched, and whispered to. There are ghosts in the bathroom, on the stage, in the caretaker's apartment, near the bucking bronco, in the main bar, and in the basement. It is a spirited establishment that still caters to those who like music, dancing, and the spirits who remain behind.

Address:	44 Licking Place, Wilder, Kentucky 41076
Phone:	606-431-6588
E-mail:	bmackey@aol.com
Contacts:	Bobby and Janet Mackey
Business Information:	open Friday and Saturday night from 7:30 P.M.-2:30 A.M.; cash only; wheelchair accessible
References:	Personal communication, Bobby Mackey's; Dennis William Hauck, *The National Directory: Haunted Places: A Guidebook to Ghostly Abodes, Sacred Sites, UFO Landings, and Other Supernatural Location*; Troy Taylor, *Ghosts of the Prairie*; Ghost Research Society, *Ghost Trackers Newsletter* (February 1992); Susan Michaels, *Sightings: Beyond Imagination Lies the Truth*; *FATE Magazine,* Patricia Bowskill, "The Haunted Honky- Tonk," April 1997; Douglas Hensley, *Hell's Gate: Terror at Bobby Mackey's Music World* (1994).

Gratz Park Jnn

Lexington is Kentucky's second largest city and the commercial center of the Bluegrass Country. Originally a hemp producing city, it became a major tobacco producer after the Civil War. Today, Lexington is the country's chief producer of blue grass seed and white barley, and it continues a long tradition of raising Thorough-bred horses.

The picturesque colonial revival building isn't officially located in the Gratz Park Historic area. In 1912 one of the founders of the Lexington Clinic, Dr. William Bullock, purchased the Bodley-Bullock house at 200 Market Street, which was in turn bought by General Thomas Bodley for his family of twelve children, shortly after being built by Thomas Pindell.

Construction of the building was begun in 1916 for Dr. Waller O. Bullock, Dr. David Woolfolk Barrow, and Dr. Barrow's father, Dr. David Barrow. Inspired by the Mayo Clinic, the three doctors began a joint practice in 1916. They commissioned Frankel and Curtis of Lexington to construct the colonial revival two-story Upper Street front and matching one-story Second Street wing. The practice grew, and in 1920 nine doctors, including the original three founders, opened the Lexington Clinic. The clinic enlarged the wing on Second Street and added a number of rooms to accommodate the increase in patients.

During 1958, as the Lexington Clinic relocated to Harrodsburg Road, the Fuller Engineering firm began occupying the building. After Fuller Engineering moved out in 1976, the building sat vacant until 1987, when renovation began on what is now the Gratz Park Inn. In addition, a third story was added to the original building. Restoring the building literally turned it around—the new address was now 120 Second Street. The change in address, as well as the complete renovation of the former clinic building, must have stirred up a number of otherworldly clientele. It was shortly after the opening of the Gratz Park Inn that its spirited past came to life.

Since it opened as an inn, staff and guests have reported a number of strange sightings and events that have taken place inside. One shaken guest reported seeing a little girl playing with her jacks in front of the elevator. When the guest called out to the child, she laughed and ran around the corner. The guest gave pursuit, but when he turned the corner the child had simply vanished into thin air. From that moment on, the child was given the name Anna. She has been frequently sighted throughout the hotel, particularly on the second floor, by staff and guests. She has been described as cute, very young, dressed in Victorian clothing, and usually laughing, singing, playing with her dolls or jacks, and trying to engage anyone she can in a game of hide-and-seek. As people give chase, Anna will duck into closets, hide behind doors, and disappear as a corridor makes a left or a right turn. After the frustrated chase is concluded, many individuals will hear her childish laughter echo through the empty rooms and down deserted corridors. The more people play with Anna, the more the sightings increase.

Another, more mischievous spirit has been called John. It seems this spirit likes to put a little scare into guests by awakening them in the middle of the night. He has been credited with turning on the television or turning the volume on the radio way up when guests are just lying around or already in bed. His laughter has been heard reverberating down deserted hallways, and he has been known to appear as a filmy shadow. No one is sure whether it is John or Anna who is responsible for causing cold gusts of air to brush by unsuspecting people, playing with electrical appliances, causing unexplained footsteps, or emanating a strong energy force that causes people to look around as if they are being watched or followed.

On the third floor, guests have periodically complained of hearing people pacing around in a room above theirs, or they have reported to the main desk that a loud party is in progress in a room next to theirs. A majority of the time the polite staff members have to tactfully point out that either there is no one staying above them, since the third floor is the top floor of the hotel, or that the

room next door is unoccupied. The staff is quite used to respond-
ing to the ghostly pranks.

A final Gratz Park Inn phantom is a strange black man who
sometimes wanders into the laundry room, standing almost at
attention without speaking as housekeeping is doing their chores.
He has given many a housekeeper a case of the jitters, especially
when he vanishes in front of them. In the early 1900s the laundry
room was the county morgue, and perhaps the man died there or
assisted in some manner. The former Lexington Clinic turned
Gratz Park Inn has something for everyone, including a few spirits
who refuse to leave their favorite haunt.

Address:	120 W. Second Street, Lexington, Kentucky 40507
Phone:	606-231-1777
Fax:	606-233-7593
Toll Free:	1-800-678-8946
Amenities:	Complimentary continental breakfast; afternoon tea; evening cordials; limousine service; daily paper; dining and distilled spirits in the Tap Room
Accommodations:	38 guestrooms and 6 suites, each individually deco-rated in the nineteenth-century antique reproduc-tions, mahogany four-poster beds, and artwork from the region

Payment:	Most major credit cards are accepted
References:	Personal communication, Gratz Park Inn; Robin Mead, *Haunted Hotels: A Guide to American and Canadian Inns and Their Ghosts* (1995)

Old Absinthe House Bar

On a conspicuous corner of Bourbon and Bienville in New Orleans's French Quarter stands a famed antique building known as the Old Absinthe House. This square building of plaster and brick was visited by Mark Twain, Oscar Wilde, William Thackeray, Walt Whitman, and Aaron Burr.

The building was constructed in 1806 by two Spanish importers, Francisco Juncadella and Pedro Font. It continued as a commission house for various foodstuffs until 1820, when it was turned into an epicure and then a bootshop. Finally, in 1846, the ground floor corner room became a saloon known as Aleix's Coffee House, run by Jacinto Aleix and his brother, who were nephews of the widow of Juncadella.

Absinthe was being sold from this building as early as 1826. In 1869 the Aleix brothers hired Cayetano Ferrer, another Catalan, who had been a barkeeper at the French Opera House, to work for them. In 1874 Cayetano himself leased the place and renamed it the Absinthe Room because of the numerous requests he had for the drink, which he served in the Parisian manner. The building in which the drinking establishment was located was later called the Old Absinthe House.

After the doors to the bar were nailed shut by the U.S. Marshal during Prohibition in 1926, Pierre Casebonne bought the cash register, the paintings on the wall, the old water dripper, and the marble topped bar from which absinthes had been served and moved them to what is now the Old Absinthe House Bar at 400 Bourbon Street (at Conti). The original Absinthe Room is still a bar, called Jean Lafitte's Old Absinthe House, named after the myth that the pirate Lafitte used to hold clandestine meetings here.

Psychics agree that the Old Absinthe House Bar is filled to the brim with spirits. The Battle of New Orleans was planned in the building, and its colorful history is filled with good times and violence—so much so, that spirits from every time period seem to roam the bar and dining areas. In particular, the ghost of renowned pirate Jean Lafitte has been frequently sighted walking on the second floor and then vanishing in front of startled staff members. The pirate has also been known to show himself in a vanity mirror.

One fall day an employee named Jeff went up to his apartment on the third floor to change his attire. As he was standing in front of the mirror, a bright light flashed in the background, and to his amazement, a man was suddenly standing behind him. Jeff noted that the strange-looking man was wearing a feathered hat, an open shirt, and something tied around his waist. The figure just stared at Jeff as if inspecting the clothes he was trying on. By the time Jeff got up the courage to turn around, the image had vanished. He searched the room for several minutes but to no avail. He also recalled that when the apparition appeared the room had become icy cold.

On another occasion, a lone employee was closing up late at night. After completing his tasks, he decided to sit in the dining room while grabbing a late snack. All of a sudden, a blustery wind filtered through the dining room, and the two doors that separated the kitchen from the dining area blew back and forth as if someone had just walked in or out of the room. It was 4:00 A.M., and the brave employee immediately decided to check the place out just in case someone had broken in. There was no one but him inside the

cold, eerie bar and dining room—at least that he could see. He quickly downed his food, locked up, and left.

Several psychics have felt a strong male energy at work inside the establishment, and there have been reports of apparitions, strange power outages, plates being tossed, of chairs being moved by unseen hands, and of guests and employees being touched or gently pushed when no one else is around. The scent of perfume has been known to accompany a sighting, and putting the furniture back in place after it has been moved during the night continues to be an on-going problem.

Another sighting of Jean Lafitte occurred by the stairs near the bar area in 1997. A member of the staff was going through her usual closing routine by first securing the second floor and then coming downstairs to secure the bar area. There is a dining area located behind the bar, obscured from view by a white tile counter, similar to an oyster bar, approximately five feet high. As the woman was facing the bar, it seemed as if time suddenly stood still. The air was still, and a deathly silence engulfed the area. Walking directly toward the staff person was a strange-looking man who was smiling at the woman. He had very tanned skin, almost leathery, his eyes were brown, with an almost mischievous expression, he was thirty-five to forty years old, with a long, curved, waxed mustache covering his lip. The gentleman was wearing royal blue pants and a fine red shirt with a bandoleer bullet holder draped over it. As the man approached, the staff person stood frozen. Their eyes were fixed on one another, as the man walked right through the bar and just vanished.

On other occasions parties have been held on the second floor while employees were cleaning up downstairs. It was after hours each time, and no one knew what to make of the merriment. It sounded as if forty to fifty people had suddenly arrived out of nowhere and began having the time of their lives. Each time the staff investigated, there was no physical form to the laughter and myriad voices. Most of the time when the staff investigated, a few chairs had been moved, and occasionally one or two would be found lying on the floor, but other than that, it was a ghost party that no one could see or join in.

A ghostly woman, a lost child, phantom partygoers, Jean Lafitte, and many other characters seem to like the upstairs dining area and basement bar area. The tunnels that have been found leading under the structure have also been a source of mysterious voices, noises, and shadowy figures from the days when pirates used to bring their bounty into town in the dead of night by way of underground passages. One thing all the ghosts of the old structure have in common, there is an absinthe of malice—no one has ever been threatened or harmed.

Address:	240 Bourbon Street, New Orleans, Louisiana 70116
Phone/Fax:	504-523-3181
Contacts:	Jeannette Moran, and Kristin Rosen
Payment:	All major credit cards are accepted
References:	Personal communication, Old Absinthe House

Commander's Palace

The Commander's Palace is nestled in the middle of the Garden District. The building is a turquoise-and-white Victorian fantasy of a building, complete with turrets, columns, and gingerbread. Since 1880 Commander's Palace has been a New Orleans landmark known for the award-winning quality of its food and a number of dining rooms.

In the early 1800s, when Louisiana officially joined the nation, eager young Anglo-Saxons flocked to this promising territory to make their fortunes. Since the Vieux Carre was the stronghold of the proud Creoles, these "Americans" (as they were referred to by the Creoles) sought a residential section of their own. Thus was born the Garden District, with its stately Greek Renaissance homes and quiet tree-lined streets.

In the Garden District, George W. Cable entertained Mark Twain, and Jefferson Davis spent his last days there. Also in 1880 Emile Commander established the only restaurant patronized by the distinguished neighborhood families. He chose the corner of Washington Avenue and Coliseum Street, a site that had been part of the J.F.E. Livaudais Plantation. In 1854 it was swallowed by the growing city of New Orleans, and by 1900 Commander's Palace was attracting gourmets from all over the world.

Under different management in the twenties, riverboat captains frequented Commander's, and sporting gentlemen met with beautiful women for a rendezvous in one of the private upstairs dining rooms. However, the main dining room downstairs, with its separate entrance, maintained respectability for family meals after church and family gatherings. In 1944 Frank and Elinor Moran bought Commander's Palace, refurbished it, and carried on its tradition of excellence.

When Ella, Dottie, Dick, and John Brennan took over personal supervision of the restaurant in 1974, they provided the splendid old landmark with a new look. It was decided to design rooms and settings indoors that complemented and enhanced the beautiful outdoor setting. Therefore the decor was planned for a bright, casual airiness. The solid walls were removed and replaced with walls of glass. Trellises were handmade for the garden rooms, and paintings were commissioned for each room to complement and accent a room's particular color and design. After a new spirit was instilled in the Commander's Palace, an old spirit came out of the woodwork, Emile Commander.

The Commander's Palace is believed to be haunted by the spirit of the original owner of the restaurant. The Commander frequents one of the upstairs dining rooms known as the Sun Porch.

One night the table was set for a dinner party of twelve guests. The host wanted the staff to pre-pour the wine so it could breathe for a while before the guests arrived. About an hour later, when the party was escorted into the dining room, the doors to the balcony overlooking the cemetery across the street (Lafayette #1) were opened, and one of the glasses of wine was completely empty. No one had entered the room between the time the tables were set and the time the guests arrived—it was a mystery.

Every now and again unexplainable occurrences take place in the Sun Porch dining room, as well as other areas of the establishment. Dishes and silverware are rearranged by unseen hands, chairs are moved from one location to another, and an occasional full glass of liquor is mysteriously consumed. Staff was reluctant to talk about unexplained footsteps that can be heard walking the building late at night and the occasional door that will open and close by itself. Certain lights also seem to have a mind of their own, but all of the activity is quite benign.

There is little doubt that the Commander still considers this his home, so essentially everyone in the building is his guest. All he asks is that you enjoy yourself and perhaps either raise a glass in his memory or better yet, save a glass for him to consume.

Address:	1403 Washington Ave., New Orleans 70130
Phone:	504-899-8221
Fax:	504-891-3242
Contact:	Lisa Kuebel
Business Information:	Lunch (Monday-Friday) 11:30 A.M.-1:30 P.M./Jazz Brunch (Sunday) 10:30 A.M.-1:30 P.M. (Saturday) 11:30 A.M.-12:30 P.M./dinner hours: Sunday-Thursday 6:00-10:00 P.M.; Friday-Saturday 6:00-10:00 P.M.; closed: Christmas Eve, Christmas Day, and Mardi Gras Day; the restaurant is wheel-chair accessible on the first floor
Payment:	All major credit cards accepted
References:	Personal communication, Commander's Palace

The Delta Queen

The *Delta Queen* is one of three stern-wheel paddle steamers that still operate year round on the Mississippi, Cumberland, and Ohio Rivers from New Orleans, Minneapolis/St. Paul, and Pittsburgh. The authentic *Delta Queen* is a national historic landmark. Once, thousands of paddle wheelers cruised up and down the Mississippi River. Today, there are only a few that still make the river voyage, and the *Delta Queen* is one of those throwbacks to an all but forgotten era.

The *Queen* had an illustrious career after its stint on the Mississippi, operating a shuttle along the Sacramento River from the mid-1920s until 1940. During World War II, the navy painted the *Delta Queen* gray and used it to ferry military personnel to and from ships docked in San Francisco Bay. The boat was later moved to Pittsburgh to undergo complete refurbishment. The *Delta Queen* offers visitors a chance to relive an unforgettable historic American waterway journey by offering three- to fourteen-night excursions along the Mississippi, Ohio, Tennessee, Arkansas, Atchafalya, and Cumberland Rivers. It also gives tourists a chance to meet one of only two qualified female pilots on the Mississippi, Captain Mary Greene. The interesting thing is, Captain Greene is dead.

Captain Mary Greene was in charge of the *Delta Queen* when the ship was first moved from San Francisco to the Mississippi in 1947. Her picture still hangs in the ship's Betty Blake Lounge—an irony, because she did not allow alcohol on board while she was alive. She died in 1949 in what is now Cabin 109. Before passing away, Greene said she loved every single day she sailed the *Queen* and had no regrets. After Mary Greene's death, the owners of the *Delta Queen* quickly opened the ship's first bar in the forward passenger lounge. It was the end of an era but not the end of Mary Greene.

Hundreds of unexplained events have taken place aboard the *Delta Queen* since she was accidentally rammed by a giant barge

that operated along the Mississippi. Oddly enough, the barge was named the Mary Greene. Engineers were finally able to separate the two ships, but since that time the spirit of its former captain lingers aboard ship, perhaps to make sure nothing bad ever happens to her ship again. She is frequently sighted near the lounge, the bar, and in Cabin 106. Her ghost has been known to open and close the transoms in the forward passenger lounge, attend parties, open and close doors as she enters and leaves, wander the corridors, and even pay visits to certain passengers.

Captain Greene was once seen in the Betty Blake Lounge by a female passenger who slept in one of the cabins facing the lounge. The woman had left her room during the night to get a book, when she was confronted by a very real-looking, green, glowing image of a woman wearing a housecoat. The female figure didn't speak but smiled, nodded sympathetically, and walked away, as the passenger went back to her room. The next day the passenger told her story to the captain after she realized that she had not seen the woman in a green housecoat prior to or after the incident. The captain listened intently, then took the woman to the wheelhouse where he showed her a picture of Captain Mary Greene. The passenger instantly confirmed that this was the woman she not only saw, but also spoke to. Captain Greene apparently was still taking an interest in the wellbeing of her passengers.

Other passengers have seen Mary Greene on holiday cruises, including a flu-ridden and feverish woman who was on board with her mother-in-law. While resting during the day in a cabin near the Betty Blake Lounge, she was going through the worst of her illness, when she was visited by someone she thought was her mother-in-law, who soothed her brow and offered her aspirin. Much to the surprise of the sick passenger, her mother-in-law later said she had been onshore all day and could not have possibly come into her room to comfort her. The woman knew someone had tended to her, and she knew she did not dream the encounter. She told her mother-in-law that she remembered the woman who came to her aid wore a green housecoat. The two women later learned that the description of the helpful lady fit Captain Greene perfectly.

Mike Williams had a strange experience aboard ship in 1982. He was sleeping in his bunk around 2:00 A.M. when he was suddenly awakened by someone next to him trying to get his attention by whispering in his ear. When he turned on the light and looked around the room, there was no one there. Brushing the incident off, he tried to go back to sleep. Within seconds the same whispering sound forced him out of bed. Rather than have the voice wake him up again, he decided to see who might be the cause of this annoying game. As Williams left his room, he heard a door in the aft cabin lounge slam shut in front of him. Chasing the sound, he continued below deck and reached the engine room. To his surprise, water was gushing in from a broken, rusted pipe. Had the phantom whisperer (Williams believed it to be Captain Mary Greene) not alerted him, the *Delta Queen* most likely would have sunk.

Calls have come into the front desk from rooms that are unoccupied. There is a feeling sometimes of being watched when no one else is around. And late at night in the lounge and in some of the corridors, guests have sighted Mary Greene still keeping an eye on her ship. She usually floats by without taking notice of the passengers; however, sometimes she is there to lend a guiding hand or simply to reassure passengers that everything is safe aboard the *Delta Queen*.

A cruise aboard the ship is like taking a step back in time, and Captain Mary Greene is sometimes there to lend a helping hand in case you have any questions or may be in need of some comforting. It's still her ship, you know.

Address:	Robin Street Wharf, 1380 Port of New Orleans Place, New Orleans, Louisiana 70130-1890
Phone:	504-586-0631
Fax:	504-585-0630
Toll Free Number:	1-800-678-8946
Contact:	Terri Monaghan
Facts:	Length: 285 feet, 174 passenger capacity, crew: 81, one ghost
Accommodations:	87 authentically appointed outside staterooms feature period furnishings, patchwork quilts, collectibles, brass fittings, and wood-shuttered windows to view your trip up the Mississippi; rates include room, meals, and entertainment
Amenities:	Betty Blake Lounge, Forward Cabin Lounge, Gift Shop, Orleans Room, Texas Lounge.
Payment:	All major credit cards are accepted
References:	Personal communication, *Delta Queen*; Robin Mead, *Haunted Hotels: A Guide to American and Canadian Inns and Their Ghosts*; National Trust for Historic Preservation (1996), Historic Hotels of America, Washington, D.C.; *The History Channel*– "Haunted History, New Orleans" (1998); Dixie Franklin, *Haunts of the Upper Great Lakes*

Royal Cafe

The Royal Cafe is also known as the LaBranche House and is considered one of the most photographed buildings in New Orleans. The structure is located in the French Quarter at the confluence of the world-famous Royal and St. Peter Streets. The property dates back to 1796 when Marianne Dubreuil, a free woman of color, owned the property. Structures built prior to 1794 were destroyed in the fires of 1788 and 1794. The property was then sold to several other free people of color until a four-story structure was built in 1832 by a wealthy sugar planter, Jean Baptiste LaBranche (known as Zweig in his native Germany).

Jean Baptiste married Marie Melanie Trepagnier, and they had three sons: Jean Louis, Euphemon, and Cyprien. Using the finest materials and craftsman, he created a showplace of craftsmanship and elegance. In 1842 Mrs. LaBranche added the wrought iron balconies that exist today. She sold the building and all its additions to Paul Napoleon Rivera in 1866. Between 1866 and 1996 this property was sold over thirty times. After nearly one hundred seventy-five years of hurricanes and other disasters, the building endures. A philanderer most of his married life, after LaBranche died in 1842 his wife found her dead husband's mistress and murdered her.

The Royal Cafe is said to be haunted by the ghost of LaBranche's mistress, as well as Mrs. LaBranche. It is believed that LaBranche's mistress is responsible for moving tables, chairs, and other furnishings around the restaurant offices and has been known to throw a coffee cup across the sales manager's desk. A number of guests and staff have encountered the strong presence of Mrs. LaBranche on the second floor of the restaurant. Too often to count, individuals have commented on feeling as if someone was watching them or standing next to them; however, there is never anyone there when people look around. Manifestations of Mrs. LaBranche are rare, yet she has been spotted in the restaurant wearing a dark blue dress, with long, styled, black and gray hair. She has also been sighted wearing a tasteful selection of jewelry.

The International Society for Paranormal Research (ISPR), now located in Los Angeles, California, conducted an intensive investigation that revealed the presence of two entities in the LaBranche building. A search of the first floor resulted in no anomalies. The second floor, however, was an entirely different matter. A thorough walk-through produced the energy of a young woman in her early twenties, with long, light brown to blonde hair, and wearing a long, plain, white dress. The third floor was even more intense.

When ISPR investigated the two suites on the third floor, the energy from a female named Melissa was very intense in the first suite. The second suite was very negative and agitated and

seemed to belong to Mrs. LaBranche, who walks the entire floor. The ISPR research team believed that Mr. LaBranche was having an affair with the young girl named Melissa. A short time after his death, LaBranche's wife found the girl, brought her to the attic, chained her to an outside brick wall, then starved her to death. This represents the same location as the renovated office. Numerous anomalies have occurred since the renovations, including problems with the computer system and other electrical conveniences. There have also been cold spots reported, along with unexplained footsteps, doors opening and shutting on their own, and an occasional light switch that is toyed with by the playful spirits of this restaurant. The Royal Cafe is a famous New Orleans landmark with a colorful past that includes several spirits who continue to make the place their home.

Address:	706 Royal St., New Orleans, Louisiana 70116
Phone:	504-528-9086
Fax:	504-528-9235
Contact:	John Stern
Accommodations:	Executive suites conveniently located in the center of the French Quarter
Amenities:	Each suite boasts its own balcony with a magnificent view. Exquisite eighteenth century antiques fill each room. A private, ninety-foot covered balcony wraps around the building, affording one of the most spectacular views of the Vieux Carrel.
Payment:	Most major credit cards accepted
References:	Personal communication, Royal Cafe; Daena Smoller, *The Official ISPR Self-Guided Ghost Expedition of New Orleans*

Dauphine Orleans

A red light still burns in the hotel's courtyard next to May Bailey's Place, a reminder of a time when the building served as a house of ill repute. Today guests are provided with a copy of the license issued to May in 1857, when prostitution was legal in New Orleans. Records of the Dauphine Orleans' site date from 1775, and several of the original structures survive, including what is now known as the Audubon Cottage where, from 1821-22, John James Audubon painted his noted "Birds of America" portraits. The restored cottage serves as the hotel's main meeting room.

Fourteen spacious patio suites, located across from the main hotel, were initially built in 1834 as the home of a prosperous merchant, Samuel Hermann. The original building contract outlines Mr. Hermann's detailed instructions right down to the size of the nails and the number of coats of paint required to complete the job. Hermann also demanded only the best country brick, sand, and cypress be used in the construction of his residence.

In 1991 the cottages were renovated, revealing the brick walls and wooden posts used in the initial house construction. The handmade nails are believed to have come from the Old Jean Lafitte Blacksmith Shop. Stone fireplaces and the original pecky cypress and pine beams had also been covered by sheetrock. Today, they are an integral part of the suites' unique decor. The

property's initial owners were among the first families of the area. Some of those early inhabitants who used the building are still hanging around.

Between 1985 and 1986 the International Society for Paranormal Research (ISPR) conducted a number of paranormal investigations at the Dauphine Orleans Hotel. The cottage on the corner (Audubon Studio - #401 Dauphine) was used as a saloon and pool hall in 1896. There has been quite a bit of paranormal activity at the hotel over the years. ISPR witnessed a white male entity in the hotel lounge (called May Bailey's). The spirit was approximately 5'7" or 5'8" and noticeably thin. A bartender also saw the apparition of a white man with gray hair and wearing a white suit and a Panama-tyle hat, floating through the lounge area. This ghost has been responsible for knocking books off the shelves in the lounge library when he seeks attention or is upset.

Suite 111, located above the bar, has also been a paranormal hotbed of activity. Objects have been reported moved from their original location, and when guests forget to lock the front door after leaving, some otherworldly force does it for them. On a few occasions people have reported seeing the spirit of a black man in the room, a ghost that has been named George.

Suite 110 has also had its share of strange occurrences. The door has refused to open when people have tried to enter, as if someone on the other side did not want people entering—that someone is a ghost. Lights have failed to work or have gone on and off on their own. There is also the pervasive feeling of being watched by an unseen force while staying in the room. The curtains in the room are frequently found pulled to one side, as if yanked hard to the side by someone. Of course, this happens most often when the room is unoccupied and housekeeping comes in to perform their routine.

The courtyards have also been known to entertain a dark-complected male entity of possible Spanish or French decent. He is frequently described as thin, with long hair, and wearing a dark blue uniform with red and white trim (reminiscent of a soldier from the War of 1812). A female entity named Estelle or Estella had been sighted with long hair and wearing a long dress with no shoes. She has been seen on a number of occasions playfully dancing around the courtyard. A visit to the Dauphine Orleans is sure to provide more than a good night's sleep, a good dinner, or a pleasant conversation at the bar. You may be treated to its resident spirits.

Address:	415 Dauphine Street, New Orleans, Louisiana 70112
Phone:	504-586-1800
Fax:	504-586-1409
Toll Free Number:	1-800-508-5554
E-mail:	reservations@dauphineorleans.com/ dohfq@aol.com
Amenities:	A palm-filled courtyard and pool; welcome cocktail upon arrival; enhanced continental breakfast; afternoon tea; fitness and exercise room; complimentary drink with lunch or dinner; guest library; coffee lounge open every morning from 6:30 until 11:00; May Bailey's serves as the bar of the Dauphine Orleans Hotel
Accommodations:	111 guestrooms; 15 suites—some feature Jacuzzis
Payment:	Most major credit cards accepted
References:	Personal communication, Dauphine Orleans Hotel; International Society for Paranormal Research (ISPR)

Antoine's Restaruant

Antoine's, the world-famous New Orleans restaurant serving French/Creole cuisine, was established in 1840 and is now fifth-generation family owned. There are fifteen dining rooms, each with their own personality.

Antoine Alciatore came to New Orleans in 1840 after trying to establish a restaurant in New York. It was on St. Louis Street that twenty-seven-year-old Alciatore started Antoine's. After a brief period in the kitchen of the grand St. Charles Hotel, Antoine opened a pension, a boardinghouse, and a restaurant. After the Pension Alciatore was firmly established, Alciatore made arrangements for his fiancée to join him from New York. She came to New Orleans with her sister, and she and Antoine were married. Together they worked to build up their pension with culinary emphasis. New Orleans' gentility was so taken with the restaurant that it soon outgrew its small quarters, and Antoine's moved down the block and eventually, in 1868, to the spot on St. Louis Street where the restaurant stands today. In 1874 Antoine, being in ill health, took leave of his family and returned to France where he died.

Jules served as apprentice under his mother's tutelage for six years before she sent him to France where he served in the great kitchens of Paris, Strassburg, and Marseilles. He returned to New Orleans, becoming chef of the famous Pickwick Club in 1887 before his mother summoned him to head the house of Antoine.

Jules married Althea Roy, daughter of a planter in Youngsville in southwest Louisiana, and Marie Louise, the grand dame of the family, was born. A son, Roy Louis, was born in 1902 and headed the restaurant for almost forty years until his death in 1972. Roy Alciatore managed the restaurant through the Prohibition era and World War II. Marie Louise married William Guste, and their sons, William Jr., former attorney general of Louisiana, and Roy Sr., became the fourth generation of the family to head the restaurant. In 1975 Roy's son, Roy Jr., became proprietor and served until 1984. He was followed by William's son, Bernard "Randy" Guste, who heads the restaurant today. At least one of the family members remains behind to oversee things from the other side.

Several spirits are rumored to haunt Antoine's, the most famous being the original owner, Antoine Alciatore. Guests and staff confirm the presence of Alciatore's ghost, since sightings of the man bear a striking resemblance to early photographs of the man who founded Antoine's. Even the descendants of Alciatore have come across their deceased ancestor, who they say is still checking up on the family business to see how it is running—just fine thank you.

On one occasion a family member was making some prepara-
tions just outside the Japanese Room, when he chanced to look up

and see what he thought was a busboy enter the room. As he followed the person, who was dressed in a white uniform, he reached for the door, but it was locked from the outside. Extremely curious at this point, he quickly unlocked the door, entered the room, and found no one; there was no other way in or out.

Another time a relative was carrying important documents to an upstairs office. As he was about to ascend the stairs, he looked up to see a glowing figure, without discernible features, standing on the landing. As he stood dumbstruck, he watched as the glowing figure vanished in front of him.

A staff person claimed to have seen Alciatore enter the Mystery Room. At first he thought the strange-looking man was the headwaiter, so when the man entered the room, he quickly followed, since he had a question that needed answering. Upon entering the room, he looked around and there was no one there. Returning to the front, he saw the headwaiter and asked him why he disappeared so quickly in the Mystery Room. Disappear was the operative word, for the headwaiter claimed to have never left his post. The other waiter then described in detail what the other man looked like. The headwaiter smiled and told the man that he had just witnessed the spirit of Antoine Alciatore, who had a habit of going into that room and then vanishing. The young waiter vowed never to go into the Mystery Room alone again.

A cashier has also spotted a man wearing a tuxedo and standing in the dining room. The cashier did a double take because the unusual-looking person was almost transparent. Within a second or two, the figure completely disappeared and was nowhere to be found inside the restaurant.

Address:	713-717 Rue Saint Louis, New Orleans, Louisiana 70130
Phone:	504-581-4422
Fax:	504-581-3003
E-mail:	info@antoines.com
Business Information:	Open for lunch and dinner on Monday through Saturday. Lunch seating is from 11:30 A.M. to 2:00 P.M. Dinner seating is from 5:30 to 9:30 P.M. The restaurant is closed on Sundays, Mardi Gras Day, Memorial Day, July 4th, Labor Day, Thanksgiving,

	Christmas, and New Year's Day. No jeans or shorts. A coat is required for dinner!
Payment:	American Express Card, Diners Club, Visa, Master Card, and Antoine's house accounts
References:	Personal communication, Antoine's; *FATE Magazine* ("Haunted New Orleans," by Charles Coulombe, October 1998)

Le Pavillon Hotel

Located on the site of one of the area's first great plantation homes, Le Pavillon is situated in the heart of historic New Orleans. Opened in 1907, it received instant international acclaim as one of America's most notable new hotels. It has been exquisitely restored.

Originally owned by the Sieur de Bienville (founder of the city), it was then purchased by the Jesuits. After the Jesuits were forced to leave, the land was bought by Mr. Jean Gravier, a wealthy sugar cane and indigo plantation owner. The early 1830s witnessed the birth of the New Orleans and Carrollton railroad, the oldest in the city. When the railroad depot was no longer utilized, the structure was remodeled and was a showcase for circuses, traveling shows, and other attractions.

In 1867 the National Theater, often called the German Theater, was built. In the 1870s the property was owned by Philip Werlein, founder of the famous music store, and the theater became known as Werlein Hall. It was destroyed under mysterious circumstances in 1889. In 1899 ownership of the property went to La Baronne Realty Company. They built a hotel soon to be known worldwide for its modern amenities and splendid luxury. The New Hotel Denechaud was completed in 1907 and was the first building in New Orleans to have hydraulic elevators installed, as well as the first building ever with a basement. In 1970, under new ownership, the hotel was restored and was renamed Le

Pavillon. On June 24, 1991, Le Pavillon was placed on the National Register of Historic Places.

During August of 1996 the International Society for Paranormal Research (ISPR) investigated the hotel. In the restaurant dining room, they recorded a high electromagnetic energy field, and two psychic investigators sensed the presence of a male and female energy near the buffet tables. A third cold spot was also recorded and remained for roughly thirty seconds.

The second floor by way of the staircase yielded high electromagnetic readings, and a majority of the investigators felt the sensation of heat while they were in that location. While walking through the second-floor hallway, the entire team and hotel management experienced a strong sulfur smell, which seemed to pass through the group. Once again, the presence of the couple was detected.

Some group members witnessed an apparition of a young man in a dark suit on the third floor. On the fourth floor everyone experienced the smell of sulfur. The man in the dark suit was seen again on the sixth floor. As soon as everyone emerged from the stairwell onto the ninth floor, the energy of a sixteen- to nineteen-year-old girl named Eva, Ava, or Aida was sighted. She was wearing a long blue dress of empire design from the 1830s or 1840s. Investigators believe she may have died nearby.

Le Pavillon has been beautifully restored and would be worth a visit or stay, even if it wasn't haunted. But it is, and that makes the visit even more enticing.

Address:	833 Poydras Street, New Orleans, Louisiana 70112
Phone:	504-581-3111
Fax:	504-523-7434
Toll Free:	1-800-678-8946
Accommodations:	219 guestrooms, seven suites
Amenities:	Valet parking; heated rooftop pool; fitness center; dining in the Crystal Room; Gallery Lounge; seven versatile meeting rooms for 12 to 300 guests; complete business services
Payment:	American Express/Carte Blanche/Diners Club/Discover/MasterCard/Visa
References:	Personal communication Le Pavillion Hotel; International Society for Paranormal Research (ISPR)

O'Flaherty's Irish Pub

The two buildings that now house O'Flaherty's Irish Pub were constructed in 1798. Originally the buildings accommodated businesses downstairs and living quarters on the upper floors. During the period when epidemics ravaged the French Quarter, the second floor was used as a quarantine house for those waiting to die. In 1806 Mary Wheaton from New Jersey married Joseph Bapentier, who owned a general feed store. He and his wife lived on the second floor over what is now called the Ballad Room.

In 1810 Bapentier murdered a young female acquaintance named Angelique on the property. He threw her from the third-floor window, then dragged her body across the courtyard and threw it into a sewage well. The well was located just to the left of the steps leading to the elevated courtyard level. Bapentier later hanged himself from the third-floor window. His wife, Mary, inherited the building and resided there until her death in 1817. Since there were no heirs, the property was auctioned off. If tragedy begets ghosts, the grounds on which the atmospheric Irish Pub stands certainly should have its share of spirits—and it does not disappoint.

The ghost of Mary Bapentier has been sighted a number of times from the courtyard looking out of the second-floor window over the staircase, adjacent to the Ballad Room. Many witnesses saw Mary's ghost sitting on the balcony level of the Ballad Room when it was closed to the public. She was always described as wearing a long gray dress and sporting shoulder-length black hair.

The spirit of Angelique has also been spotted over the years. She has been seen walking around the courtyard before vanishing, and cold spots have also been known to signal her presence. She seems to be drawn to young men and children, and she enjoys stroking their hair or holding their hands. Angelique manifests at the youthful age of twenty, with waist-long, straight brown hair. Her tragic death, according to the International Society for Paranormal Research (ISPR), has left a moving cold spot about the size

of an adult hand, two inches above the brick planter, which was formerly the well where her body was thrown.

The troubled spirit of Joseph Bapentier has been seen and felt often in the courtyard. His spirit, however, is not as friendly as Mary's or Angelique's. Joseph is said to create a somber and friction-based mood when he is encountered. People have begun fighting near the spot where his energy is most focused for no apparent reason. The ghost has even scratched and pushed people when his spirit is restless.

An ISPR investigator was once attacked by the spirit of Joseph in the courtyard, and visible strangulation marks appeared around the psychic's neck as the investigation was taking place. Re-enactments of Bapentier's suicidal hanging have been frequently observed by guests and employees in the courtyard—a brief glimpse of a troubled spirit who can't seem to find peace. The lives of the three principal spirits who haunt O'Flaherty's Irish Pub were tragic in life, and perhaps that is what keeps them mired in the same spot through time.

Address:	514 Toulouse Street, New Orleans, Louisiana 70130
Phone:	504-529-4570
Payment:	Most major credit cards accepted

References: Daena Smoller, *The Official ISPR Self-Guided Ghost Expedition of New Orleans* (1988), International Society for Paranormal Research (ISPR)

Oak Alley Plantation, Restaurant & Inn

Vacherie is an old settlement located on the west bank of the Mississippi River. In French, it means a "place where cows are kept." It is also an almost magical place where the Oak Alley Plantation is situated. Here, you can stroll the grounds or take a long walk on the levee and watch the mighty Mississippi River roll by.

Sometime before the 1718 founding of New Orleans as the colonial seat of government, a French settler selected the site of the present-day Oak Alley Plantation as the location to build his dream home. He planted twenty-eight live oak trees in two rows of fourteen each, eighty feet apart, to form an avenue of trees a quarter mile in length leading to the Mississippi River. The French settler died, but his oak trees continued to grow.

In the early 1830s Jacques Telesphore Roman, a wealthy Creole sugar planter from the French Quarter in New Orleans, met and courted Celina Pilie, whose prominent family lived on Royal Street. They were married in June of 1834. As a wedding gift for his bride, Jacques purchased from his brother-in-law, Valcour Aime, a plantation in St. James Parish that riverboat captains would later dub "Oak Alley," due to an alley of quite stately live oak trees leading to the river.

Construction was begun on the Greek-revival style mansion in 1837, the most notable feature being the twenty-eight classic columns surrounding the house. In 1839 the home was completed, but additions and improvements continued until 1841. Celina Roman christened her new home "Bon Sejour" (pleasant sojourns), but travelers along the Mississippi began calling it Oak

Alley because of the line of oak trees—Oak Alley stuck! The Roman family resided at Oak Alley throughout the Civil War. Jacques died of tuberculosis in 1848. In 1866 Henri, the only surviving Roman son, was forced to sell the plantation for $32,800.

Antonio Sobral, a Portugese immigrant, purchased Oak Alley in 1881. He and his family lived and worked on Oak Alley for nearly twenty-four years and, with four sons and three daughters, raised sugar cane. Sobral was forced to sell in 1905. When Jefferson Davis Hardin Jr., of New Orleans, bought the plantation in 1917, he replaced the old roof on the mansion, restored the overseer's cottage, and converted the old jail into living quarters for his family until the big house was ready for occupancy.

Floods, fire, and costly litigation resulting from a train derailment forced the Hardin's to sell it in 1924. The purchase of the plantation in 1925 by Mr. and Mrs. Andrew Stewart turned the sad ruins of a once gracious mansion into a home again. Josephine Steward outlived her husband by twenty-six years, and shortly before her death in 1972, she created a nonprofit foundation, the Oak Alley Foundation, in order to insure that the home and twenty-five acres of surrounding grounds would always remain open for all to share—including the plantation spirits.

Louise Roman, the daughter of Jacques and Celina Roman, seems to be the most notable spirit of Oak Alley. Louise was a well-bred Creole girl, who unfortunately fell in love with a drunk. One day the drunken lover showed up at the mansion, and Louise ran up the stairs to her room to escape an embarrassing scene. As she climbed up the stairs, her heel caught in her petticoat and she fell. The fall caused a gaping leg wound, and her leg had to be amputated below the knee. An embittered Louise entered a nunnery in St. Louis and later founded her own convent in New Orleans where she died. She was buried with her amputated leg beside her.

The ghost of Louise has been frequently spotted by staff in one of the bedrooms. Her image has also been captured in a photograph, seated on a chair in an empty room. Tourist guides report something pinching their legs as they go up the stairs, whereupon small bruises show up below the knee—interesting coincidence considering Louise had an amputated leg.

There is the pervasive feeling of being watched or followed in various areas of the house. Guides and staff persons have repeatedly heard unexplained footsteps following them or coming from the floor above. Psychics say that Louise is not the cause of all that goes awry in the old plantation home. Other spirits also inhabit the mansion.

The voices and laughter of phantom children are often heard in the hallways and bedrooms. There is also the ghostly sound of a horse and carriage pulling up to the front porch. Psychics confirm the strong paranormal activity in the house. In addition to Louise, former owner Mrs. Stewart, who died in 1972, has been sighted wearing dark clothing as she makes her way down the hallway and into the room where she passed away.

The most impressive spirit of Oak Alley seems to belong to none other than Celina Roman, who is frequently sighted dressed in a black crinoline and black flowing veil on the widow's walk, the balustraded gallery right on the crown of the roof. She has also been spotted galloping on horseback down the avenue of trees toward the levee, and she has been seen on the second and third floor balconies, areas that are not open to staff or to visitors. She may be looking for her husband, Jacques, after all this time. Oak Alley Plantation offers food, overnight accommodations, and ghosts galore.

Address:	3645 LA Highway 18, (Great River Road), Vacherie, Louisiana 70090
Phone:	504-265-2151
Fax:	504-265-7035
Toll Free Number:	1-800-44ALLEY
E-mail:	oakalleyplantation@worldnet.att.net
Accommodations:	Turn-of-the-century Creole cottages are located close to the mansion.
Amenities:	A full country breakfast is included in the rental rate, and is served at the Oak Alley Restaurant. Breakfast is served from 8:30 to 10:00 A.M.; lunch from 11:00 A.M. to 3:00 P.M. The restaurant is not open for dinner.
Payment:	Visa, MasterCard, Discover, American Express
References:	Personal communication, Oak Alley Plantation; Robin Mead, *Haunted Hotels: A Guide to American and Canadian Inns and Their Ghosts*

Ormond Plantation

Destrehan, with a population of around 8,000 inhabitants, lies on the outskirts of New Orleans. This oil refinery town was established in 1914, but it lies within the Destrehan Plantation grounds. The world-famous Destrehan Plantation on River Road is one of the oldest homes in the lower Mississippi Valley. Not far behind in age and notoriety is the Ormond Plantation, which is listed on the National Register of Historic Places.

The Ormond Plantation was built before 1790 on a tract of land granted to Pierre d'Trepagnier by the Spanish governor Don Bernardo de Galvez. The main building was completed shortly before 1790 and was occupied by Mr. and Mrs. d'Trepagnier and their children. d'Trepagnier became wealthy growing indigo and sugar cane. The house is built in the Louisiana Colonial style and is modeled after the sugar plantations of the West Indies. The house was constructed using bricks between cypress studs on the front and rear walls and a type of adobe filling on the side walls. Round cemented brick columns support the front porch, or gallery, with wood columns on the second floor supporting the roof.

The home frequently served as a social focal point for entertaining important officials. In 1798 Pierre d'Trepagnier was summoned from a family meal by a servant to meet a Spanish gentlemen. After speaking briefly to his wife, Pierre d'Trepagnier left with the man, and no trace of him was ever found.

On June 25, 1805, Colonel Richard Butler bought the plantation from Mrs. d'Trepagnier. Butler had fallen in love with the South, and he named his new home Ormond after his ancestral home, the Castle Ormonde in Ireland. On August 7, 1809, Butler became a business partner with Captain Samuel McCutchon and sold him one-third share in Ormond Plantation. On June 29, 1819, Richard Butler turned over all of his holdings to Samuel McCutchon and moved to Bay St. Louis, where he and Mrs. Butler died of yellow fever in 1820. Butler was forty-three.

The two existing wings, or garconnieres, were constructed by either Richard Butler or Captain McCutchon between 1811 and 1830. McCutchon filled his home with furnishings from Great Britain, France, and the Orient. His eldest son, Samuel B., married Adele d'Estrehan, the daughter of the owner of neighboring Destrehan Plantation. Samuel B. and his brother James William took over the plantation after the death of Captain McCutchon and continued its tradition. Like other southern plantations, the Ormond fell on hard times after the Civil War, changing hands twice before being sold at public auction in 1874 and again in 1875.

The Ormond Plantation was bought on December 1, 1898, by State Senator Basile LaPlace Jr. He bought Ormond with hopes of profiting from its rice production. Unfortunately, on October 11, 1899, Basile LaPlace Jr., who had made enemies with the Ku Klux Klan, was shot to death one evening and his body hung from a large oak tree, which stands on River Road in front of the plantation home.

Ormond passed from LaPlace's widow to his mother and then to the Schexnaydre family during 1900. The five Schexnaydre brothers (Joseph, Emilien, Barthelemy, Albert, and Norbet) each held an undivided one-fifth share of the property. Emilien was selected to move his family into Ormond. Emilien died in 1910, but his children continued to live and raise their families at Ormond. At one time there were five families living under the roof of Ormond. The Schexnaydres held the property until 1926 when it was turned over to the Inter-Credit Corporation. The house fell in disrepair by the late 1930s, with its walls and ceilings crumbling and the porch sagging.

Fortunately, beginning in late 1943, Mr. and Mrs. Alfred Brown, owners of the Brown's Velvet Dairy in New Orleans, undertook major restoration and renovations to the plantation home. They added modern indoor plumbing, gas, and electricity. After the death of Mrs. Brown, Mr. Brown sold Ormond to a real estate developer, who began making changes in the house but stopped in 1971. In 1974 Johnson and Loggins sold the house and seventeen acres of land to Mrs. Betty R. LeBlanc. Through the late 1970s and early 1980s, Mrs. LeBlanc began restoring the house. Unfortunately, cancer struck and quickly took Mrs. LeBlanc's life in June 1986. Ormond is presently under the care of Ken Elliott, son of Mrs. LeBlanc and executor of her estate. Mr. Elliott now carries on the work of restoring Ormond and at the same time opening the home to the public for the first time in its history.

The following ghost story was provided by management and was taken from an article published in the *Times Democrat*.

Of the innumerable traditions about ante-bellum residents, there is one that should be related. Perchance the central scene of the tale is the Ormond house, which you see a short while after turning your face up the road from the Red Church.

Having already described a few of the ante-bellum mansions, it is only necessary to say that the Ormond house is a residence characteristic of the country seats of the past. Looking through the intervening yard, which is overgrown with rare trees and flowers, you discern that it is a large, quaintly proportioned two-story structure, with an annex, or wing, on either side, each stretching across the yard to slightly elevated spots of ground, beneath which are darksome wells, well-walled and well-domed with bricks and cement. The house obstructs the view of the grange in the rear. But go upstairs, through the corridors and to the rear of the balcony of the right wing and then you see the old brick Negro quarter houses, the stables, barns, and ante-bellum pigeon houses, the large, old-fashioned fireplaces looming through the shattered portals of the backyard buildings.

Far away are the ruins of the old sugar house, one of the first sugar mills erected in Louisiana. A tottering chimney and crumbling walls, the last of the sugar house, are reflected in the pool beyond the ruins. In old times, runs the legend, when the splendor and glory of the plantation were in bloom, some ghostly being came gliding into the house. Night had fallen, and the bats were coursing erratically in the gloom of the trees and the weeping moss, occasionally swooping about the chimney tops and gibbering at the wind, which moaned at every corner. A steamboat appeared, slackened its speed, then landed at an old warehouse that stood a short distance above the house yard. A Negro was sent to ascertain the object of the landing. When he reached the landing place the boat was speeding away. He looked about in vain, for nothing was there. Returning by a road under the trees in the pasture he ran almost into something that was darker than the night. He started back. The blackness vanished. He ran frantically into the plantation house and swore that he had seen a ghost.

A portion of the house wondered over these events. Strange it was, that landing of the boat, and a ghost? A gust of wind swept down the gallery in front, struck a stairway that led to the balcony of one of the wings, then rumbled into the garret, entering an open trapdoor. The noise reverberated on and on, as though it rolled into some deep, noisome chasm. Ha, ha, ha! A ghost! What was that in the adjoining room? Was there really something moving? Horrors! What thing was that obstructing the dim light seen through the transom above the front door? The ghost, like all other ghosts either had a "passe partout" or had passed through the keyhole. The man became unnerved and was in the hand of a merciless terror; yet he lay motionless and silent. Slowly did the dark figure move. The man knew not just where, yet he knew that it was gliding about in the room. Then a cold shivering almost fleshless hand touched his face. A cry of horror broke from his lips.

According to the present owner, the plantation is quite
haunted. A number of strange events have taken place since renovations began. The spirits appear to be restless, with unexplained
footsteps, cold spots, and mysterious voices heard by staff and
guests alike. A visit to this historic structure may provide more
than just a trip down memory lane courtesy of a history lesson.
The history just may come to life in the form of a ghost of one or
more of Ormond's previous occupants.

Address:	13786 River Road, Destrehan, Louisiana 70047
Phone:	504-764-8544
Fax:	504-764-0691
E-mail:	info@plantation.com.
Contact:	Ken Elliott, manager
Amenities:	Restaurant La Garconniere; catering; club lun-cheons; private parties; banquets; a bottle of wine and a fresh fruit and cheese tray served in the eve-ning; a plantation style breakfast is served on the porch, or in the restaurant dining room; No pets!
Accommodations:	Guestrooms are located inside the ante-bellum home, and they are furnished in period antiques. Each room has its own private bath, air condition-ing, and heating.
Payment:	Visa, MasterCard, American Express
References:	Personal communication, Ormond Plantation

The Myrtles

The two-story, wood-frame bed and breakfast inn is located
three miles north of St. Francisville, Louisiana, on Highway
61. The two-hundred-year-old plantation has been described by
the Smithsonian as America's Most Haunted House.

St. Francisville is a small town in the middle of what is called
"English Louisiana." Settlers were primarily of English descent
who came from Colonial America. They did not mix with their

French neighbors, so they kept their Anglo-Saxon heritage intact over the years.

General David Bradford, the leader of the Whiskey Rebellion, built the twenty-room mansion in 1796 atop sacred burial grounds of the Tunica Indians. The Native Americans were said to have put a curse on the house. Perhaps the curse had something to do with so many deaths associated with this building. The mansion is now a bed and breakfast, and guests have sworn they have been visited by ghosts and heard the children's cries in the night, as well as many other strange occurrences.

Janet Roberts, a psychic who is the treasurer of the Louisiana Society for Psychical Phenomena, believes that The Myrtles has many ghosts, and except for the ill-tempered ghost who will occasionally hurl a clock or drop a candlestick, they are harmless. A former owner finally got used to the nocturnal footsteps, the door slamming, and strange voices echoing through the rooms and corridors. Ghostly photographs have even been taken of what many believe to be Chloe and the two children. The fact that ten murders have taken place at The Myrtles is the key to why paranormal activity is so pronounced at the mansion.

Judge Clarke Woodruff bought the plantation in 1818. His eldest daughter, Octavia, was later killed in the French day room because she was the illegitimate daughter of the judge and Chloe, a black governess to Woodruff's children as well as his mistress.

Chloe was caught eavesdropping one day and had her left ear severed. In retaliation, she boiled oleander leaves and baked the arsenic-like residue into a cake. Woodruff's two youngest daughters died from that lethal treat in their nursery, the Twin Room. Chloe was subsequently hung by her own people outside the mansion.

In the 1820s a man named Louis Sterling planned to marry Octavia but went back on a gambling debt and was knifed to death. He died in the doorway between the dining room and the foyer.

Kate Winter, the granddaughter of one of the Stirlings who lived with her parents in the house in the mid-1830s, died there of yellow fever in the Peach Room, even though a voodoo priestess had been summoned to cure her.

Kate Winter's father, William Winter, was shot to death on the verandah of the house and died in his wife Sara's arms on the seventeenth step of the main staircase.

Three Union soldiers were shot here during the Civil War.

An overseer of the plantation was stabbed in a robbery attempt.

There have been so many ghosts sightings over the years that a book in the hallway of the house affords guests the opportunity to write down their haunting experiences as they happen. Guests and staff have often heard the noises of children laughing and playing, as well as their pitiful cries. Guests staying in the house during May and June have encountered a young, badly wounded Confederate soldier in one of the bedrooms, and the figure of a frock-coated man is seen staggering backward from the front door as if shot, then making his way up the stairs before collapsing on the seventeenth stair.

There is still a dark bloodstain in the polished wood that no amount of work can remove. A happy spirit has been known to tuck guests into bed. Add a phantom ball where people are heard laughing, clinking glasses, and talking when the house is shut tight, and you have the haunted Myrtles which has been featured on *Sightings*, The *Wall Street Journal, USA Today, Life* Magazine, *Southern Living*, and *Family Circle*.

A number of television networks have also done features on this house. According to the U.S. Tourist Bureau, The Myrtles is also one of the authenticated haunted houses of America, and it has sometimes been called America's most haunted house. Psychics, paranormal investigators, ghost hunters, and scientists continue to explore the spirited mansion, hoping to obtain irrefutable evidence of life after death. If they can't find proof at The Myrtles, then it probably doesn't exist. Spend a night at what many consider America's most haunted house, have a bite to eat in the on-site restaurant, or get in the spirit by taking a tour.

Address:	Highway 61, P.O. Box 1100, St. Francisville, Louisiana 70775
Phone:	504-635-6277
Fax:	504-635-5837
Contact:	Jenny Melcanon or John and Teeta Moss
Accommodations:	Nine guestrooms are richly furnished. Guests dine under Baccarat chandeliers and take their coffee and after dinner drinks on the Long Gallery.
Business Information:	Guided tours daily from 9:00 A.M. to 5:00 P.M. Friday and Saturday evening tours; restaurant on the grounds
Payment:	All major credit cards accepted
References:	Personal communication, The Myrtles; Dennis William Hauck, *The National Directory: Haunted Places: A Guidebook to Ghostly Abodes, Sacred Sites, UFO Landings, and Other Supernatural Locations*; Ghost Research Society, *Ghost Trackers Newsletter* (October 1991); Elizabeth Hoffman, *Here a Ghost, There a Ghost*; Nancy Roberts, *Haunted Houses: Tales From 30 American Homes*; Nancy Roberts, *Haunted Houses: Chilling Tales From Nineteen American Homes*; Robin Mead, *Haunted Hotels: A Guide to American and Canadian Inns and Their Ghosts*; Christy L. Viviano, *Haunted Louisiana*; *Life* (November 1980); *FATE Magazine* ("A Night in Louisiana's Most Haunted House," by Marjorie A.E. Cook, October 1998)

Mississippi

Natchez

King's Tavern Restaurant and Lounge

The King's Tavern is listed on the National Register of Historic Places. The establishment is said to be the oldest house in the Natchez Territory and is situated on the historic Natchez Trace. The three-story structure was made out of brick and hand-hewn timbers of cypress and poplar and fitted together with wooden pegs. The ground floor is made of brick, rising from the present sidewalk, and may have served as stables with two smaller rooms originally functioning as slaves quarters.

The first United States mail delivered to the region was carried via the Natchez Trace by Indian runners and brought to King's Tavern where a small room on the first floor served as the post office. Aaron Burr and Andrew Jackson were visitors to the tavern, which also serviced a rambunctious crowd—bullet holes are still embedded in the heavy doors, and the imprints of both bear and cougar paws can be seen in the floor.

The earliest legal record for the tavern found to date indicates that the land was part of a grant made to a man named Prosper King on May 31, 1789. The grant references the outlying grounds and buildings, suggesting that the tavern pre-dates 1789 and King's ownership. King operated the tavern from 1789 until 1820, serving as a stop-off point for weary travelers on their return from New Orleans. The Natchez Trace was infested by thieves and bandits, and travelers often banded together at the tavern before proceeding up the Trace.

When the inn was used as a rest stop, the attic was often rented to poorer travelers for a small pittance. In 1823 the Postlethwaite family purchased title from King and used the building as a residence until 1970 when it was bought and restored by the Pilgrimage Garden Club. During its use by the Postlethwaites, rooms were added and other changes made to the structure. Also in the early 1900s, after the chimney collapsed, a jeweled Spanish dagger was found, and in 1930 three skeletons were recovered from the ground floor—two were men and the third was a sixteen-year-old girl. This is the stuff ghost stories are made of.

Local legend has it that an Indian chief appears at midnight in the Tap Room when the moon is full. Another legend tells that original owner, Richard King, had a young mistress named Madeline, who was also his serving girl. She was rumored to have died on the property, supposedly killed by King's jealous wife.

Laura Carter, an employee, said that one night two ladies, a little girl, and a man came in the restaurant. She greeted them, as she does most visitors, and sat them at table number five. She immediately put down four menus and went to get them their water. When she returned with their water and asked to take their drink order, the man was gone. She assumed that he had left to go to the restroom. Carter asked the lady if she knew what her husband would like to drink. The woman, taken aback, replied that her husband was not with her tonight. The woman then asked Carter why she put down four cups of water when there were only three of them. Half ignoring the question and still curious about the strange man, Carter once again asked her if there wasn't a man with them when they first came in. This time there was an emphatic No. Carter had no idea who or what followed the three women into the Kings Tavern and actually sat down.

The primary phantom is believed to be Madeline, Richard King's mistress. However, after reading various accounts, it seems as though Madeline can appear as either a young woman or

a child—either that or the ghost of the young child belongs to an as-yet-unidentified spirit. There are also a number of other spirits haunting the King's Tavern.

One employee recalled sitting at one of the tables after hours and hearing a ball bounce, followed by someone walking upstairs. The upstairs area had been closed down, so no one could have been up there. A quick check of the area confirmed that fact. On another occasion, two employees were taking the garbage out, and the upstairs lights had been turned off. When they were outside, they looked up and noticed that all of the upstairs lights were on. As they quickly raced upstairs and reached the light switch to turn the lights off, someone else had already taken care of it. On numerous occasions the staff has stood in silence as the bar lights dim, or they hear unexplained footsteps pace throughout the place when there is no one else in that area of the restaurant.

The staff has also noticed puddles of water appear out of nowhere on the floor. Several people have complained that while they are on the second floor, water will begin dripping on their heads, and no matter where they move, it will continue dripping for several seconds. The spigot behind the bar has also been known to turn itself off and on. Sometimes when the water is dripping, an employee will reach over to turn off the faucet only to find that it's already off! Sometimes the water will run hot or the pipes will feel hot to the touch after water has been running, even though there is no hot water line into those particular pipes.

On a number of occasions hot water has flowed from pipes that have been disconnected, even when a startled plumber has been present. Madeline has also been blamed for alarms that go off in the wee hours of the morning. Although the police have been summoned, there is never any evidence of an intruder. Several times a locked inside door on the second floor has been found open. The locked door could not have been reached unless the outside doors and windows had been tampered with—they never are.

Madeline enjoys playing with the heavy door leading to the waitress station. The door has been known to swing open on its own, stop in midswing as if someone is holding it, then swing shut after a few moments. This is sometimes accompanied by the feeling of being touched by an invisible passerby. Workers once found small footprints in an upstairs bathroom that began next to the bathtub as if someone had taken a bath and stepped onto the floor. Of course, no one had been in the bath because spider webs were still untouched inside the tub, and there was no evidence that the water had been turned on.

One time a guest came in late and ordered some wine. Since the wine was kept upstairs and the liquor storeroom was locked up for the night, the waitress had to apologize for the fact that she couldn't get the patron his wine. Suddenly they heard the dumbwaiter make its way down from the second floor and inside was the bottle of wine the man had ordered! Was Madeline playing waitress?

One thing for sure, Madeline does not like people in "her" attic, and she sometimes puts out the lights to avoid intruders in her space. One night she must have been very upset, because she blew every light out on the second floor. Madeline also plays tricks on women in the restroom mirror, occasionally appearing and conforming to the outline of the women who is looking to freshen up. By the time the ladies realize it is not their faces they are applying lipstick to, but instead, the ghostly countenance of a young woman with reddish hair whose lips are not exactly the same proportion as their own, it is too late. Usually Madeline's little prank has made them look like clowns.

At closing time one evening a table was still occupied. When a brazen waiter called out for Madeline to make herself known, all the lights suddenly went out. After checking the main breakers, which were still on, the staff noticed that only the lights in the dining room were out. Not only that, but the candles used for temporary lighting would not stay lit.

One waitress, while alone in the Tap Room, happened to glance into the mirror she was standing in front of. To her amazement, she saw a woman wearing a blue Victorian-style dress staring back at her! The same woman, while working the register at closing, noticed what appeared to be the only other waitress still on shift enter the main dining room. Calling out to her fellow worker, she noticed that the woman kept right on walking without saying a word. A few minutes later the other waitress walked by again. When the first waitress asked why she didn't respond a few minutes prior, the second waitress said she hadn't been anywhere near the dining room.

Another time a waitress was walking through the main dining room and saw a man in a black coat and hat standing beside the fireplace trying to keep warm. Thinking the man a little odd looking, she did a double take only to have the man vanish in a wink of an eye. This tall spectral man, wearing a black top hat, has been spotted a number of times near the fireplace or standing near the old Hoosier cabinet in the tavern.

For those staff persons working late, closing up has been no simple task. Normally, the employees begin the process by shutting off the lights, securing the upper-floor rooms, then heading downstairs. However, on a number of occasions, the upstairs lights, after being turned off, will suddenly go right back on, and the doors that were just secured will be unlocked. This little game sometimes lasts until either the staff or the spirits get tired of playing.

Many times the chairs in the dining area are found moved back from the tables. Doors will open and close on their own; lights will go on and off by themselves; the sound of footsteps will echo from a deserted part of the building; and cold drafts of air will blow through the tavern even though all the windows and doors have been tightly shut.

One evening a waitress seated two men and a young girl. When the men ordered, the waitress asked if the little girl wanted anything. The confused men looked at one another and replied that there was no little girl with them. Short on time and patience, the waitress didn't think their joke was funny. She knew that she had seen the two men arrive with the little girl with a long ponytail and blue dress. Returning to the kitchen, the waitress told the others about the practical joke the two men were playing on her. Much to her chagrin, the other employees swore they did not see a little girl enter with the two men either. This happened a third time until the waitress realized she had just witnessed the ghost of a younger version of Madeline, an apparition she had heard about but did not believe in until now.

The ghostly young child has been spotted numerous times, either walking in with guests or joining a group of unwary customers. In some instances only one waitress would see the girl, while other times the phantom child was seen by several staff members at the same moment.

One night, when a large group of people were dining, the owner glanced over toward one of the tables as the group of people was ready to leave. The owner witnessed a very touching scene. One of the guests wearing a top hat picked up a little blonde-haired child wearing a blue dress and held her close to his chest. The man had his back to the waitress so she focused on the beautiful child. As the man and child left with most of the others, the owner couldn't help but walk over and tell one of the remaining group members that she hadn't noticed the child when the group was first seated. The response was, "There was no child in the group." When the owner asked the other waitresses in the dining room about the strange man in the black top hat and little child, they all swore they saw no one fitting that description enter or leave that night.

Madeline's ghost is not the only spirit in King's Tavern. The ghost of an Indian in full war bonnet has been spotted by employees in the portion of the tavern that was once used as the post office. There have also been reports of a man with a red hat spotted in the barroom mirror—possibly the spirit of a Native American who helped bring the mail down the Trace.

Another unsettling phenomenon that occurs on a regular basis is the sound of a baby crying. The poor child is heard by a number of staff, and although the exact location cannot be pinpointed, some think the sounds come from behind the wall in the old postroom, or the wall behind the dumbwaiter. One afternoon the owner was sitting at her desk in the kitchen with the cook and a waitress when they all heard a baby crying. Looking everywhere, they were unable to find the source of the sound. Another time three women were alone in the building when the baby began crying. Again, no one was able to find the source. Usually within a day or two of a visit to the attic by a staff member, the baby's cry is heard.

A story is told of a baby who was killed in the mailroom by outlaw Big Harpe. The outlaw was in the adjoining tavern and didn't like the distraction of the crying child, so he grabbed the child from the mother and cruelly slammed it against the wall, killing it instantly.

One morning a female psychic visited the tavern just as it was opening for business. The psychic walk-through produced startling revelations. Unfamiliar with the history of the tavern and never having been there before, she walked into the Tap Room and immediately picked up on a tragic death involving a baby. She also sensed that six bodies had being buried under the tavern (three had already been recovered). When the psychic closed her eyes, she described a little girl with a ponytail, wearing a blue dress, who was dancing around the Tap Room. The name she picked up on was "Madeline."

The kitchen area has seen its share of flying utensils, as well as a coffee pot slamming into a brick wall. The bar area is not exempt from strange events and ghostly apparitions. On one occasion, after a loud group of patrons had finished celebrating at the bar, a lone waitress was responsible for cleaning up. As she was finishing the cleanup work at the inside tables on the hot summer night, she glanced outside just in time to see a tall man wearing a long coat walk along the upstairs outside porch area. She immediately became frightened, thinking it was an intruder. Hurriedly, she checked all the inside doors and windows to make sure the place was securely locked. From inside she was able to see the entire porch area, and after a careful search she was unable to find a living soul fitting that description inside or out. Then it dawned on her that not only was the man strangely attired for summer, but also when he walked along the outside porch it should have made a loud creaking sound—but she never heard footsteps as the man passed by. Venturing outside, she was stunned to see the only access to that area was securely locked!

A holiday season also had its share of strange occurrences. After Christmas, the decorations were being taken down, which meant that someone had to take the tree and boxes with decorations into the attic, the most haunted place in the tavern. Two of the staff were designated to deliver the goods to the "haunted attic." Both reluctant employees wanted to get in and out of the place as quickly as possible. As they reached the top of the stairs, the male employee refused to enter the attic door, while the female employee just wanted to get the job done as quickly as possible.

Using the tree as leverage, she pushed open the unlocked door. As she did so, an overwhelming sensation of fear engulfed her. She felt as if the life was slowly being drained from her body. Terrified, the male employee ran downstairs for help. In those few moments that the female employee was paralyzed in front of the attic door, she felt intense pressure applied to her body. Her mouth was completely dry from fear, she was losing her sight, and she had the intense feeling of blood flowing from her mouth and nose. With her remaining energy, she hurled the tree through the door, broke away from the force, and ran down the stairs in horror. After regaining her composure, she swore she'd never go in that room again.

Finally, a reporter and her husband decided to tempt fate and spend a night in the tavern. The only guest suite is on the third floor, and people who choose to spend the night are left alone. Skeptical about the purported hauntings, the reporter, prior to being left alone, listened to the detailed history of the place delivered by the owner. Afterward, the reporter began snapping photographs of the painting of Madeline that hangs on the wall. However, each time she attempted to do so, the painting would begin swaying back and forth. Finally, the uncooperative portrait was placed on the bar so it wouldn't sway, and a photograph was taken.

As the reporter had her own picture taken, a chain dangling from the wall near her began swinging slowly back and forth, then in a circle. When the owner called out to Madeline to make the chain swing straight, the chain suddenly began swinging back and forth once again. The reporter was thoroughly "spooked" at that point. As the reporter sat down at a nearby table to recover, the table began to vibrate. That was only a warm-up for the tavern spirits.

After the tavern closed, the reporter and her husband were left alone to spend the night in the third-floor suite. After settling in, the reporter decided to step outside the room to check out the hallway as her husband took photographs inside the room. As she did so, she was immediately confronted by a ghostly shadow on the wall about ten feet in front of her. She made out the slender form of a woman who stood defiantly with her hands on her hips. The reporter knew it wasn't her shadow because her arms were at her side. The apparition remained for several seconds, then vanished.

The thought of leaving the place crossed the reporter's mind, but she reluctantly decided that the story was more important than her fear. The rest of the night was sporadically interrupted by a few squeaks, rattles, and rapping noises, but nothing else major happened. Perhaps Madeline, after making her point to the skeptic that she and other spirits *do* haunt the historic structure, decided to let the couple rest in peace the remainder of their stay.

Address:	619 Jefferson Street, P.O. Box 1613, Natchez, Mississippi 39121
Phone:	601-446-8845
Fax:	601-446-8878
Innkeeper:	Yvonne Scott
Payment:	Most major credit cards accepted
References:	Personal communication, King's Tavern Restaurant and Lounge; Dennis William Hauck, *The National Directory: Haunted Places: A Guidebook to Ghostly Abodes, Sacred Sites, UFO Landings, and Other Supernatural Locations*; Sylvia Booth Hubbard, *Ghosts! Personal Accounts of Modern Mississippi Hauntings*; *The Natchez Democrat* ("Ghost Stories From The Tavern," article by Maria Giordano); *The Enquirer* ("Face-to-Face With A Ghost," article by Sylvia Hubbard)

North Carolina

Asheville

The Grove Park Inn Resort

Many famous names have appeared on the early guest registers of the Grove Park Inn, including Thomas Edison, Harvey Firestone, Henry Ford, Woodrow Wilson, the Roosevelts, General Dwight Eisenhower, and F. Scott Fitzgerald, who spent the summer of 1936 at the inn while his wife Zelda was in Asheville's Highland Hospital. The inn is listed on the National Register of Historic Places.

A hotel was the dream of Edwin Wiley Grove (1850-1927) of Tennessee, owner of a pharmaceutical firm in St. Louis that produced Grove's Bromo-Quinine and Grove's Tasteless Chill Tonic. He came to Asheville one summer and found the climate so beneficial to his health that he bought land on Sunset Mountain. The idea of building a unique resort overlooking the mountains he had come to love soon became a reality. He consulted many architects, but none could grasp his idea, so he turned to his son-in-law, Fred L. Seely, for help. Without an architect or a contractor, this remarkable man built an edifice considered to be the finest resort hotel in the world of its time.

The hotel was constructed of Sunset Mountain boulders, which were hauled to the site by wagon trains and fitted into place

111

by Italian stonemasons and hundreds of local laborers. Built in eleven months and twenty-seven days, the opening date was July 12, 1913, with William Jennings Bryan delivering the official address.

The lobby, or "Big Room," which was 120 feet long and 80 feet wide, was constructed with elevators running through the chimney rockwork and massive fireplaces large enough to burn twelve-foot logs. A superb orchestral organ, with 7,000 pipes, was built for the inn by Ernest Skinner of Boston. It was sold in 1927 for $75,000.

Mr. Grove leased his hotel from 1914 to 1927 to his manager, Mr. Seely, whose policies, though appreciated by his conservative clientele at the time, would seem a bit austere now. Children were discouraged, pets forbidden; only low tones and whispers were permitted after 10:30 P.M.; and slamming of doors was not allowed. As the hotel literature stated, this was all necessary to maintain a place where tired, busy people could get away from all annoyances and rest their nerves.

During World War II, the inn was leased by the U.S. government. In 1942 Axis diplomats were interned here while awaiting repatriation. Though completely cut off from the outside world, they were treated as ordinary guests, paying their own expenses. At the end of 1942, the Navy Department converted the inn into a rest center for Navy personnel. From 1944 until the end of the war, the hotel was part of an Army Redistribution Station where soldiers back from overseas service rested before being reassigned to further duty.

The inn changed hands many times until 1955 when it was purchased by Dallas entrepreneur Charles A. Sammons. The Fairway Lodge and North Wing were added in 1958 and 1964 (since removed), and in 1976 the adjoining Country Club of Asheville with its 18-hole golf course, pool, and clubhouse was purchased.

A new era began in 1982, when a multimillion-dollar expansion program was launched. The Main Inn was renovated, the Sammons Wing added, and the Country Club remodeled. In 1984 the once-seasonal resort opened year round. Further expansion has included the addition of an indoor sports center and the luxurious ten-story Vanderbilt Wing, which opened in 1988, the year the inn celebrated its 75th anniversary. The 202-room Sammons Wing was refurbished in 1994 and the Historic Main Inn in 1995.

Because of the vision and efforts of Charles Sammons (1898-1988) and his wife, Elaine, who is currently chairman of the board, Dr. Grove's dream has become a reality. Now restored and expanded, the Grove Park Inn Resort is ready for the twenty-first century and the admiration of generations yet unborn.

According to accepted lore, on a chilly November night in late 1919 or early 1920, a young woman staying at the hotel and wearing a long, pink gown went to her room in the Palm Court, the center of the Main Inn where six levels of rooms surround an atrium, two stories below. Some time during the night she plunged to her death. To this day, no one knows whether the fall was suicide, accidental, or murder. Additionally, her real identity remains a mystery. Yet, ever since the event took place, employees and guests have been reporting unexplainable phenomena throughout the historic building. The Pink Lady appears most frequently in room 545, two stories above the Palm Court atrium floor where she is said to have fallen to her death.

Since the first documented occurrences around 1940, people have encountered everything from a pink phantom gliding through the hotel, to a rash of mischievous and unexplainable events. Occurrences range from small events such as objects moving around, doors of vacant rooms being locked from the inside, elevators being sent to empty floors, and typewriters typing by themselves, to larger events like bellmen being physically pushed by invisible force and the lights in every guestroom being turned on at once, even though the hotel was closed for the winter. The witnesses include people from all walks of life. In every case, the spirit or spirits have been benevolent—never has anyone been harmed.

A handyman who worked in the hotel from the 1950s through the 1980s said that during the late 1950s or early 1960s, while the hotel was shut down during the winter, repairs were made to the building. On one cloudy and very gloomy winter day, he was checking on the progress of his crew. As he approached room 545, he got cold chills, which became more intense the closer he came to the door—his fear prevented him from going into the room. For the remainder of his time at the hotel, he never ventured into the room, always sending another worker in his place.

Over thirty years later, in 1995, the hotel's engineering facilities manager had a similar experience. While on his way to check a bathtub resurfacing project in room 545, he stopped dead in his tracks as he approached the room. His hair suddenly stood up on his scalp as well as his arms. Almost instantly, he felt extremely uncomfortable, and what seemed like a rush of cold air passed through his entire body. Like the handyman, he didn't go in and hasn't gone back in since—he didn't know of the handyman's experience before having his encounter.

A two-year-old son of a Florida college professor, who dozed on consecutive afternoons in an empty Main Inn guestroom, asked the manager who the nice lady was that he saw and where she might have gone—there was no one fitting that description there at the time of his visit.

The manager of Elaine's, the Grove Park Inn's nightclub, has seen the Pink Lady several times since 1992. Her gentle spirit usually appears as a glowing, pinkish, pastel, dense smoke. It's there one minute, then the haze vanishes before her eyes. The chief of police of Kitty Hawk, North Carolina, swears somebody or something sat down next to him on his Main Inn guestroom bed while he was telephoning home. Two Grove Park Inn employees, standing outside the hotel while it was closed and locked up for the winter, saw all the sixth-floor guestroom lights come on, then turn off, followed by all the Main Inn lights doing the same thing. The president of the National Federation of Press Women experienced several unexplainable events in her Main Inn guestroom. At 4:00 A.M. one New Year's Eve, the Pink Lady was sighted in the inn's accounting office. The Pink Lady was spotted by two employees who heard someone come in the back door after an office party. They saw a woman in party clothes quickly pass by them. Thinking it was a guest who was lost, they got up to assist her— within seconds she just vanished.

Joshua P. Warren, a North Carolina writer and ghostbuster, came to investigate the famous legend of the Grove Park Inn. At approximately 5:30 A.M. on December 30, 1995, Warren captured a strange image in a photograph he had taken of a chair in the lobby. He was using Kodak 1000 speed film and a 35mm camera at the time. He snapped a photo of a gray mist hovering over the chair. At the time the photograph was taken, there was no visible indication of an apparition, and instrumentation registered no anomalies. After the photo was developed, it was examined by four photographic experts. None of them could give him a conventional explanation for the image.

Warren, with intermittent help from several colleagues, stayed in a total of twenty rooms at the Grove Park Inn over a period of ten nights between December 29, 1995, and May 27, 1996, to monitor potential anomalies using scientific instrumentation and techniques. Several photographs revealed an unexplainable image, while strong, fluctuating electromagnetic fields were also recorded. Conventional sources for the energy in most cases were never found. Over the course of the investigation, two events significantly affected his research. A photograph taken by an elevator operator of Warren and a friend showed an unusual orange glow outside of room 545.

Deciding to investigate further, the team attempted to enter room 545 with the maid's key. It repeatedly malfunctioned, as did a guest key. Finally, security had to open the door. Once they were inside, massive, fluctuating energy fields were measured throughout the room. The first night revealed little. During the second night, however, an electromagnetic field meter was set up on the arm of a chair in the room. The meter showed fluctuations, and the three investigators took a number of photographs. They also felt strange physical sensations near the chair—something unseen was there with them.

The night of January 20, 1996, represented another major event, this time in Elaine's, the hotel's nightclub. There had been countless sightings in the club. Not long after setting up the equipment, measurable electrical discharges were observed. An unexplainable white streak was witnessed by a researcher. A photograph developed later confirmed that a white, illuminated streak was visible in the upper right-hand corner. Perhaps the Pink Lady was providing proof for the ghost hunters that she is still around and intends to stay. Why not. It's hard to imagine a more beautiful setting to haunt.

Address:	290 Macon Avenue, Asheville, North Carolina 28804-3799
Phone:	704-252-2711
Fax:	704-253-7053
Toll Free Number:	1-800-438-0050
E-mail:	jgraves@groveparkinn.com
Contact:	Jessica Graves or David Tomsky, media relations
Accommodations:	510 rooms: 142 guestrooms in the Main Inn; 202 guestrooms in the Sammons Wing; 116 guestrooms in the Vanderbilt Wing (including 12 suites); and 28 rooms on the private Club Floor
Amenities:	Lounge with complimentary continental breakfast, and cocktail service; the Blue Ridge Dining Room; Carolina Cafe; Horizons; Sunset Terrace; Great Hall Lobby Bar (Main Inn); Magnolia Lounge (Sammons Wing); Elaine's (Vanderbilt Wing); and Pool Cabana (Country Club); 40 meeting rooms;

two ballrooms; an 18-hole Donald Ross golf course; 9 tennis courts (3 indoor and 6 outdoor); 2 pools (indoor and outdoor); sports center with tennis, aerobics, racquetball, squash, Nautilus, whirlpool, and saunas

Payment: All major credit cards are accepted

References: Personal communication, The Grove Park Inn Resort; Joshua P. Warren, *Haunted Asheville*; *FATE* Magazine (June 1997)

Richmond Hill Inn

The mansion was built in 1889 for Richmond Pearson and his wife, Gabrielle. An ambassador and congressman, Richmond Pearson had his home designed by James G. Hill. The mansion became one of the most elegant and innovative structures of its time, with running water, ten master fireplaces, a communications system, and a pulley-operated elevator for transporting baggage from one floor to the next.

The Richmond Hill estate was a center of social and political activity for many years. The Queen Anne-style mansion, with its grand entrance hall and spacious rooms, could accommodate large gatherings, and Richmond's beautiful and vivacious wife, Gabrielle, was a gracious hostess.

Gabrielle and Richmond had three children: Richmond Jr.; Marjorie Noel; and James Thomas. Richmond Jr. born in 1886,

The children of Richmond Hill: James Thomas,
Marjorie Noel, and Richmond Pearson Jr.

excelled in his studies and seemed destined for a bright future. Unfortunately, he died in 1900 of scarlet fever at the tender age of fourteen. Marjorie, born in 1890, spent most of her life traveling abroad and died at Richmond Hill in 1972. Thomas was born in 1893, served in World War I, graduated from Princeton in 1915, and died in 1963.

Gabrielle Thomas Pearson was born on September 7, 1858. She married Richmond Pearson on March 30, 1882. After an illness, she died in New York on December 17, 1924. Richmond Pearson was born on January 26, 1852, studied law at Princeton, was a U.S. Congressman, built Richmond Hill, and died at Richmond Hill in 1923 at the age of seventy-one.

Gabrielle Pearson

After ninety-five years of political and social acclaim, the Richmond Hill Mansion faced demolition when the Pearson heirs sold it. The Preservation Society saved the house, and it was moved 600 feet to its new location. It was finally purchased by the present owners, Dr. and Mrs. Michel. Following substantial historical research and a three-million-dollar restoration, the estate was reopened as an inn in 1989.

According to management and staff, at least two spirits call the Richmond Hill their home. From all indications, the spirits are those of Gabrielle Pearson and her son Richmond. Gabrielle died of malaria, and young Richmond died at fourteen of scarlet fever. The fact is, several family members lived and died in this wonderful mansion, so the likelihood that other members may remain behind is high. Time and continued paranormal research efforts will most likely answer some of these questions.

Sounds of children talking and playing are often reported throughout the mansion. Several times people have felt something brush by them in the hallways, followed by giggling and occasional doors opening and shutting. Also, the apparitions of Gabrielle and Richmond Jr. have been reported on the second floor. Lights that turn on and off by themselves, moving cold spots and drafts, and other phenomenon have been reported by guests and staff since the mansion opened for business.

All of the mystifying events that have taken place are what you might expect from the well-educated, well-respected family who once occupied the mansion—benign and happy. It seems as if some of the original family members wish to continue enjoying the comforts of home, even in the afterlife.

Address:	87 Richmond Hill Drive, Asheville, North Carolina 28806
Phone:	828-252-7313
Fax:	828-252-8726
Toll Free Number:	800-545-9238
Contact:	Susan Michel
Accommodations:	The Mansion has 12 guestrooms; the Garden Pavilion has 15 guestrooms; and the Croquet Cottages have 9 cottage rooms.
Amenities:	Gabrielle's Restaurant; spectacular views, fine antiques
Payment:	Most major credit cards
References:	Personal communication, Richmond Hill Inn

South
Carolina

Pawleys Island

Evans Pelican Inn

Plowden Charles Jeannerette Weston was the original owner of the house on Pawleys Island now called the Pelican Inn. As the story goes, Plowden wanted to marry Emily Frances Esdaile of England. After both families approved of the wedding, a quarrel broke out as to who could give the couple more financially. Plowden's father won that battle, and the two were married in August of 1847.

They lived on the Hagley Plantation, a gift from Plowden's father. The residence was located close to Pawleys Island, just off-shore. The young couple built a house on the island—now called Pelican Inn. Near the end of the Civil War, Plowden developed tuberculosis, and he died in his wife's arms at Conway, South Carolina. His body was brought back to Hagley.

Tying the story together, people believe that because Plowden cared so much for his home, servants, and neighbors in peacetime and during war, his spirit remains behind to continually warn people when danger approaches.

According to Dennis William Hauck, sometimes on the second-floor piazza of the Pelican Inn or along the deserted dunes nearby, the thin figure of a man wearing a gray fishing cap and in working clothes is encountered by startled tourists. But locals know and welcome this phantom they call the Gray Man.

This faceless apparition always warns locals of approaching dangerous storms. His first appearance was followed by a fierce gale in 1804. Thereafter island residents headed for the safety of the mainland whenever someone witnessed the Gray Man. According to local lore, he has appeared just before the devastating hurricanes of 1806, 1822, 1893, 1916, 1954, 1955, and 1989 and is credited with saving thousands of lives. His specter has also appeared at the home of certain residents, as well as being sighted walking the beach.

Staff and guests at the inn, although they believe in the ghost of the Gray Man, are positive that someone else haunts their establishment. A number of witnesses have seen a lady watching them in the kitchen as they do their chores. She stands with her arms folded, and her gaze is intently fixed on those busy in that area of the house. Just as an unsuspecting staff person catches a glimpse of the woman, she vanishes. Apparently she leaves after being satisfied that people are doing their task right.

The lady has also been sighted in other parts of the house, usually wearing a gingham, gray-and-white checkered dress, with her bodice fronted with pearls and an apron tied around her waist. Guests have seen the strange woman walking up the stairs from their position on the sitting room sofa, only to have her fade away before making it all the way to the top. The female phantom also tugs at people's clothing, opens and closes doors, turns on lights and other appliances, and walks around upstairs when that area is unoccupied by staff or guests.

Both the Gray Man and the mysterious 1800s lady are quite comfortable on Pawleys Island and at Evans Pelican Inn. Drop in some time, but if you see the Gray Man, the suspected ghost of Plowden Charles Jeannerette Weston, you'd better not plan to stay for very long.

Address:	P.O. Box 154, Pawleys Island, South Carolina 29585
Phone:	864-237-2298
Contact:	Mrs. Theodore R. Evans
Business Information:	Open every day May through September from 9:00 A.M. to 10:00 P.M.
Amenities:	American plan includes breakfast, midday dinner
Payment:	Visa, MasterCard, Discover, American Express, Diners Club, Carte Blanche
References:	Personal communication, Evans Pelican Inn; Dennis William Hauck, *The National Directory Haunted Places: A Guidebook to Ghostly Abodes, Sacred Sites, UFO Landings, and Other Supernatural Locations*; Jean Anderson, *The Haunting of America*; Rosemary Guiley, *The Encyclopedia of Ghosts and Spirits*; Hans Holzer, *Great American Ghost Stories*; Hans Holzer, *The Phantoms of Dixie*; Nancy Roberts, *Ghosts and Specters of the Old South*; Nancy Roberts, *Ghosts of the Carolinas*; Beth Scott and Michael Norman, *Haunted America*; Elizabeth Robertson Huntsinger, *Ghosts of Georgetown*

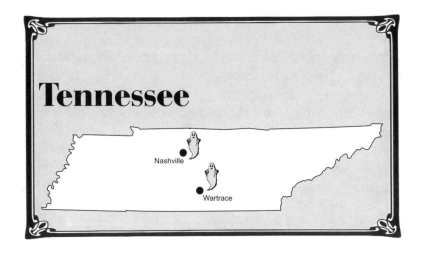

Tennessee

Nashville

Wartrace

Walking Horse Hotel and Shops

The Walking Horse Hotel is located in south central Tennessee, Bedford County, Wartrace, Tennessee, midway between Shelbyville and Manchester on Highway 64. The hotel is listed on the National Register of Historic Places.

While the history of the Walking Horse Hotel only goes back to the early twentieth century, the history of this area goes back much further. Undoubtedly this area attracted many Native Americans with its fertile land, mild climate, and abundant streams and rivers. The earliest Europeans were probably hunters, trappers, and mountain men. The first recorded land grants were bestowed shortly after the Revolutionary War. Some of the proud descendants of those early settlers still live in the area. The railroad has always figured prominently in the development of this area.

The first narrow gauge rail line was completed in 1852. The engines and cars were much smaller than we are accustomed to seeing today. The following year the town of Wartrace Depot was chartered. Eventually Depot was dropped, and the town became simply Wartrace. The early railroad transported passengers and freight of all kinds in and out of the region. The early trains were powered by coal-fired steam engines. A spring known as Coffee

Spring located north of the hotel on Spring Street was the source of water to produce the steam.

During the Civil War, control of the railroad was of vital importance. Many battles and skirmishes were fought in this area, frequently for control of the railroad. After the Civil War, life achieved some measure of normalcy, and the economy boomed. Over the years, Wartrace has had three banks (two of the safes from those banks are still in use), general mercantile stores, hotels, restaurants, a livery stable, tannery, stockyard, and other establishments.

The hotel was built by Jesse and Nora Overall in 1917. By 1938 Floyd and Olive Carothers had bought it. Floyd Carothers enjoyed a reputation as a first-rate horse trainer. Early in 1939 he purchased a workhorse and trained him to show in the Tennessee Walking Horse shows, which were gaining popularity. That horse, Strolling Jim, won the first National Celebration held in 1939 in Shelbyville and was named the World's Grand Champion Tennessee Walking Horse. He was sold several times but returned to Wartrace in 1947. He died in 1957 and is buried in the pasture at the rear of the hotel.

The ghost of Floyd Carothers is said to wander the hallways of the hotel. The misty white apparition of Carothers has been seen by a former owner, staff, and guests, walking or standing on the stairway. A photograph taken in the hotel dining room in the early 1980s showed a former owner and a guest seated at a table in the dining room, with two indistinct, slightly glowing figures standing behind the chairs.

Another photograph was taken of what should have been an empty table with place settings. Unbelievably, four specters are visible in the photograph. One phantom figure is sitting comfortably in each chair. An expert in New Bedford, Massachusetts, studied the photographs and authenticated them.

The pesky spirit of Floyd Carothers has frequently interfered with the hotel's security cameras and has also been responsible for other unexplained anomalies. The ghost assisted in the delivery of a horse named Lucky Chance at 1:30 A.M. on July 2, 1991. At around the same time Lucky was born, Floyd's wife, Olive, passed

away. Some of the people who worked at the hotel during this period said that when Olive Carothers passed away, Floyd joined her, and the ghostly sightings stopped.

However, not all the staff and management were convinced that Floyd was the sole spirit who inhabited the hotel, especially if the various photographs of several specters are to be believed. Some people swear that at least one other male ghost, possibly belonging to a member of the Wright family who was killed on active service in the Far East while serving in the Navy, still hangs around the place.

During Thanksgiving or Christmas, a picture was taken of the family, minus the young man who had died, and was developed. Seated in the empty chair, left for the war hero since his passing, was a clear outline of a man in naval uniform. If Floyd Carothers did finally join his wife in the afterlife, then perhaps another ghost still haunts this hotel, the spirit of a young man who died in battle and, even in death, returns to happier times.

A visit to the Walking Horse Hotel may prove to be more than just a visit to a place with an interesting past. The interesting past may in turn come and visit you. When you visit, judge for yourself as to whether Floyd, a former member of the Wright family, or someone else haunts this hotel.

Address:	P.O. Box 525, 101 Spring Street, Wartrace, Tennessee 37183
Phone:	931-389-7050

Fax:	931-389-7030
Toll Free Number:	1-800-513-8876
Contact:	John and Bea Garland
Accommodations:	Six deluxe rooms on the third floor
Amenities:	Strolling Jim Restaurant and lobby on the first floor; 12 shops including a barbershop and souvenir shop on the second floor; suites on the third floor; the guestrooms have queen-size beds, cable television, phone, and private baths
Payment:	Visa, MasterCard, Discover, American Express, Diners Club, Carte Blanche
References:	Personal communication, Walking Horse Hotel; Dennis William Hauck, *The National Directory: Haunted Places: A Guidebook to Ghostly Abodes, Sacred Sites, UFO Landings, and Other Supernatural Locations*; Dale Kaczmarek, "National Register of Haunted Places," Ghost Research Society; Robin Mead, *Haunted Hotels: A Guide to American and Canadian Inns and Their Ghosts*

The Westin Hermitage Suite Hotel

Over the years famous visitors to this hotel have included cowboy star Gene Autry and his horse Champion. Dinah Shore made her singing debut in the Oak Bar in 1946. The only example of a commercial Beaux Arts structure in Tennessee, the Hermitage opened its doors in 1910. The hotel served as the headquarters for the suffragette movement in 1920, as the state cast the deciding ballot allowing women the right to vote. Italian Sienna, Grecian, and Tennessee marble were used for the exterior and lobby. Circassian walnut and cut glass adorn the dining room. Completed in 1995, the exquisite restoration is evident from the spectacular lobby, with its three-story arched ceiling and skylight to the guest suites.

Management, staff, and guests are aware of the otherworldly at this incredibly beautiful hotel. Let's face it, who wouldn't want to haunt this tourist treasure. There seem to be at least three ghost guests who frequent the hotel. They have been reported in several rooms and have been blamed for turning on the water in front of a startled housekeeping staff, as well as guests. One of the spectral visitors includes a lady in white who is frequently spotted throughout the hotel, floating around or just standing still and gazing at people. Reports are that this woman caught her husband cheating on her and was subsequently found dead. The details are shrouded in mystery, as is the woman's identity.

A bellman entered the ninth floor one evening and approached one of the rooms (number 910 to be exact). He was alone and carrying a guest's luggage to the suite. As he reached the door and was about to open it, the bellboy heard the distinct sounds of a baby crying inside. As is customary in these situations, he knocked first. The crying continued inside, and not receiving a response after knocking repeatedly, he cautiously entered. The crying ceased the moment he entered the room. A thorough search of the entire suite failed to produce the source of the child's moans. He was so frightened that he left the luggage outside the door and ran out of the room. He subsequently resigned from his position, leaving the hotel and the phantom baby for good.

The director of security also reported an encounter with the unknown. It was late at night at the base of the steps to the main ballroom. People were still dancing and having a great time, when a chill, followed by an odd queasy feeling overcame him. First looking toward the ballroom and then toward the front lobby, the man was stunned as he beheld a vision of radiance and beauty approaching him. She was a young, gorgeous woman, a "knockout," with dark hair and a gown right out of *Gone with the Wind*. When she finally walked up to him, his body was covered in goosebumps. He hesitated, then asked her if he could be of some assistance.

Before receiving a response, something distracted the man, causing him to turn his head for one brief moment. Quickly turning back to the woman, he was astonished to see that she had vanished into thin air. He spent the rest of the night trying to find out who the mysterious, gorgeous woman was, but to no avail. He asked around, but no one had seen her but him. Perhaps she came for a party that only she was invited to and then walked through a door to another dimension to join it. Her ghost has also been sighted on the mezzanine level railing overlooking the lobby.

These are only a few of the stories that exist pertaining to the Westin Hermitage Suite Hotel. As time goes by, more stories will most certainly surface, and perhaps a psychic or paranormal investigative team can produce some names or more detailed information about the phantom lady, the crying child, and possibly other spirits, and why they remain behind. Until then, a visit to this historic hotel is worth it even without the possibility of running into the attractive but elusive female phantom.

Address:	231 6th Avenue, North Nashville, Tennessee 37219
Phone:	615-244-3121
Fax:	615-254-6909
Toll Free Number:	1-800-678-8946
E-mail:	kim.ferguson@westin.com
Accommodations:	120-one and two bedroom suites

Amenities:	Each suite has a refrigerator, wet bar, two televisions, and three telephones; The Capitol Grille, named one of the Top 25 New Restaurants in the United States by *Esquire* magazine, for creative cuisine and old world charm; light fare in The Veranda; drinks in the Lobby Bar and Oak Bar; The Grand Ballroom accommodates groups of up 300; three intimate conference suites and two private dining suites
Payment:	Visa, MasterCard, Discover, American Express, Diners Club, Carte Blanche, personal check, travelers check, cash
References:	Personal communication, The Westin Hermitage Suite Hotel

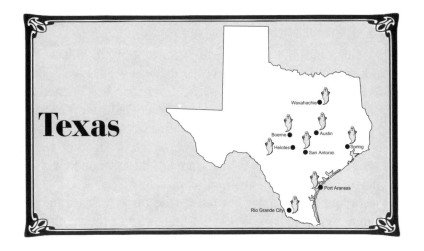

Texas

The Alamo Street Restaurant

The present-day restaurant was formerly called the Alamo Methodist Church, which served San Antonio Methodists until 1976 when the small size of the congregation forced the church to close down. The first level of The Alamo Street Restaurant contains the dining room and the kitchen. The second level hosts theater performances, concerts, and weddings (the theater area used to serve as the old chapel).

Mr. Beverly Spillman designed the mission-style building, and construction was completed in 1912. The congregation disbanded in 1968, merging with another congregation east of San Antonio. As the building lay vacant for eight years, it deteriorated and was vandalized. In 1976 Bill and Marcia Larsen purchased the building to create the Church Dinner Theater as a bicentennial project. The Larsens continued restoring the building, funded in part by the sale of cookbooks, display items, and an occasional private donation.

During 1977 the Larsens earned the coveted San Antonio Conservation Society award for their work in restoring this wonderful landmark. Retiring from the theater aspect of the building in 1982, the couple focused on restoring the rest of the building.

During this time, the second level was used by the Alamo City Theater. (Jerry Pollock operated the theater portion from 1984 to 1987.) During 1988 the Alamo Street Restaurant was opened and operated in conjunction with the Alamo Street Theater. The same year, the building was listed on the National Register of Historic Places, being the first known church building of this type to feature a sloped floor in the sanctuary area. Bill Larsen died in 1996, but Marcia continued the restoration process.

According to a booklet put out by the owner, "you can't see 'em, but our visitors have ways of letting us know they're around: Cold spots suddenly develop in the air; lights go on and off by themselves; cooks are shoved into the refrigerator; washed and draining dishes suddenly move back into the dishwater by themselves; doors open and close . . . or lock and unlock themselves; and unusual noises persist."

Regardless of who or what is responsible for these occurrences, the restaurant staff pays little heed and just seems to work around the ghosts. Once in awhile a cook will shout, "Now you just stop that!" and everyone knows there's an otherworldly visitor in the place. If you're skeptical (who isn't?), ask to see the photos of the "lady-in-white" caught on Polaroid film by an out-of-state guest one summer day in 1990! "We can't explain our visitors! We're not sure we want to. But we do know one thing for sure—our visitors are definitely Friendly Spirits!"

According to Docia Schultz Williams, psychics have confirmed that there are at least four resident spirits in the building, and they apparently are so happy there, they probably will be staying for a long time. While the best known spirit seems to be a woman in a white Victorian dress, who is frequently glimpsed in the former choir loft or out in the audience during productions, there are three other interesting personalities in this former house of worship.

Williams says, "The restaurant is the regular beginning point for my 'Spirits of San Antonio' tours." After a delicious home-cooked meal, the tour participants are regaled with great stories about the escapades and antics of "Miss Margaret," the white-clad actress spirit. There is also "Little Eddie," a youngster who loves

to play mischievous pranks on the cook; and the elderly seamstress, "Henrietta." Last and certainly not least, there's Al Martin, the tall man in the dark suit, and then an elderly man who doesn't do much but "hang out" in the belfry, sometimes waving to passers-by.

Management has taken the time to discuss each spirit: Miss Margaret is a graceful lady and the restaurant's most frequent visitor. She is always spotted wearing a white Victorian-style dress, complete with high lace collar, leg-o-mutton sleeves, and a full-length skirt. She wears her hair swept up into a bun on top of her head. Because she is most often seen appearing during a stage production, she is believed to be Miss Margaret Gething, a charming, beautiful young singer and actress, who lived with her mother on Guenther Street. When a touring show came to San Antonio in the early 1900s, Miss Gething stepped into a part vacated by an ailing actress. She performed in New York and Europe, once starring on Broadway with Clark Gable. Margaret died in 1975 and the lady-in-white began visiting the building one year later.

Little Eddie is a mischievous spirit, playing pranks and practical jokes on the long-suffering kitchen help. He is less frequently observed than Margaret and his age is thought to be between eight and twelve. Like most kids, he is known to get rather bothersome until he receives attention. One local psychic said his name was

Edward (although he preferred Eddie), while another linked his death to a long-since vanished playground. A third psychic believes the youthful spirit came to the place by way of an antique rattan wheelchair that was once used as a prop for a play.

Other apparitions include an elderly man and woman who appear on or near the stage or on the bell tower at the front of the building. Psychics have come up with the name Henrietta for another of the female spirits. She may have been a servant or employee of Miss Margaret who did her sewing. She has been blamed for costumes appearing and disappearing.

The elderly man is believed to be Alvin, an actor in one of the Alamo City Theater plays performed long ago. Alvin, who was a partner in a gallery at Blue Star, two blocks down from the theater, was cast in a performance of *Born Yesterday*. On opening night he thought he might have the flu and stayed home. The next evening he didn't show up for the actors call. When the stage manager went to his home to find him, he was almost comatose. Days later Alvin passed away in the hospital from an unknown virus, never getting a chance to perform. Perhaps that's why he remains behind in the theater. The trouble is, Alvin's ghost is still late for many of the rehearsals—but at least he shows up.

The active spirits are responsible for a number of unexplained events including shelves suddenly being pulled out of the refrigerator and microwave. During lunch, silverware has risen up off the steam table, levitated across the room, and landed on the carpeted floor among the dining tables. An occasional plate is taken and thrown from a waiter delivering food. Washed and draining dishes suddenly move back into the dishwater on their own. Unusual noises persist for a while, then dissipate, and discarnate voices whisper employees' names. As the cover of a pamphlet by the owner states, "Great Food and Friendly Spirits, from the Most Haunted Eatery in San Antonio."

Address:	1150 South Alamo Street, San Antonio, Texas 78210
Phone:	210-271-7791
Contact:	Marcia Baer Larsen
Payment:	Most major credit cards accepted

References:							Personal communication, Alamo Street Restaurant
								and Alamo Street Theater; Docia Schultz Williams,
								*When Darkness Falls: Tales of San Antonio Ghosts
								and Hauntings*; Docia Schultz Williams and Reneta
								Byrne, *Spirits of San Antonio and South Texas*;
								*Great Food and Friendly Spirits: A Collection of Pri-
								vate Recipes*, and "Spirited Tales from Marcia Baer
								Larsen's Alamo Street Restaurant"

Victoria's Black Swan Inn

Artifacts illustrating Native American occupation of Salado Creek for several thousand years have been found by archaeologists along the creek banks and in the open fields near this inn. On September 19, 1842, a battle took place on Holbrook Road in proximity to the Black Swan Inn, between a Mexican army of 1,400 soldiers directed by a French general and 200 Texans, along Salado Creek. Sixty-one Mexican soldiers and a lone Texan died in the battle. A historic marker commemorates the battle and is located just beyond the entry gates to the inn.

Heinrich Mahler and his wife, Marie Biermann Mahler, immigrated to America from Germany in 1870, soon after their marriage. They found their way to Texas and purchased 200 acres of land on what is now the corner of Rittiman and Holbrook Roads, on January 14, 1887. The Mahlers then built their first house overlooking the creek. In 1897 Mahler extended his holdings by purchasing 240 acres that adjoined his property to the north. After buying this additional land, the Mahlers built a new residence and moved there in 1901.

This one-story farmhouse sat atop a knoll, overlooking the creek. Heinrich Mahler had farming and ranching interests and also grew cotton, but his main business was dairy farming. The dairy barn, water tank, windmill, and stables are still situated on the grounds. The Mahlers had four children: Sam, Daniel, Louise, and Sarah. Marie Mahler died in 1923 at age seventy-three, and Heinrich was eighty-three when he passed away in 1925. Both are buried in the St. John's Lutheran Cemetery.

Heinrich left Daniel the house, silo, and milk barn while Sam was given the corner property. Each daughter received one of the houses the Mahlers owned in San Antonio. During the mid-1930s the Mahler farms were sold. Sam's property was purchased by Paul F. Gueldner, father-in-law of Sophie Mahler Gueldner, and was later again resold. Daniel's property was bought by the Woods and Holbrooks.

Since both families planned to reside in the house, changes were made. The main portion of the house was converted into one extremely large drawing room, which looked out onto the long front porch. Several walls, which had divided up smaller rooms in the original residence, had to be knocked out. Two long wings were added to either side of the center section, each wing having one large and one smaller bedroom. Each wing had a large bathroom and numerous closets. A kitchen and dining room were added, and the remodeled house was now called White Gables.

The Holbrooks had no children; the Woods had a daughter, Joline. She lived in the house with her parents, aunt, and uncle until she married. Her husband, Hall Park Street Jr., was locally famous. After the Holbrooks and Mr. Woods passed away, Mrs. Woods remained in White Gables with Joline, Park Street Jr., and their children, Hall Park Street III and Joline. A second story was added and the house expanded to sixteen rooms and 6,000 square feet of living space. Joline Street died of cancer in her late thirties, leaving a daughter of nineteen. Mrs. Woods continued to live in the house with Hall Park Street Jr. and the grandchildren after the death of her daughter.

Park Street finally remarried and lived in the house with his new bride. On August 4, 1965, Street's wife found him dead at age fifty-five, strangled, a belt looped around his neck, tied to a bedpost. After Park Street's death, his daughter, Joline Woods Street Robinson, and her family moved into the house with her grandmother. They remained there until she passed away. Finally, in 1973, the house was sold to Mrs. Ingeborg Mehren. She decided to

sell the property and take on other endeavors in 1984. Today the residence is known as Victoria's Black Swan Inn.

The Black Swan is definitely haunted. Former owners, staff, and guests have reported a number of strange incidents that have led to this conclusion. Doors that have been securely locked find a way to unlock themselves. Lights in the outside hallway have turned on without the aid of human intervention. A man dressed in a white shirt and wearing dark trousers, usually with his hands on his hips, has been frequently sighted standing at the foot of one of the beds before suddenly disappearing. An elderly, wrinkled man with an unpleasant demeanor has been seen peering in an upstairs bedroom window, even though there is no way humanly possible for someone to climb up to that part of the house. There have been numerous cold spots reported in the house. Some doors will not remain locked, while others, especially the bathroom doors, will lock themselves from the inside. Lights, especially in the south wing of the house, have come on by themselves—this area of the house has made a number of people feel uneasy. An oversized closet located in the largest room of the house, at the end of the wing, is so eerie that people are reluctant to go there alone because they get chills or feel as if they are being watched by some form of unseen energy. During a television filming, all the lights in the south wing came on by themselves. A grand piano in the drawing room has been known to start playing a few notes by itself. The sounds of a music box can sometimes be heard echoing throughout the house, and the distinct sound of hammering has been heard downstairs, although the source has never been found.

Then there is the gift shop on the premises, which has a number of dolls on display. On more than one occasion, the dolls have been mysteriously rearranged and the doll buggy moved from its original position, as if an invisible child has been playing. A beautiful dollhouse still lies toward the back of the house, which the Streets built for their daughter, Joline, when she was young. Perhaps the daughter's spirit likes to play with the reminders of a more pleasant time in her life.

A former owner, upon purchasing the house, was told by several local residents that the house was haunted by a beautiful lady who was frequently seen in the largest of the upstairs bedrooms wearing clothing reminiscent of the 1920s. Could it be the ghost of Joline Woods, who once traveled to Washington, D.C. to represent San Antonio at a gala ball. A period photograph showed Joline wearing clothing similar to the apparel the ghost often wears.

A reporter and camera crew from the Sci-Fi Channel's television show *Sightings* visited the Black Swan Inn during December of 1996. Peter James, a renowned psychic consultant, agreed that the place is literally overrun with spirits. During his investigation,

James was able to pick up the energy of a woman on the stairway, another energy form in the main reception room, two spirits in the south wing, and another force in a hallway. He also witnessed a man looking in the house from an outside window. James finally remarked that the spirit of a little girl who pulls the pranks with the dolls at Justin's shop is named Sarah but commented that she was always called "Suzie."

The renowned psychic also told JoAnn Rivera that former owner Park Street Jr. has been trying to contact her for quite some time. It seems he wants her to find something important he left hidden in the house—at last report this has not occurred. The findings of the renowned psychic only solidifies the opinion of many that Victoria's Black Swan Inn is one of the most spirit-filled places in Texas, if not the United States.

Address:	1006 Holbrook Road, San Antonio, Texas 78281
Phone:	210-590-2507
Fax:	210-590-2509
Contacts:	Katie or JoAnn Rivera
Business Information:	Restaurant hours are from 9:00 A.M. to 5:30 P.M., Tuesday through Friday (later appointments can be made for Tuesday and Wednesday); full service catering; seminars; luncheons; private parties; weddings; receptions
Payment:	Most major credit cards—no American Express
References:	Personal communication, Victoria's Black Swan Inn; Docia Schultz Williams, *When Darkness Falls: Tales of San Antonio Ghosts and Hauntings*; Docia Schultz Williams and Reneta Byrne, *Spirits of San Antonio and South Texas*; Paramount Studios, Ann Daniel Productions, *Sightings* (1996)

The Menger Hotel

The oldest hotel in San Antonio lies directly across the street from the Alamo. The Menger lies on a portion of the 1836 Alamo battlefield. A number of famous people and celebrities have visited the Menger including O. Henry, Lillie Langtry, Sarah Bernhard, Anna Held, Beverly Sills, Teddy Roosevelt, Robert E. Lee, presidents Taft, U.S. Grant, McKinley, Nixon, and Truman, Cornelius Vanderbilt, Oscar Wilde, and Roy Rogers and Dale Evans.

The original two-story, fifty-room hotel was built out of limestone. The hotel quickly became so popular that a three-story addition was built directly behind it. A list of major events in the history of the Menger Hotel follows: 1871 - William A. Menger died; 1874-75 - additional property was acquired to the north; 1881 - the hotel was sold to Major J. H. Kampmann. The kitchen was relocated and a third story added to the Alamo Plaza portion, along with a three-story addition to the north; 1887 - a fourth story was added to Blum Street side, and improvements included the addition of an artesian well, steam laundry, electric lights, and a steam elevator; 1897 - the kitchen was remodeled and new fixtures and furnishings were added to the dining room; 1899 - a fifty-room addition was built; 1909 - noted architect Alfred Giles made extensive changes to the hotel. An ornamental marquee of ground glass and iron was added to the interior, and the original (south) lobby was embellished with a new marble floor; 1912 - architect Atlee B. Ayres was commissioned to renovate the dining room and add thirty rooms; 1943 - the hotel was purchased by W. L. Moody. Jr.; 1949-50- a four-story, 125-room addition, new lobby, and pool were added. The bar was installed on the Crockett Street side; 1953 - the Menger Patio Club and swimming pool was added; 1966-67 -a five-story addition was built; 1988 - restoration of the hotel was completed. A new ballroom, several meeting areas, and thirty-three rooms and suites were added; 1990 - the Colonial Dining

Room was restored; 1992 - extensive renovation and restoration was done on the original 1859 building.

In 1887 manager Hermann Kampmann decided that a new tap-room should be built within the hotel as a replica of the House of Lords Pub in London. The architect, who was sent to England to examine the pub, installed a paneled ceiling of cherrywood, booths and beveled mirrors from France, and decorated glass cabinets at a cost of $60,000. It was in this bar that Teddy Roosevelt recruited many of his Rough Riders as volunteers for the Spanish American War. A number of volunteers were members of New York's elite, including Cornelius Vanderbilt. During Prohibition the bar was moved, piece by piece, to its current location.

The modernization of the Menger may have occurred to counter the two new hotels built in 1909, the St. Anthony and the Gunter. Many elaborate balls and parties, hosted by San Antonio's social and political elite, were held in the Colonial Dining Room. The room has been in continuous use since it was opened. Many of the Menger chefs came from Europe to create dishes that reflected the German, Mexican, French, and American blend of cultures found within San Antonio. The Menger's famous mango ice cream has remained on the menu for over a hundred years. Throughout its illustrious career as one of San Antonio's premiere hotels, there were rumors of ghosts inhabiting the building.

One hotel manager was convinced the Menger was hauntingly alive and said he is certain that Teddy Roosevelt's ghost has come back several times to visit the bar. Maintenance men have talked about doors that will not stay closed after they were locked and relocked. Staff members have heard musical sounds and marching footsteps in various parts of the hotel.

An *Express News* article stated that guests had reported seeing a "woman in blue" walking silently through the hallways on a number of occasions. Historian David Bowser also wrote about the Lady in Blue and the fact that a housekeeper had seen the phantom while cleaning a room. The woman was too convincing and detailed in her description of the incident to be summarily shrugged off. The account suggested that after the maid entered the room and began her daily cleaning routine, she began sensing that someone else was in the room with her. Thinking it was one of the guests, she quickly turned and was stunned to see a woman in an old-fashioned, long blue dress, sitting peacefully in a chair a few feet away from her. The female apparition was described as an attractive woman, with blondish shoulder length hair worn in a style of the 1930s or '40s. The awe-struck employee was still gazing at the figure when the apparition suddenly disappeared—along with the housekeeper who immediately ran out of the room seeking the company of people she could see, touch, and talk to.

Rumors of odd occurrences in a dimly lit hallway and a second-floor room in one of the old sections of the hotel are frequent.

Several of the hotel's personnel assigned to this particular room have experienced bizarre incidents. There have been reported gusts of cold air, strange noises, room lights flicking on and off inexplicably, doors closing of their own accord, and a general feeling of being watched, all coming from this room.

Another long-time housekeeper is also convinced that the hotel is haunted. Although she has never seen the elusive Lady in Blue, she knows others who have. Several times maids and guests have smelled cigar smoke in the no-smoking bar. The smell comes and goes and is most noticeable in the early morning hours while the staff is busy cleaning and preparing for the next busy day of work.

Another restless spirit roams the long halls on the third floor of the original building. The wraith has been sighted wearing a full, floor-length skirt and a scarf or a bandanna tied around her head. A long necklace of beads has been seen dangling around her neck, and she sometimes wears an apron. The ghost is said to be Sallie White, a chambermaid who worked at the Menger in 1876. People who have seen her believe she likes to return to the place where she spent so much time. Her life was cut tragically short on March 28, 1876, when she was shot by her husband in a fit of rage. She hung on to life for two agonizing days before expiring on March 30. An old hotel ledger entry by Frederick Hahn states that he paid $32 cash for Sallie's burial—$25 for a coffin and $7 for a grave.

A famous ghost guest who stayed at the Menger when he visited San Antonio was Captain Richard King, founder of the famous King Ranch, south of San Antonio. The King Suite is still furnished with period furniture used during his visits there, including the old four-poster bed complete with canopy. The Captain died at dusk in August of 1885. He loved the hotel so much that his funeral service was conducted in the big front parlor.

A former security guard, while patrolling the hallways of the older section of the hotel, saw a man walking down the hall late at night. The man wore old-fashioned, western-type clothing, including a string tie and broad-brimmed black hat. The curious guard pursued the man to where the hallway turned. The startled guard watched as the bizarre-looking man kept walking—right through the wall! On other occasions, the same guard stated that when he rode up the elevator it frequently stopped on the third floor, no matter what button he pushed.

There is also the matter of the room-service bell at the front desk. Although it has been disconnected for quite some time, it periodically rings quite loudly, startling the staff! The desk staff is convinced it's the ghost of Teddy Roosevelt demanding the prompt service he enjoyed while he was visiting the Menger. Teddy Roosevelt as well as one or two of his "rough riders" has also been sighted in the Menger Bar, a favorite hangout and a place Roosevelt used for recruiting purposes. Bar personnel, employees, and custodians have reported a number of strange encounters there.

One morning in April, before the bar opened, a custodian entered the double doors to perform his routine tasks. He was youthful and afraid of few things in life. Business as usual, he wheeled his cleaning cart into the bar area and placed a doorstop to hold the heavy entrance doors in place. As he began to clean, he happened to glance over toward the bar where a chair was lying on the floor. Usually during closing, all of the barstools are laid face down on top of the bar. However, that wasn't his only concern. There, at the end of the bar, he caught sight of a patron whom he initially thought had managed to elude the staff in order to remain for a few more toasts.

The usually fearless but now quite concerned employee suddenly froze in his tracks when he realized that his bar contact was not wearing modern-day attire, but rather an old-fashioned military uniform. Furthermore, after a few seconds it dawned on him that if the man was not there when he first walked in, where did he come from—did this stranger just materialize out of thin air? The young custodian's curiosity soon turned to fear, and fear gave way to panic when the man at the bar attempted to beckon the young man over with his index finger. That was all the custodian needed—he tried beating a hasty retreat after realizing that the bar patron was a ghost!

The spirit would have the last word, however, by slamming the double doors shut before the custodian could reach them, then locking them before he could leave. After what seemed like an eternity, the frantic custodian raised such a ruckus that the night manager and a night security guard rushed to his rescue. All the while, the ghostly visitor calmly sat on the barstool and stared at the frightened custodian, who had no means of escape.

The poor, distraught boy was finally rescued, and he collapsed in a lobby chair. His rescuers feared that he might be having a heart attack, since he was gasping for breath and shaking violently. They called 911 as the custodian blurted out that he had seen a ghost. As he was taken to a local clinic for precautionary measures, the night manager and security guard searched the bar for any sign of an intruder—or ghost. No spirit materialized and no flesh and blood intruder was found. The young boy never came back to the Menger as an employee or to the bar as a patron. The once fearless lad now had great respect for the unseen.

Another custodian working in the bar around 1:30 A.M. felt as if he were being watched. He glanced up at the balcony area and noticed a man dressed in a dark gray suit and wearing a small hat. The strange-looking man sat at the railing on the side closest to the Alamo for a few minutes. The startled custodian tried to elicit the help of a fellow employee, but by the time he returned with help, the apparition had disappeared. Again, another employee quit rather than take a chance on meeting a Menger Bar ghost again.

During September of 1996 a couple remained in the Menger Bar until closing time. As they got up from their table and were preparing to leave, the woman was standing in the center of the bar, while her husband stood off to the side. Just then the husband saw a man enter the bar and take a few steps toward his wife. Since the man appeared to ignore the husband and moved closer and closer to his wary wife, the husband tried to intervene. To their amazement, as the husband stepped in the path of the man, the visitor vanished!

Other unusual events included four men who watched in silence as the front doors of the bar suddenly swung open, yet no one walked in. Because of their weight, the heavy brass and glass doors can't open by themselves. There was no wind that night, and the doors are on the inside of the building in a protected entryway.

Another time a women operating the gift shop off the main lobby reported witnessing a display of little shot glasses lift off the counter. The glasses moved from the left side of the counter to the right side, then were carefully placed back down on the counter by an invisible force.

One hotel guest reported seeing a male figure appear just before stepping into an elevator on the top floor. She had pressed the elevator button, while glancing over her shoulder. She saw the figure of a man wearing a jacket with big, puffed sleeves and a hat from another era approaching her. Just a few feet away from the woman, the figure suddenly vanished in front of her.

A man who was checking out of the hotel, questioned a number of telephone calls billed to his room—he swore he made no such calls. Upon closer inspection it dawned on him that the phone number seemed vaguely familiar. Then he remembered that it belonged to his mother. Unfortunately, she had been dead for ten years! Was his mother trying to reach him for an otherworldly emergency or just calling to see how his stay was at the Menger?

A waitress who worked the early morning shift saw the figure of man whom the staff called "Mr. Preston." He appears as an old man who frequents a bench in the patio area, always wearing a top hat and a dapper dress suit of the late 1800s era.

One morning, Fox TV National News Service personnel, hotel manager Ernesto Malacara, and Tom Brady, the hotel's chief of security were walking down the corridor that leads to the hotel parking garage when they spotted a man sitting in the office. The offices had not yet opened for the day, so they did a double take only to find that the man had completely disappeared!

During a convention, a woman and her husband were assigned a room in the original building. Upon entering the room, the woman immediately felt a presence or force watching over them. After arriving, she took a nap and immediately after dozing off, had vivid dreams of two skulls. Later that same evening, whatever was in the room when they arrived, as well as the instigator of her dreams, became a little more brazen—it, or they, began pawing at the bed sheets, and she felt as if she were being touched all over her body. She told her husband all about the occurrences and wanted out of the room immediately. He loved the accommodations and didn't wish to leave, so she took her credit card and checked into another room by herself. She wasn't bothered again by the pesky spirit. Perhaps it had turned its attention to her husband, although he had no complaints the next morning. That, or the ghost just likes women.

While checking out, another woman lodged a complaint. Apparently the night before, after she went to sleep, the television suddenly came on. She dutifully got up out of her cozy confines and proceeded to turn off the set, attributing it to an electrical problem. Once again she climbed into bed, and as she was about to go to sleep, the television turned on again! This happened several times before it ceased—perhaps the spirit had become tired of this game, or the show it was watching was over.

On another occasion, a repairman was busy at work on the hotel's video system. There are three steel lockers that house the video players, with eight units per locker. As he was working on one locker, the door to an adjacent one suddenly flung open and out popped a tape. The movie that flew out happened to be *The Devil's Own*.

Several women who have operated the hotel PBX over the years often complained that they felt as if someone was watching them while they worked. On numerous occasions they have turned in the direction of where they felt a presence and encountered a face that seems to dissolve before their eyes. No one has a clue as to the identity of this mystery person.

Another housekeeping person, whose job it is to remove the prior night's trays left in front of hotel rooms before sunrise, has heard her name called out several times by an invisible guest. Every time she checks the area the sound emanated from, there is no one around.

The door to the main hotel entrance is notorious for swinging open unassisted. It's not electrically powered, and the massive door is made of around 160 pounds of brass and glass, so the fact that it's heavy, constructed away from the street, and recessed in the building's facade makes it impossible for wind to cause it to suddenly open. The startled staff oftentimes looks on incredulously as the doors open and then close as if some unseen guest or guests have just entered the building.

Two women spending the night in one of the "haunted" rooms said that one of them was awakened at 6:30 A.M. by the sound of someone walking across the carpet at the foot of her bed. The woman who was awakened described the sound as a heel-to-toe walking motion, making its way slowly across the floor. She immediately sat upright in bed and focused on the area where the sound was coming from. At first, she thought her roommate had gotten up early. She was startled to look over and find her friend sound asleep. At that point, she did the only normal thing a person could do when confronted by the unknown, which was to quickly pull the covers over her head and pray that whatever it was would go away—it did!

Be sure to check out the Menger on your own in search of spirits. Have some food, a drink at the bar, spend the night, or simply browse this historic wonder. Or, you can take a fabulous tour of the Alamo and local haunts.

Address:	204 Alamo Plaza, San Antonio, Texas 78205
Phone:	210-223-4361
Fax:	210-228-0022
Toll Free Number:	1-800-345-9285
Contact:	Ernesto Malacara
Accommodations:	350 guestrooms
Amenities:	Air-conditioned rooms; Colonial Room Restaurant; Menger Bar; Victorian Lobby; Renaissance Room; receptions, meetings, and conferences; swimming pool; gardens
Payment:	Visa, MasterCard, Discover, American Express, Diners Club, Carte Blanche
References:	Personal communication, The Menger; Docia Schultz Williams and Reneta Byrne, *Spirits of San Antonio and South Texas*; Docia Schultz Williams, *When Darkness Falls: Tales of San Antonio Ghosts and Hauntings*; *Welcome to the Historic Menger Hotel: Historic Hotels of America, A Self-Guided Tour*. The Menger Hotel, San Antonio; Robert

Wlodarski and Anne Powell Wlodarski, *The Haunted Alamo: A History of the Mission and Guide to Paranormal Activity*; Robert Wlodarski and Anne Powell Wlodarski, *Spirits of the Alamo*; Jen Scoville Ghost City Texas, http://www.texasmonthly.com/travel/virtual/ghostcity/hunt.html; Docia Schultz Williams, *Best Tales of Texas Ghosts*

The Holiday Inn Crockett Hotel

Using photographs of the existing structure, the architects uncovered original brickwork, windows, and storefront structures; cleaned and repaired trim and cornices; and restored the lobby to its original condition. In addition, an atrium was constructed, guestrooms added, and others refurbished. As a result of this careful renovation, the Crockett Hotel is listed on the National Register of Historic Places, and architects Ford, Powell, and Carson received a Historical Preservation Certification from the U.S. Department of the Interior.

In 1718 Governor Martin de Alaroon founded the Mission of San Antonio de Valero near the San Antonio River, the first Spanish mission in the area. In 1724 the mission moved east to its present site, and an acequia was constructed to provide water to the mission fields. The land occupied by the Crockett Hotel is situated between the two branches of that Acequia Madre, just south and east of the mission property. It was not until 1758 that the mission was built. By 1773 refugees from an abandoned mission in East Texas arrived and petitioned for the distribution of mission lands in order to support their families.

In 1793 a decree was finally carried out, and the land was given to Juan Bautista de la Zerda to be used for agriculture cultivation over the next fifty years. This uncultivated land stood just east of the Alamo, the famous "Cradle of Texas Liberty." In fact, the grounds of the Crockett Hotel were part of the Alamo battlefield.

During the night before the Battle of the Alamo, hundreds of troops moved into the area where the hotel pool and courtyard are now situated. The southeast palisade fronting the chapel was defended by Davy Crockett, for whom the hotel is named.

A prosperous French-born merchant, Augustese Honore Grenet, purchased the property in 1874 and operated a general merchandise store on the site. G.B. Davis bought the land in 1887 as part of a judgment for the estate of Honore Grenet. The land changed owners three more times before being sold to the International Order of Odd Fellows on January 30, 1907. This fraternal organization built the lodge hall and hotel (now the Crockett) in 1909. Oddly enough, one of the five men who formed the San Antonio Lodge #11 of the International Order of Odd Fellows in 1849 was John James Giddings, who owned the land fifty years before the lodge was constructed.

The celebration of the ninetieth anniversary of the Independent Order of Odd Fellows and the laying of the cornerstone of the San Antonio Odd Fellows Temple took place with great ceremony on April 26, 1909. The 275 brothers dedicated the top two floors of the six-story structure for lodge purposes, with the first four floors to be used as a hotel. The hotel's first proprietors were F. Peck and William Nagel. In 1927 a west wing was added, a seven-story addition done by architect Henry T. Phelps of San Antonio. The Independent Order of Odd Fellows maintained ownership until 1978 when it was purchased by an investor from British Columbia. In 1982 San Antonio native John Blocker bought the Crockett at the urging of his wife, Jeanne, whose sister, Mary Ann Castleberry, was a past president of the San Antonio Conservation Society. At that time the property was renovated in order to be faithful to the original building, and it is still a San Antonio architectural wonder and a historic Texas landmark, with 202 spacious and beautifully decorated guestrooms. The Texas landmark is also haunted.

Ghostly activities have centered in the lobby where the entrance doors will occasionally open and close without being triggered by a human being. The bar area and certain rooms in the hotel are also places frequented by the spirits of the Crockett. The ghosts seem to enjoy whispering to staff persons, as well as guests, although the noises sound more like other-dimensional mutterings rather than specific requests.

There are also those pesky moving cold spots, unexplained footsteps, which, although often heard walking through the corridors, rooms, and lobby area, are never accompanied by a human figure. There are also reports, which have circulated over the years, of the figure of a man who appears in the executive offices section of the hotel. This apparition has been sighted by several staff persons, who have watched in amazement as the man vanishes in front of them. The offices are located in the modern two-story section of the Crockett that encompasses the swimming pool and patio areas.

Renowned ghost story author, tour guide, and psychic investigator Docia Williams, who toured the Crockett in 1996, related the following incident from her book *When Darkness Falls: Tales of San Antonio Ghosts and Hauntings*: "Dave Mora, the reservations manager, decided to tag along. He had actually seen the figure of a man clad in a dark blue jacket as he moved into the small kitchen area adjoining the boardroom. Mora recalled the day he had come around the corner from the area where the offices are located and spied the figure of a sturdy man with dark brown hair as he moved into the kitchen. A quick check into that room revealed that it was empty. Yet Mora was convinced he saw the man quite clearly. He added that other hotel staff members had seen him at various times."

According to psychics and staff, there is yet another spirit that haunts the Crockett, although further investigation is needed in the future to ascertain the possible identity of the spirits who reside at the hotel. The playful spirits of the Crockett seem to affect the functioning of the air-conditioning units; are the cause behind the whispered conversations that are heard in unoccupied areas of the hotel; cause curtains to suddenly move in rooms that are being cleaned; open the electronic doors at the front entrance; are responsible for disembodied footsteps that are oftentimes heard near the entrance to the building; and various other minor sounds, and events that frequently happen.

Considering the Crockett's proximity to the Alamo and the fact that the building lies in the heart of the 1836 battlefield, it's not surprising that the hotel is haunted. But who are these restless spirits? Soldiers, defenders, or ordinary people who once spent a memorable time in this timeless place.

Address:	320 Bonham Street, San Antonio, Texas 78205
Phone:	210-225-6500
Fax:	210-225-6251
Toll Free Number:	1-800-292-1050
Accommodations:	206 guestrooms, five junior suites, two suites
Amenities:	Cable television; air conditioning; outdoor swimming pool; 7th floor sun deck with Jacuzzi, laundry and room service, complimentary morning coffee in the lobby; meeting space; Landmark Restaurant; Ernie's Bar and Grill

Payment:	Visa, MasterCard, Discover, American Express, Diners Club, Carte Blanche
References:	Personal communication, The Best Western Crockett Hotel; Robert Wlodarski and Anne Powell Wlodarski, *The Haunted Alamo: A History of the Mission and Guide to Paranormal Activity*; Docia Schultz Williams, *When Darkness Falls: Tales of San Antonio Ghosts and Hauntings*; Robert Wlodarski and Anne Powell Wlodarski, *Spirits of the Alamo*; Jen Scoville Ghost City Texas, http://www.texasmonthly.com/travel/virtual/ghostcity/hunt.html

The Camberley Gunter Hotel

In the early 1900s the 301-room, eight-story building was the largest hotel in San Antonio, as well as the center of social life. "Black Jack" Pershing, Will Rogers, Max Baer, John Wayne, Harry Truman, Tom Mix, B.C Forbes, Mae West, Rogers Hornsby, Gene Tunney, Nancy Reagan, Lady Bird Johnson, and hundreds more celebrities, politicians, and dignitaries have visited and continue to visit this historic hotel in the heart of San Antonio.

The Gunter Hotel, when completed in 1909, was the largest building in San Antonio, a palatial structure with marble floors, walnut paneling, and chandeliers. The history of the Gunter Hotel began in 1837 when the Frontier Inn was built on the site of the present-day hotel. In 1851 the site became the United States Military Headquarters; from 1861 to 1865 it served as Confederate Headquarters; in 1872, as the Vance House; and in 1886, was renamed the Mahncke Hotel.

The Gunter Hotel became a reality because of real estate developer L.J. Hart and twelve local investors, including Jot Gunter who purchased the site from Mary E. Vance Winslow in 1907. The Gunter survived the major floods of 1913 and 1921; a ninth story was added in 1917; in 1926 three more stories were

Seiterle Group acquired the Gunter in 1979 and began restoration, which was achieved from 1982-1984.

With its fame and notoriety came the inevitable stories of hauntings. Room 636 (now changed) became legendary as the location of one of San Antonio's greatest unsolved mysteries, which tragically concluded at the St. Anthony Hotel in room 536. The murder room at the Gunter is reportedly haunted. Docia Williams, in several of her books, discusses the murder in detail and the subsequent investigation involving a blonde, a man registered as Albert Knox, and a body that was there one minute and disappeared the next.

Blood was found everywhere in room 636, indicating someone had been brutally murdered, even butchered, but there was no body ever found. The only suspect who may have been able to solve the mystery was a man named Knox. Unfortunately, during the investigation, his body was found at the St. Anthony Hotel in room 536, with a bullet in his temple. The case remains open: Two people dead; blood everywhere in room 636 of the Gunter; no woman's body ever found; no motive; no confession; no missing person report for the woman—it remains one of the most bizarre crimes in San Antonio's history.

The Ballroom is another area where repeated unexplainable occurrences have taken place and psychic activity is strong. Photographs of employees and guests have been developed at a variety of functions showing guests from another time appearing as unidentifiable transparent images partying alongside the living. There have also been a number of peculiar disturbances reported in the elevators. Phantom voices have been heard in unoccupied rooms and hallways of the hotel. Ghostly parties have been reported in rooms that have not been checked into—by the living; mysterious shadows have frequently appeared on corridor walls as startled guests and staff look on in stunned silence—this is especially true in the vicinity of room 426.

A man named Buck, a long-term tenant who died in the hotel, is still seen wandering near his former room, picking up the paper, and just taking life or death one day at a time. A Lady in Blue and a Lady in White have also been seen floating through walls, as well as following staff and guests down hallways and into rooms. These are only a few of the hundreds of ghost stories drifting through this historic hotel. Dine, drink, relax for the night, or take a stroll through this vintage historical hotel, and perhaps you can add to the ghostly legends of the Gunter Hotel.

Address: 205 East Houston, San Antonio, Texas 78205
Phone: 210-227-3241
Fax: 210-227-3299
Toll Free Number: 1-800-222-4276

Contact:	Sue Baker
Accommodations:	320 guestrooms, all with private baths
Amenities:	Spacious, comfortably furnished guest rooms; cable television; data ports; a beautiful heated pool; Jacuzzi, and sundeck overlook the city skyline; a variety of dining establishments including the renowned Gunter Bakery
Payment:	Visa, MasterCard, Discover, American Express, Diners Club, Carte Blanche
References:	Personal communication, The Gunter Hotel; Docia Schultz Williams and Reneta Byrne, *Spirits of San Antonio and South Texas*; Robert Wlodarski and Anne Powell Wlodarski, *The Haunted Alamo: A History of the Mission and Guide to Paranormal Activity*; Docia Schultz Williams, *When Darkness Falls: Tales of San Antonio Ghosts and Hauntings*; Docia Schultz Williams, *Best Tales of Texas Ghosts*; Robert Wlodarski and Anne Powell Wlodarski, *Spirits of the Alamo*; Jen Scoville Ghost City Texas, http://www.texasmonthly .com/travel/virtual/ghostcity/hunt.html

Crowne Plaza St. Anthony

Officially designated as a Texas and National Historic Landmark, the Crowne Plaza St. Anthony Hotel preserves and embodies the unique history and flavor of San Antonio while providing modern, meticulously maintained facilities.

Among the many "firsts" at the St. Anthony Hotel: It was the first hotel in the nation to be completely air-conditioned (1941); the first hotel to utilize electric eye automatic doors; and the first hotel to feature a drive-through registration desk at the motor lobby entrance. The St. Anthony is also home to two very special suites—the Presidential Suite, designated in 1941, and the John Wayne Suite, named in 1978 due to the very favorable impression

Mr. Wayne made with the hotel staff during his stay while filming the movie *The Alamo*.

Named after the city and a saint, San Antonio de Padua, the Crowne Plaza St. Anthony Hotel was built in 1909 by two prominent cattlemen, B.L. Naylor and A.H. Jones, mayor of San Antonio from 1912 to 1913. In 1935 the hotel was purchased by Mr. Ralph W. Morrison, who maintained the hotel's position as a truly elegant social center for San Antonio. A world traveler, Mr. Morrison spared no expense in bringing to the St. Anthony art pieces and antique furnishings from around the world, many still on display in the hotel's Peacock Alley.

The Loggia section of Peacock Alley, characterized by French doors and windows overlooking Travis Park, was at one time an open-air porch area. It was remodeled as an enclosed area during a renovation in 1965. Among the treasures in Peacock Alley are the eight-foot Empire-style chandeliers, specially made for the hotel in 1965 by the Light-O-Leer Company of New Jersey, at a cost of $2,500 each.

From the 1920s until 1941 many of the nation's top big bands entertained in what was then known as the Starlight Terrace Nightclub situated on the roof section of the hotel. While entertaining the hotel's guests, the band concerts were broadcast live nationally every week. In 1941, during a period of extensive renovation, the Anacacho Ballroom, named after Mr. Morrison's Anacacho Ranch, was opened, and the concerts were moved into the ballroom with the live national broadcast continuing. In addition to the big band concerts of the era, guests from 1930-1967 were also entertained twice daily, seven days a week, by a string ensemble, which played in Peacock Alley.

The Peraux Room, the hotel's second social function room, was named after the Parisian artist Lionel Peraux. A large tapestry by Mr. Peraux still hangs in the Peraux Room. In 1971 Mr. William Ochse purchased the hotel from the R.W. Morrison state. It was purchased in 1981 by the Intercontinental Hotel chain, which undertook a very successful renovation of the property. Park Lane Hotels International purchased the hotel in September of 1988 and performed additional renovations in 1995. The hotel was proud to become a flag of Crowne Plaza and has been able to continue its renovations to maintain its historic character and charm.

The "spirited" side of the hotel boasts a number of friendly apparitions. On the roof (which hosted big bands from the 1920s through 1941) the sounds of children playing have been heard late at night by staff and guests. Additionally, a woman wearing a white ballgown has been frequently sighted on the roof. According to management, there are times when you swear that a party is going on, with people dancing, drinking, and having a grand time. However, when you open the door in the evening and walk outside onto the roof, a silence engulfs you, and the experience chills many to the bone—it is considered a "hotbed" of paranormal activity.

Other strange sightings have been reported along a fourth-floor corridor, the men's locker area in the basement, a kitchen corridor that is haunted by a ghostly woman, and various rooms throughout the hotel. Allegedly, a tragic event and unsolved murder connected to room 636 at the nearby Gunter Hotel ended in tragedy for the man accused of the murder, in room 536 at the St. Anthony. Staff members have, on a number of occasions, reported seeing a woman in ghostly attire in the hallways and rooms, and an elderly woman in a long, white gown in the suicide room.

Drop in for an unforgettable dining experience, or spend the night, and while you're there ask about the spirits of the hotel. Or better yet, pick up one of the books mentioned below and conduct your own self-guided tour, and see what kind of vibrations you pick up. It just might be that the staff person you think you see or the guest who breezes by you in the hallway might not be all that he or she seems. Some of the descriptions of the ghosts at the St. Anthony Hotel sound as if the only way you'd really recognize them as spirits, is if you walked right through them, or vice versa.

Address:	300 East Travis Street, San Antonio 78205-2411
Phone:	210-227-4392
Fax:	210-227-0915
E-mail:	stanthonyhotel@internetmci.com
Accommodations:	There are 350 guestrooms, including 42 suites and a Concierge Level, each decidedly European in decor and individually decorated with antique furnishings, wall fixtures, and paintings to create an Old World ambiance.

Amenities:	All guestrooms have cable television; individually controlled heat and air conditioning; direct-dial international telephone; business services for travelers; a heated rooftop pool with landscaped sundeck; fitness center; The Madrid Room for dining; Pete's Pub, where you may enjoy a light lunch, cocktails, and complimentary hors d'oeuvres; 22 meeting rooms, a 3,600 sq. ft. ballroom; and junior ballroom.
Payment:	Visa, MasterCard, Discover, American Express, Diners Club, Carte Blanche; Japanese Credit Bureau
References:	Personal communication, The Crowne Plaza St. Anthony Hotel; Robert Wlodarski and Anne Powell Wlodarski, *The Haunted Alamo: A History of the Mission and Guide to Paranormal Activity*; Docia Schultz Williams, *When Darkness Falls: Tales of San Antonio Ghosts and Hauntings*; Docia Schultz Williams, *Best Tales of Texas Ghosts*; Robert Wlodarski and Anne Powell Wlodarski, *Spirits of the Alamo*

Cadillac Bar

This establishment actually consists of two old buildings that have been joined at the hip. One building is a large stone-walled room, where the main restaurant operation is located. This structure is joined to an older two-story structure, which has two large party rooms, one on each floor.

Herman Dietrich Stumberg, a young German immigrant, left Missouri for San Antonio. He and his son George became successful in the general mercantile business. In 1870 they built a limestone building on land Herman had purchased in 1863. Their business flourished. Farmers and ranchers from across South Texas drove wagons to the camp yard behind the store, checked their guns with the storekeeper, bought supplies, and headed for the saloons to the north or maybe the red light district to the west.

The era of 1920s and early 1930s ushered in Prohibition, wild parties, and then the great Depression. It also marked the end of the Stumberg General Store, which ceased operating in 1932. After closing, the building was used for a number of purposes. In 1980 the Cadillac was left to its employees and shortly sold to "Chito" Longoria and Ramon Salido. The buildings were restored and renovated as part of a redevelopment project known as Stumberg Square. In December 1991 George Stumberg, the great-great-grandson of the German immigrant, became the operating stockholder of the Cadillac Bar in San Antonio.

According to management and patrons, strange noises, including disembodied voices and unexplained footsteps, are not uncommon in the building. Paranormal events include distinct sounds of chains rattling; heavy saddles and bridles being dragged down the stairs; screams, laughter, and other noises associated with phantom children playing inside the building; glass shattering as if a car just drove through one of the front windows; an alarm that often turns on and off by itself; serving bowls and chafing dishes flying off the shelves in the kitchen and onto the floor, although most of the time there is no debris found; and the water faucets being turned on and off during the day by unseen hands.

A number of employees have seen ghostly figures walk around the building, only to disappear in front of startled witnesses. One common sighting is that of a tall, thin elderly man with a handlebar mustache, who is spotted on the back steps leading from the kitchen to an upper storage room. He takes his ghostly stroll, as if by habit, then vanishes.

Psychics and paranormal investigators believe that at least two spirits remain in the building: One is the tall, thin man sporting a handlebar mustache; and the other, a young woman who has been described as thin, homely, with stringy dishwater blonde hair and protruding teeth. The spirits of the Cadillac Bar seem determined to stay, and given the lively atmosphere inside, they fit right in. Oftentimes, you can't tell the dead from the living when a party-like atmosphere is in session—unless they vanish before

paying their bill. Even then, it may be a friend or an acquaintance short of cash.

Address: 212 South Flores Street, San Antonio, Texas
                  78204-1011
Phone: 210-223-5533
Contact: Jesse Medina
References: Personal communication, Cadillac Bar; Docia
                  Schultz Williams, *When Darkness Falls: Tales of
                  San Antonio Ghosts and Hauntings*

Cafe Camille

ocated in San Antonio and constructed in 1910, the original residence was turned into the Cafe Camille in 1990. The first owner lived in the back portion of what is now the cafe and as of 1998, was over one hundred years old. The present owners hope the Cafe Camille lasts as long as its prior owner, as does its patrons, not all of whom you can see.

A number of unexplainable events have taken place inside this quaint-looking cafe since it opened as a restaurant. The Beckers bought one of the older houses located on East Woodlawn in an old section of San Antonio called Monte Vista. The restaurant is considered more like a bistro, with a steady patron base from the local neighborhood and surrounding area.

After renovation and remodeling, unexplainable things began to happen, and some believe that the events can be attributed to the wife of a former owner. Sometimes the doors will open and close by themselves, and then there is a strong sense of a presence, most notably in the front portion of the cafe, which has been felt by the owners, staff, and guests. A common feeling is that someone or something is watching them from a distance, yet there is never anyone standing in the area where the feeling is the strongest—at least, no one that can be seen.

On one occasion, a firmly attached mirror was lifted off the wall by some unseen force and came crashing to the floor. Another time, a hanging cupboard fell on a glass countertop, shattering the glass. If the cupboard had fallen in the direction it was hanging, nothing would have been broken. It was as though the cupboard was directed to land on the glass counter by invisible hands.

Inside the cafe, during off hours, ghostly footsteps that cannot be accounted for can often be heard pacing the floor. There are also cold spots that suddenly emerge in certain areas of the cafe, bringing a chill to the observer, then dissipate within seconds. Yes, there's something strange happening inside this bistro/cafe/restaurant that defies logical explanation. Drop in sometime, and as you open your normal senses to the great food, also see if your paranormal senses are able to contact the spirits of the Cafe Camille.

Address:	517 East Woodlawn, San Antonio, Texas 78212
Phone:	210-735-2307
Contact:	Scott and Tracy Becker
Business Information:	Open Tuesday through Thursday from 11:00 A.M. to 2:00 P.M., and from 5:00 P.M. to 10:00 P.M.; Friday and Saturday from 11:00 A.M. until 11:00 P.M.; Sunday from 11:00 A.M. to 2:00 P.M. and from 5:00 P.M. to 10:00 P.M.
Payment:	Most major credit cards are accepted
References:	Personal communication, Cafe Camille; Docia Schultz Williams, *When Darkness Falls: Tales of San Antonio Ghosts and Hauntings*

Wunsche Bros. Cafe & Saloon

The Wunsche Bros. Cafe & Saloon is a two-story, turn-of-the-century cafe and saloon that has been painstakingly restored and expanded into a down-home comfort-food eatery on the fringes of Old Town, Spring, Texas. Spring, Texas, is a small city a few miles north of Houston on Interstate Highway 45. The Harris County town was founded by German immigrants in 1840. However, it wasn't until the early 1900s that the little town began to flourish. When the Great Northern Railroad came to Spring, a building boom took place. Seven saloons and a number of small hotels sprang up to accommodate the railroad workers and weary travelers who came by train on the Galveston-Houston-Palestine line.

The Wunsches, one of the first Spring, Texas families, built their namesake hotel and saloon in 1902. When the Great Northern Railroad moved its rail yard to Houston, Spring all but became a ghost town. Fortunately, in 1982 some enterprising locals bought the property from Wunsche descendants and transformed the building into its present state. The walls of the remodeled structure are covered with old photos of Spring's golden days. The train tracks that run by the establishment occasionally bring a train or two past the cafe.

Jane and Carl Wunsche were children of German immigrants who first settled Spring, Texas. Two of their sons, Charlie and Dell, who were former railroad men, acquired a piece of property near the railroad depot in what is today called Old Town Spring. Along with another brother, William, or "Willie" as he was called, they constructed a two-storied frame structure on the property. It was the first two-storied building in Spring! The new establishment, which opened for business in 1902, was named The Wunsche Bros. Saloon and Hotel.

Spring prospered and so did the Wunsches, that is, until the Houston and Great Northern (now known as the Missouri Pacific) moved the Spring rail yard to Houston in 1923. In 1926, although most of the town's frame buildings were torn down, the Wunsches Saloon and Hotel continued to operate. The saloon was the last one to close in Harris County when Prohibition hit.

In 1949 Viola Burke leased the building, renaming the establishment the Spring Cafe. She was known for her homemade hamburgers, which sustained the railroad workers who passed through town. In time, the reputation of the Spring Cafe spread far and wide. When Viola died in 1976, her daughter, Irma Ansley, inherited the business and continued making hamburgers.

It was during this time that a gift shop was opened for cafe customers who were waiting for a meal. As the cafe clientele grew, so did the number of shops that were designed around the restaurant.

In time the building became rundown and was sold to Brenda and Scott Mitchell in 1982. The Mitchells carefully restored the building, and in the process, it became a Texas Historic Landmark and popular restaurant. They renamed the establishment the Wunsche Bros. Cafe and Saloon, which now serves only food—no overnight lodging.

In addition to great food, there is a ghost or two—the owners aren't really sure just how many spirits occupy the building. One of the spirits is believed to be Charlie Wunsche, who is rumored to still visit his former establishment. A former cook once went to retrieve a hand towel from the linen closet. As she opened the door, she was startled to hear the sound of a man's voice mumbling something from inside the closet. Since no one could have been inside the closet at the time, she did the smart thing—shut the door and quickly left. The strange voice never conveyed what he wanted, and the cook didn't really care to hear what it was, anyway. There were a number of other unexplained encounters with the Wunsche spirits as time went on, including unexplained footsteps upstairs, cold spots, and doors that would open and shut by themselves.

Another incident involving the former cook and another employee had to do with a candle-lighting spirit; perhaps it was Charlie. The restaurant routine was to light all the candles on the tables prior to the dinner rush and then extinguish them when it came time to close the place for the night. Everything worked to perfection, except for Friday nights and Saturday mornings. It seems one candle would always be lit on Saturday mornings when the two women came back to the restaurant to open up.

The two women would arrive on Saturday, grab a cup of coffee, and go into the dining area to relax before work at their favorite table. They began noticing that a lone, lit candle would greet their morning arrival—but only on Saturdays. The strange thing was, initially, the lit candle would be at a back table, but each successive Saturday the lit candle would move closer and closer to their table, as if the ghost was slowly building up courage to approach the women.

Finally, one Saturday morning they arrived as usual and were following their usual routine. As they approached their favorite table, the lit candle was on it! Once this happened, however, they never had a lit candle encounter again. Apparently the spirit finally got up the nerve to join the women and, once that was accomplished, decided to play another game or bother someone else.

According to the owners, the most intense period of paranormal activity took place when restoration was concluded and the establishment opened for business. As often happens when a place that is haunted goes through some kind of remodeling, the spirits become restless, as if their space has been invaded and the changes have upset the delicate balance between the living and dead. It was during this time the staff noted that the furniture would sometimes be moved to a different location and the chairs would rattle or shake, and strange footsteps would be heard coming from an unoccupied area upstairs.

The upstairs area, which had been part of the old hotel, was also known as a favorite haunt for one of the ghosts. Several times the apparition of an elderly man was spotted in the upstairs area used as an overflow area when the restaurant was really crowded. The gentleman was described as wearing a black hat and black suit, with long white hair that reached over his collar. Several staff members have described the apparition as looking somber and forlorn. All of the witnesses have reported being overcome by a feeling of sadness when they encountered the man. Some people have tried to communicate with the phantom man, but he simply vanishes, leaving a chilly gust of air in his wake.

Several employees have reported that packets of sugar and salt and pepper shakers would sometimes litter the floor when the place opened in the morning. And although there are dozens of pictures that adorn the walls of the place, sometimes only the same few pictures would be found tilted or off center. All of the disturbed photographs belonged to the Wunsche family members—none of the others was ever touched. Are the Wunsche family spirits watching over the establishment, like guardians? No one has been harmed or feels threatened; it's just the feeling sometimes of being watched by invisible eyes that has the staff feeling a little edgy.

Address:	103 Midway Street (Midway at W. Hardy), P.O. Box 2745, Spring, Texas 77383
Phone:	281-350-1902
Fax:	281-353-4465
Business Information:	Happy hour is on weekdays from 4:00 to 7:00 P.M.: Restaurant hours are Monday, 11:00 A.M. to 3:00 P.M.; Tuesday through Saturday, 11:00 A.M. to 10:00 P.M.; and Sunday, 11:00 A.M. to 8:00 P.M. The establishment is closed on major holidays.
Payment:	Visa, MasterCard, Discover, American Express
References:	Personal communication, Wunsche Brothers Cafe and Saloon; Docia Schultz Williams, *Best Tales of Texas Ghosts*; Docia Schultz Williams, *Ghosts Along the Texas Coasts*

The Driskill Hotel

Located in Austin, Texas, the Driskill Hotel has played host to dignitaries and heads of state, to lobbyists, legislators, and opportunists, as well as to rising socialites, honeymooners, and travelers who are just passing through.

Cattle baron Colonel Jesse Driskill built his hotel in 1886 to serve as the Frontier Palace of the South in Texas's capital city. Constructed in the Richardsonian Romanesque style from local brick and limestone, the hotel is characterized by arched windows, spacious balconies, and exceptional ornamentation. The hotel's most spectacular architectural features are the floor-to-ceiling arched doorways located at the entrance. Busts of Jesse and his two sons are placed high atop each entrance along with stylized heads of Texas longhorn steers. According to management, the ghosts of the Driskill include: Colonel Jesse Driskill, a small child, Mrs. Bridges, Peter J. Lawless, two brides who died tragic deaths, and a few other phantoms who roam about this famous and historic hotel.

Colonel Jesse was made an honorary colonel by the Confederate army during the Civil War. He built the hotel at a cost of almost $400,000—an unheard of price at that time. People told him he was foolish to spend that much money on a hotel, and he proved them right. He went bankrupt and lost the hotel in a high stakes poker game. Three years later, in 1890, he passed away. It is said that since he was not able to enjoy his namesake creation, he haunts the hotel to this day. He makes his presence known by smoking his cigars in guests' rooms and playing with their bathroom lights.

"The Small Child"—According to Driskill lore, a U.S. senator was visiting Austin and staying here. While he was attending an event on the mezzanine, his four-year-old daughter was playing with a ball near the grand staircase. She slipped, fell, and tragically died at the base of the stairs. Some nights she can be heard

bouncing the ball down the steps and giggling. If she makes too much noise, she can only be shushed by the front desk staff.

Mrs. Bridges—Mrs. Bridges worked the front desk for several years in the early part of the century. Though she didn't die here in the hotel, she can often be seen late at night. She is clothed in a Victorian dress, and she is usually seen walking from the vault out into the middle of the lobby, the site of the old front desk. She seems to fuss with the flower arrangements that would have been there.

Peter J. Lawless—This gentleman lived in the hotel from 1886 until 1916. During these three decades the hotel was closed several times, but he stayed on, often without staff. He had a key to his room as well as the key to the front door. He is sometimes seen on the fifth floor traditional side near the elevator. When the doors open, he checks his pocket watch.

Tragic Bride #1—This story goes back about thirty years. The wedding was scheduled to take place in the hotel, and she was staying there as well. The bride-to-be was told by her fiancé, the night before their wedding that the engagement was off. She ran up to her room and took her life by hanging herself. This is one of the most active ghosts. She can be seen on the fourth floor traditional side in her wedding dress, walking the hallways. She is most often seen by guests who are here for a wedding or bachelorette party. It is usually considered good luck for brides to see her before their wedding (possibly as a warning sign to not be overcome by the wedding details).

Tragic Bride #2—This event was as recent as the early 1990s. The woman was a Houston socialite and engaged to be married. When her fiancé, called the wedding off, she took a vacation to Austin to recuperate. She booked a room for an entire week and went on a shopping spree with her ex-fiancé's credit cards. After maxing out all his cards, she returned to the hotel and took her life in her room. She was later found by a houseman, who is still employed with the hotel. She has often been seen in the hallways in a modern wedding gown, gun in hand. She is normally seen around Halloween time. A few years back she was seen in the restrooms on the balcony level. A woman went into the bathroom while her husband stood outside the door. While she was in there, an unknown female leered at her from under the door. The woman screamed and her husband came running in. He felt someone move past him, but he saw no one. When his wife described the woman she saw to the front desk staff, they recognized the description of the Tragic Bride #2.

Although these are the only spirits the Driskill has names for, it is believed that several other entities float around hallways and corridors. The spirits are said to be both helpful and mischievous. Housekeepers have reported that several times the elevator doors have opened without buttons having been pushed, and the button to their destination floor is already lit. Also, the elevators will run without a guest, operating apparently on their own.

Little occurrences here and there are also attributed to the Driskill spirits. Guests have called the front desk in the middle of the night to say that they awoke to the sensation of someone pushing them out of bed. Other guests claim that they sometimes find their furniture has moved during the evening. Annie Lennox, before a concert, was staying at the Driskill. Before taking a shower, she laid two dresses out to decide between for the concert. When she got out of the shower, one of the dresses had been put away. Lead singer Johnette Napolitano wrote a song about her ghostly experience in the hotel. The song is named, "Ghost of a Texas Ladies Man." It is assumed by the lyrics that this was the colonel.

Address:	604 Brazos Street, Austin, Texas 78701
Phone:	512-474-5911
Fax:	512-474-2214
Toll Free Number:	1-800-678-8946
Accommodations:	178 newly restored guestrooms and suites
Amenities:	Access to the health club; breakfast, lunch, and dinner served in the Driskill Grill; the Lobby Bar features casual fare, and piano stylists at the cocktail hour; meetings can be held in the historic newly restored Driskill Ballroom, Governor's Board Room, and Maximilian Room, plus 11 other meeting rooms, and will accommodate groups up to 500.
Payment:	Visa, MasterCard, Discover, American Express, Diners Club, Carte Blanche, Travelers checks, Gift certificates, cash, personal checks
References:	Personal communication, Driskill Hotel

The Catfish Plantation Restaurant

The town of Waxahachie is thirty-five miles directly south of Dallas on Interstate 35, with approximately 20,000 inhabitants. The house now containing the restaurant was constructed in 1895 by a man named Anderson, and he had a daughter named Elizabeth. According to legend, Elizabeth was strangled in the house, by either her lover or the groom, on her wedding day in the early 1920s. Elizabeth apparently died in what is now the ladies room. A second woman named Caroline Jenkins Mooney died in the house in 1970, at the age of approximately eighty. She had lived there with her husband and their family. The third spirited occupant is believed to be a farmer named Will, who lived in the house during the Depression and died in the 1930s.

The ghosts of the Catfish Plantation Restaurant are well known and have been noted by management, staff, guests, journalists, and psychics. The triad spirits have been blamed for a number of strange events including numbing cold spots that move through the house and slamming doors. A big stainless steel iced tea urn was found sitting on the floor, and all the coffee cups had been taken off the shelf and piled inside the urn, although no human was responsible; coffee cups have flown across the rooms. People have felt as if they've been hit, yet there is never anyone near the person. Freeze-dried chives have been lifted off a shelf and thrown across the room, crashing to the floor in front of several startled people. Many staff have seen shadows move out of the corner of their eye. A stereo in the dining room has frequently changed stations from one end of the band to the other when no one was near the radio. Lights have been known to go on and off by themselves, refrigerator doors will open and shut in front of surprised staff, and a fresh pot of coffee was made by the ghost for one of the owners.

Elizabeth's spirit seems to confine her activities to the dining room, and she likes to touch people; Will's apparition is often seen on the front porch; Caroline's disturbed spirit is often noted in the kitchen.

A psychic visited the restaurant one time and held a seance. It was supposed to be a simple procedure and a fun experience. The assembled group of young people who worked there began trembling, some grew very pale, and the girls began crying. There was tapping on the walls; dishes rattled in the kitchen; the candle on the table lit up by itself; and the kitchen door flew open on its own, bringing with it an apparition of a young girl wearing a sort of wedding gown. The ghost was identified as Elizabeth, one of the three ghosts who are reported to inhabit the Catfish Plantation.

Other psychic investigators who have visited the establishment have also picked up on the names of Elizabeth, Caroline, and Will. One pair of investigators said that Elizabeth's last name was Anderson, and her father built the house. Caroline was said to have died of a stroke, and her last name was Mooney, but her

maiden name was Jenkins. The ghost of Will was said to be that of an old farmer who lived on the land during the 1930s and likes wearing overalls.

Psychics concluded that Caroline enjoys throwing and slamming things, since she spent a lot of her life in the kitchen, preparing dinner for her family. If people do not respond when she wants them to sit at the table, she throws a tantrum. Caroline has been known to break wine glasses, slam doors, and throw coffee cups. Elizabeth, on the other hand, is a quiet soul who often makes herself known as an apparition standing in the front bay window that looks out on the street. Will is known as the quiet one who frequents the porch. Police have reported seeing a man standing on the porch. When they walk up to investigate, the strange man just vanishes. He is also responsible for occasionally triggering the security alarm system. All three spirited phantoms are responsible for the various cold spots felt throughout the building.

The following article, "The Ghosts at Catfish Plantation" was e-mailed by Pat Cody to Melissa Baker at the restaurant:

> I've investigated at Catfish Plantation three times now and have intriguing photos of the place that our experts evaluate as inexplicable. On my first visit, I heard

distant knocks, as if from overhead and under the floor and felt the usual cold spots of "active" sites. A friend felt as if the floor tilted in the ladies' room, a feeling like Californian earthquakes, which she's quite familiar with! During that same visit, I felt a "cold collar" encircle my throat as we sat in the original dining room of the house talking with Tom Baker. He was telling us about the death of the first owner's daughter, and I interrupted to say I thought I knew how and where she had died. Yep. She was strangled, somewhere in the general area where we sat, he said, on her wedding day in the 1920s. We got permission to stay on after closing to watch for the dancing blue lights on the ceiling that Melissa had described. As we sat, necks craned, looking upward, loud sounds emanated from the kitchen area. Though we all heard them differently, the sounds included slow, heavy footsteps and a great clatter. When I called out to Tom, the sounds stopped. We waited a bit and they resumed, louder and more complex in variety than before. Again, I called to Tom, but this time the sounds continued. The lead author bravely advanced on the door, with me hoping she wouldn't go in—meaning I'd have to back her up or call myself a coward forever. As soon as she pushed open the door, the sounds stopped.

Visit the Catfish Plantation for some delicious food or just to browse around, and keep an eye and all your senses peeled for the other-worldly presences including Elizabeth, Caroline, or Will. Perhaps they will find you first!

Address:	814 Water Street, Waxahachie, Texas 75165
Phone:	972-937-9468
Contact:	Melissa Baker
Business Information:	Open Thursday from 5:00 to 8:00 P.M.; Friday from 11:30 A.M. to 2:00 P.M., and 5:00 to 9:00 P.M.; Saturday from 11:30 A.M. to 9:00 P.M.; Sunday from 11:30 A.M. to 8:00 P.M.
Payment:	Most major credit cards are accepted

References: Personal communication, Catfish Plantation Restaurant; Dennis William Hauck, *The National Directory Haunted Places: a Guidebook to Ghostly Abodes, Sacred Sites, UFO Landings, and Other Supernatural Locations*; Arthur Myers, *The Ghostly Gazetteer: America's Most Fascinating Haunted Landmarks*; Lissa Proctor, "Three Ghosts Haunt Catfish Plantation," The *Antique Traveler* newspaper, February 1990; Judy Williamson, "Spirited: Restaurant Offers Remarkable Fare," The *Dallas Morning News*, Sunday, December 6, 1987

Country Spirit

Members of the German colony of Bettina, students of the classics who founded a number of settlements in Texas, first settled the area in 1849, designing their farm after Cicero's country home, Tusculum. The town was patterned after some European communities. Boerne was the home of George Wilkins Kendall, who owned much of the land in what is now Kendall County.

The Country Spirit building was one of Boerne's first two-story houses and, because of its size, was known as the Mansion House. The house was built in the 1870s by French architect Frank LaMotte. In 1883 the property and house were sold to Matilda E. Worcester for $2,800. The gracious building has been a home for many of Boerne's prominent families including the Rudolph Carstanjens, Charles Gerfers, Henry Grahams, and Gilma Halls.

During the early 1900s it served for several years as an annex to the Phillip Manor Hotel across the street, and a drugstore was located in a portion of the ground floor. Augusta Phillip Graham owned the home from 1923 to 1943. The Mansion House was completely remodeled with respect for its historical architectural integrity by Sue Martin and opened as the Country Spirit in the fall of 1984. The inside of the Country Spirit is a retreat into the 1800s.

According to management, the Country Spirit is home to several spirits including Augusta Phillip Graham, David, and Fred. According to psychic investigators, management, staff, and guests, the restaurant is a very spirited place. One spirit is that of a young boy named David, who prefers the upstairs men's restroom, located in one of the old bathrooms with an old-fashioned bathtub. Local lore suggests that David was an orphan in his early teens who frequented the Mansion House. The cook gave him hand-outs, and the boy was allowed to play with the other children of the household. It seems that sometime in the late 1880s, while playing in the driveway, David had a accident from which he subsequently died. Since it became the Country Spirit restaurant, a number of strange things have been reported throughout the building.

A candle was once seen moving unassisted from one side of a table to the other side as stunned guests looked on. A man sitting at the bar in the rear portion of the building watched in amazement as four glasses suddenly flew off the shelves, one at a time, and hit the floor in front of him. The beer spigot has been known to turn itself on, as if unseen hands are operating the equipment. Spoons have flown across the kitchen; the lights in the bar will sometimes go out by themselves; people have been heard partying and laughing downstairs when it is unoccupied; footsteps are sometimes heard in the upstairs portion of the restaurant when it is unoccupied—usually late at night.

Psychics also say the ghost of Augusta Phillip Graham has been sighted in the women's bathroom, usually as a reflection in the mirror, although she has also been spotted standing inside as women walk in. A third spirit that has been sighted is called Fred, and he has been seen eating at table 13 or just sitting at the table watching people pass by.

A trip to the Country Spirit will most certainly liven your spirits, and perhaps it will spark some otherworldly entertainment from the three patrons who, although deceased, still have a great time in the restaurant.

Address: 707 South Main Street, Boerne 78006
Phone: 830-249-3607
Contact: Sue Martin
Business Information: Open Sunday through Thursday from 11:00 A.M. to
                      9:00 P.M.; Friday and Saturday from 11:00 A.M. to
                      10:00 P.M.; closed on Tuesday.
Payment: Visa, MasterCard, Discover, American Express,
                      Diners Club, Carte Blanche
References: Personal communication, Country Spirit; Docia
                      Schultz Williams and Reneta Byrne, *Spirits of San
                      Antonio and South Texas*; Randy Mallory, "Haunted
                      Places in Texas," *Texas Highways*, October 1997;
                      Roy Bragg, "Supernatural Guests Welcome at
                      Boerne Restaurant," *San Antonio Express News*,
                      Metro Section, Wednesday, January 7, 1998

Ye Kendall Inn

Ye Kendall Inn is both a Texas and a national landmark, located in Boerne. The building has provided shelter to many famous people including Jefferson Davis, President Dwight D. Eisenhower, and Robert E. Lee.

Some little known, interesting facts about the inn include evidence in the cellar of a tunnel, which is said to connect the old hotel with another building a block away. The tunnel was used for protection from wandering bands of hostile Indians. There is a staircase of native hewn stone down in the cellar. The cellar, however, is not open to the public.

The main structure is constructed of native rock walls, which are twenty inches thick. The front porch facing south has excellent exposure for staying cool in the hot summers. The property extends down to the Cibolo Creek and consists of approximately five acres. A hand-dug well was discovered under a pile of rubble while restoration work was in progress. At twenty feet deep, ice cold water was found.

The history of Ye Kendall Inn begins April 23, 1859, when John James sold the land to Erastus and Sarah Reed for only $200. The Reeds built the center section of the inn as their home, bringing the Southern Colonial style of architecture to the Texas Hill Country. Since there was no regular hotel for travelers in these early days, the few homeowners of the town shared their spare rooms. The Reeds began the hotel tradition by renting out their spare rooms in The Reed House. Harry W. Chipman leased the property from the Reeds. He rented accommodations to horsemen and stagecoach travelers. The grounds around the house served as a wagon yard for ranchers, who penned their cattle in what is now the city park, awaiting other cattle for a big drive up the trail.

Col. Henry C. King and his wife, Jean Adams King, purchased the inn on May 4, 1869. While Col. King served as state senator and covered his district on horseback, Mrs. King ran The King Place. In 1878 C.J. Roundtree and W.L. Wadsworth of Dallas purchased The King Place and renamed it The Boerne Hotel. These new owners added the two long wings on either side of the original house to accommodate the large number of health seekers attracted to Boerne's climate. In 1882 Mr. Edmund King and his wife, Selina L. King, and children came to Boerne from England and leased The Boerne Hotel.

Mr. King was killed in a hunting accident in back of the hotel on September 26, 1882. The Boerne Hotel served as an authentic stagecoach inn throughout the 1880s. Dr. H.D. Barnitz purchased the hotel in 1909 and adopted the name Ye Kendall Inn after George W. Kendall. From 1922 to 1943 the Kendall Inn was owned by Robert L. and Maude M. Hickman, who began restoring the building. The inn was purchased by Ed and Vicki Schleyer in April 1982, and after extensive restoration, the inn reclaimed its position as a local architectural masterpiece.

Restoring the old building to its former grandeur also resuscitated its spirit or, as many believe, spirits.

According to various reports from the owners, staff, and guests, a number of unexplained events have taken place inside to suggest the spirits of Ye Kendall Inn are alive and well. Many witnesses have heard heavy footsteps on the upper floors when the space is unoccupied. A worker fell through the floor as he attempted to install a bathroom fixture. The claw legs kept falling off the old bathtub. Doors have frequently opened then slammed shut when no one else was in the area where it occurred, and doors that have been securely locked beforehand will open on their own. There are frequent moving cold spots in the building.

Staff working in the restaurant have reported that crystal prisms have fallen off the chandelier a number of times. The door-knob between the restaurant and the shop will often rattle as if someone is trying to enter, yet when the area is inspected, no one is there. The electricity, in particular lights, seem to have a mind of their own, frequently turning on and off without human assistance. A guest witnessed an elderly woman, wearing Victorian clothing, who told the visitor that she was Sarah before vanishing in front of the startled woman—the first owner's wife was named Sarah Reed.

The Marcella Booth room, named after a woman who was born at the inn, frequently shows signs of spirited activity. The bed, after being made, exhibits signs of someone having just sat or slept on it by leaving a noticeable impression. And then there is the unsettling feeling that you are not alone in that room, as well as in other areas of the house.

The spirits of Ye Kendall Inn are not harmful according to the owners. They are just playful ghosts who seem to enjoy lingering in their beautiful surroundings. This house of spirits is truly a pleasure to visit, whether you have a ghostly encounter or not.

Address:	128 West Blanco Road, Boerne 78006
Phone:	830-249-2138
Fax:	830-249-2138
Contact:	Shane & Vicki Schleyer
Accommodations:	17 guestrooms and suites
Amenities:	Private baths; air conditioning; cable television; some rooms with phones; continental breakfast; a restaurant is located in the west wing of the building.
Payment:	Visa, MasterCard, American Express, cash, or personal check

References: Personal communication, Ye Kendall Inn; Docia
Schultz Williams and Reneta Byrne, *Spirits of San
Antonio and South Texas*

LaBorde House Inn

Following a meticulous and complete restoration program, the
historic LaBorde House Inn opened as a luxurious, full-service
hotel in April 1982. Early-day guests included those traveling to
Texas political events, riverboat and wagon travelers, cattle bar-
ons who sold their herds on nearby river docks, and military
officers on their way to California.

The LaBorde House was designed in Paris in 1893 by French
architects, and the plans were refined by San Antonio architects at
the building site in 1898. Construction was completed in 1899.
The house was originally the home of Francoise LaBorde. Restoration criteria for the hotel were established from the original
records and photographs and through consultation with the Texas
Historic Commission and the U.S. Department of Interior. The
hotel is now listed on the National Register of Historic Places.

A number of sightings of the gentle spirits of the LaBorde House have occurred over the years. The lovely historic inn has its share of phenomena including doors that open and shut on their own; lights that turn themselves on and off; soft, cold breezes that blow through certain areas of the building, although their cause cannot be determined. Occasional laughter can be heard in unoccupied areas of the inn, and an infrequent shadow is seen by staff and guests.

The owner wants to assure everyone that her spirits are harmless and probably remain behind because the authentic restoration of the house has brought back memories of happier bygone days.

Address:	601 East Main Street, Rio Grande City, Texas 78582
Phone:	956-487-5101
Contact:	Margaret Meade
Accommodations:	13 rooms including seven grand bedrooms and efficiency apartments
Amenities:	Each bedroom has a name commemorating a bit of local history; each room has antique furnishings; tropical courtyards and patios; parlor; a lounge and restaurant named Che's.
Payment:	Visa, MasterCard, Discover, American Express, Diners Club, Carte Blanche
References:	Personal communication, LaBorde House Inn; Robin Mead, *Haunted Hotels: A Guide to American and Canadian Inns and Their Ghosts*

Beulah's Restaurant

Beulah's Restaurant and the adjacent Tarpon Inn are located in the waterfront area of Port Aransas, Texas, a resort for visitors to Padre Island. The town of Port Aransas is situated on the northernmost tip of Padre Island, a barrier island that protects the bay and harbor of Corpus Christi which was discovered by the Spanish in 1519 on the feast day of Corpus Christi. Many well-known personalities have stayed at the adjacent Tarpon Inn and visited Beulah's over the years, including President Franklin Delano Roosevelt.

Padre Nicholas Balli acquired title to the 100-mile-long strip of sand dunes and grass from King Charles IV of Spain in 1880. Originally christened Isla de Corpus Christi, Balli established cattle ranching on the island, and over time the island became known as Padre Island. Balli also established a small town around his homestead that became Port Aransas. During the Civil War, the site of the Tarpon Inn was a barracks for Confederate troops. In 1886 the Tarpon Inn was built from materials that had been salvaged from the old barracks. The inn was named for the tarpon fish found in the waters around Port Aransas.

The first Tarpon Inn was destroyed by fire in 1900. It was subsequently rebuilt in 1904 but was once again destroyed in 1919, this time by a hurricane. In 1923 it was rebuilt to its present form, a two-story, frame building. Directly behind the inn are a garden area and two frame buildings, which make up Beulah's Restaurant. The long building at the rear of the property was once the original location for the Tarpon Inn that burned down. Beulah's was the bar for the original Tarpon Inn, then it became the Silver King. It took on the name Beulah's in mid-1992, after the head housekeeper at the inn, Beulah Mae Williams. Beulah lived in the old building that stands on a side alley behind the restaurant.

A Silver King newsletter article once stated that the Silver King (now Beulah's) was haunted. Although Beulah Mae had never encountered the ghost, she seemed to frequently hear it.

One day as Beulah Mae was walking outside the Silver King and passing by the kitchen area, she heard a lot of noise coming from inside the building. She knew the restaurant was closed, so she decided to see if someone had broken in. Once inside, and after carefully inspecting all the rooms, she found that everything was in order. Beulah Mae locked up the restaurant and stood outside for a moment, trying to come up with a logical explanation for all the commotion—she couldn't.

Other employees over the years have also remarked about the strange, sometimes loud noises that come from certain parts of the restaurant that are unoccupied. Heavy footsteps, loud pounding noises, muffled voices, and other sounds can be heard at various hours, yet the cause is never found.

An evening cook at the Silver King once witnessed an eerie haze begin to take shape in front of him. Within seconds, the mist turned into a middle-age female of medium height and faced off against the startled employee. Before he could run, the apparition abruptly turned and melted away in front of him.

A former employee also witnessed a female apparition dressed in period clothing and sporting a hairstyle reminiscent of the late 1800s. A male apparition has also been sighted in the kitchen area, and many employees feel that this may be a former cook who used to work at the restaurant. A psychic, while visiting Beulah's, ran into the male energy and came up with the name Sam, Sammy, or Samuel. On another occasion, an employee was mopping the kitchen floor. Within minutes after completing his task, large footprints appeared in the middle of the floor, followed by a smaller pair, as if someone were leading a child through the kitchen.

The kitchen ghost has been blamed for turning lights on and off, making very loud noises that can't be explained, shaking pots and pans while helpless staff stand by, colds spots that follow certain people, the strong sense of being watched or followed, and for causing doors to suddenly fly open or slam shut.

Spend the night at the Tarpon Inn, which is also rumored to be haunted, and have dinner at Beulah's, and perhaps you will catch a glimpse of the spirits of this historic establishment, where the past

sometimes intrudes on the present. So far, a male and female spirit as well as a ghost child like to call Beulah's their home. Perhaps you'll see one of them when you come to visit.

Address:	200 East Cotter, P.O. Box 2283, Port Aransas, Texas 78373
Phone:	512-749-4888
Fax:	512-749-7022
Contact:	Guy Carnathan
Business Information:	Open Wednesday through Sunday from 5:00 to 10:00 P.M.
Payment:	Visa, MasterCard, Discover
References:	Personal communication, Beulah's; Docia Schultz Williams, *Ghosts Along the Texas Coast*

The Grey Moss Inn

Originally an Indian trail, the Scenic Loop was an area where nomadic Indian tribes fought over land rights long, long, ago. The "Treaty Tree," a majestic oak located in the meadow adjacent to the inn, is said to posses a "peaceful energy" and was used by these Native Americans as a neutral, "spiritually healing" ground. It was here that treaties and alliances were negotiated and signed.

In 1821 Juan Menchaca obtained a land grant and, with his Aztec wife, began to settle the area. In the years that followed, stagecoaches from San Antonio, traveling down the road and planning to stop only for a change of horses, often met up with Native Americans and bandits who lived and hid their gold in the numerous caves located a short distance from the road. Legends persist of buried treasure still hidden in these caves.

In pursuit of these bandits and renegades was Texas Ranger Captain Jack Hayes. Hayes brought law and order to the area until he moved to Oakland. By 1872 the railroad passed through neighboring Leon Springs, as the Scenic Loop was still used by wagons and stagecoaches journeying to Helotes.

Robert E. Lee was a frequent visitor to the area, as was famed revolutionary bandit Pancho Villa. By the 1920s the area had become a popular playground and summer retreat for wealthy San Antonians. Mary Howell founded the inn in 1929. She sold homemade candy from her front porch and often cooked dinner for her neighbors. World War II ushered in a housing and beef shortage to San Antonio. The inn has never been closed and is the oldest continuously operating restaurant in Central Texas. Water is drawn from fresh spring wells, and their famous pies are made "from scratch" daily. What began as a tearoom in 1929 is now a locally famous restaurant, which happens to be haunted.

Numerous unexplained events have taken place over the years, and many are convinced that the inn is haunted by several spirits. Mary Howell's spirit seems to be the most dominant, and she frequents the restaurant, as if checking up on the quality of

food—she is not displeased. There is oftentimes a strong whiff of rose cologne, which drifts through the kitchen and in one dining room, located near the kitchen door. The rose cologne was Mary's favorite perfume in life and seems to be her favored scent in the afterlife.

On one occasion a large coffeemaker blew apart in the kitchen when no one was around. The alarm system has been known to go for no apparent reason. Tray jacks suddenly topple over, along with ice buckets, which were stationary one minute, then on their sides the next. Dishes also seem to be a phantom favorite, since they occasionally break apart on their own.

A couple celebrating their wedding anniversary had a wine bucket brought to the table. While they were waiting for their glasses to be refilled, the bucket just fell over on its own—perhaps an omen of things to come, courtesy of Mary. It turns out that within six months after the incident, the couple were divorced—coincidence?

An employee once reported that the adding machine would perform unassisted calculations. A staff person had the gates open in front of her by an invisible force when her hands were full. The computer has also been a problem—perhaps Mary doesn't like new technology. Programs have failed, hardware has continually stalled, and discs have crashed. Then there are the frequent manifestations of Mary in front of staff and guests—there one minute, gone the next.

The Garden Room may be the source of another spirit that seems much more hostile than Mary. According to the owner, years ago, after making sure all the candles were extinguished, she locked up for the evening. The next morning a fire had started in the Garden Room after hours. It only affected one table, situated underneath a giant hex sign, which stands for justice, that hangs on the wall. The place mats had burned up, the napkins on the table, the candle, and the plate beneath the candle were affected, and a tablecloth was scorched except for the area just beneath the hex sign. A basket of sugar packets on the table was not touched either. The fire alarm never sounded, and there was no smell of smoke in the building. Also, the Formica tabletop was not harmed, but the woven straw back of one of the chairs adjacent to the table had burned away. A psychic said a malevolent male spirit was responsible for the event, and his favorite area was the Garden Room.

Other events which have taken place over the years include: a shadow that is frequently sighted by a window; an apparition which materialized into a big black form that walked through a wall; water, which will sometimes literally ooze up in the patio area of the restaurant; and a tremendous clashing of cymbals which sometimes comes from the inn, setting off the alarm system. However, upon inspecting, the police never find anything amiss. The Grey Moss Inn has good food, plenty of atmosphere, and a spirit or two to add to the ambiance.

Address:	19010 Scenic Loop Road, P.O. Box 734, Helotes, Texas 78023
Phone:	210-695-8301
Fax:	210-695-3237
E-mail:	ferrariguy1@sprintmail.com
Contact:	Lou & Nell Baeten
Business Information:	Open seven days a week from 5:00 P.M.
Payment:	Visa, MasterCard, Discover, American Express, Diners Club

References: Personal communication, The Grey Moss Inn;
Docia Schultz Williams, *When Darkness Falls: Tales
of San Antonio Ghosts and Hauntings*

The Jefferson Hotel

Historic Jefferson was a bustling inland port in the 1890s, then became a ghost town overnight when the riverboat traffic ceased. Some accuse railroad tycoon Jay Gould for the rapid demise of the town. When Jefferson officials denied Gould right-of-way access for his Texas & Pacific Railroad through the town, Gould was said to have cursed the town. And when he built the line, he by-passed Jefferson.

The Jefferson Hotel was constructed in 1851 as a cotton warehouse. The rear of the hotel was once used as the front entrance of the structure. The iron door frames are still visible where large arched doors of the 1870s-era hotel faced Dallas Street. Today the front is located on West Austin Street. The cotton warehouse closed down when the steamboat port closed. The building has since been used for many purposes including a school for girls— actually it was a bordello; a Chinese laundry was downstairs in the back of the building; a hotel in the 1920s had gambling parties in a back room. The hotel has changed ownership a number of times since the 1940s.

Management, staff, and guests know about the spirits of the Jefferson. Room 19 is not the only haunted room in the hotel. At least ten of the rooms in this twenty-four-room historic hotel have had there share of cold spots, strange noises, unexplained footsteps, doors that open and close by themselves, knocks on the wall from unoccupied rooms, and shadowy apparitions. Rooms that have been prepared for the arrival of guests will be found in disarray only minutes after the maid has left the room.

Room 19, located at the end of an upstairs hallway, has its share of tales including guests who are frequently awakened by an invisible someone sitting down on the side of their bed. Other guests have reported seeing a wispy, shadowed figure hovering in the corner, or they complain that they feel as if someone is in there with them that they can't see. Usually the guests move to another room rather than face the unknown. Staff, performing simple tasks in the room, have stated that in some parts of the room, an area will turn freezing, and they will note a 20 to 30 degree change in temperature while walking around the room. Staff and guests have reported being touched, feeling goose-bumps all over their body, hearing an unseen someone breathing, or smelling a cologne or after-shave begin to permeate the room, a scent that comes from nowhere. A guest once described waking up to strange clicking and popping sounds, as well as something knocking on the walls behind the headboard of the bed. The trouble with his complaint was that the noises were coming from behind a very thick outside wall. There was no room next to his. A female guest also rolled over to face a lady with long wavy hair standing next to her. When she turned away to wake up her husband, the woman vanished.

Other paranormal rooms include room 20 where the water in the bathroom sink will suddenly come on full force in the middle of the night; room 5 where guests oftentimes hear knocking on the walls from an adjacent room that is unoccupied; room 11, where strange sounds are heard coming from inside and behind the walls; the front desk where repeated knocking is heard for several minutes when no one is anywhere around; and the hallway near room 6 where there are strange cold spots and extremely strong feelings of an unseen presence that has caused people to either turn around, expecting to see someone standing behind them, or to run out of the area in fear.

Room 2 is where a police officer, working security, had a door mysteriously slam shut behind him. When he opened the door, no once was there; however, when he tried to shut it upon leaving, he pulled against it as hard as he could but it wouldn't close. It was as if an unseen force was fighting with him for control of the door.

Finally after shutting the door, he heard a loud bang, like someone had thrown something against the door from the inside.

Room 12 is where a smoky, wispy image of a female entity came to visit a couple who later came back to the hotel and to the same room because the experience was so wonderful.

Lamache's Italian Restaurant, occupying the eastern portion of the hotel's ground floor, is not exempt from paranormal activity. Pots and pans have inexplicably flown off the shelves in front of startled clean-up personnel, and cold spots, strange voices, and unexplained footsteps are also trademarks of the restaurant.

Almost everyone at the hotel has had some kind of paranormal experience. No one tries to explain anything that happens any more; they just accept the fact that the place is haunted by several spirits and try to co-exist with their otherworldly friends. Guests have enjoyed their visits and the fact that they are in a haunted hotel. Some return over and over just for the chance to meet the spirits of the Jefferson Hotel

Address: 124 West Austin, Jefferson, Texas 75657
Phone: 903-665-2638
Toll Free Number: 1-800-226-9026
Accommodations: 24 recently renovated rooms

Amenities:	All rooms have private baths; one of the two suites has a Jacuzzi, and one a fireplace; Lamache's Italian Restaurant is within the hotel.
Payment:	Most major credit cards accepted
References:	Personal communication, Jefferson Hotel; Glenn Evans, "Hallowed Chambers," The *Marshall News Messenger* (October 25, 1998), Cindy Brown, "Have a Ghost of a Good Time at the Jefferson Hotel," *Star-Telegram* (May 17, 1998); Randy Mallory, "Haunted Places in Texas," *Texas Highways*, October 1997; Jonathan Weil, "In One Room, All The Towels Mysteriously Disappeared," The *Wall Street Journal* (October 29, 1997); Docia Schultz Williams, *Best Tales of Texas Ghosts*

La Carafe

Perhaps Houston's most beloved historic building is the Kennedy Bakery, which was built in 1861 and is the oldest commercial structure in the city. From the time Irish immigrant John Kennedy first built his bakery, it functioned as everything from a trading post and apothecary to a loan office and a Confederate arsenal. Settlers often referred to his Indian trading partners as "Kennedy's Indians."

Catherine Arnold of *Sidewalk Houston* wrote that in the mid- to late-1800s, the hub of Houston was at the intersection of what are now Congress and Travis Streets. City Hall sat on Market Square, La Carafe was known as the Kennedy Bakery, and the building next door (which isn't the same one that's there now) was Kennedy's trading post, where Indians took pelts when they came to town. During the Civil War the bakery was contracted to turn out hardtack biscuits for Confederate troops. John Kennedy, who owned a large number of slaves and several thousand acres of land in surrounding counties, was also known for running cotton through the Federal blockade.

According to management and staff, the spirits of La Carafe can occasionally get a little feisty. Given the history of the building, the ghosts could be from just about any time period. Who they are—names, dates—that's unclear; however, they do exist in this historic building, and they have been blamed for dozens of unexplained events.

As a bartender named Tyler came to work one day, he was about to walk inside when he chanced to glance up at a second floor window. The second floor area is where La Carafe's offices are. He was surprised to see a woman standing in the window, since it was early in the morning and he was always the first to come in. He tentatively walked up the stairs to the second floor area and to the location where he saw the woman. There was no one standing at the window, in the room, or anywhere else for that matter. He was alone.

On another occasion, a staff person named Tobe was closing up at around 3:00 A.M. After checking the place out, he locked the front door and strolled across the street. A gut feeling made him turn around and look back at the building. As he looked up at the second floor window, his hair stood on end and he got the chills, as a large, muscular black man was gazing down at him. Thinking that he left someone stranded on the second floor, he unlocked the door and ran up the stairs. When he reached the second floor room where he had witnessed the man standing, there was no one there. The entire establishment was empty except for him and a ghost. Management believes this is the spirit of Carl Truscott, who used to work at the Rice Hotel in the bar and died around 1990.

Other events that have been reported include exploding glasses and bottles, a painting that has flown off the wall, strange shadows on the walls, cold spots appearing out of nowhere, the feeling of being watched by invisible eyes, and disembodied footsteps heard walking through unoccupied areas of the building. Visitors are allowed to go upstairs only at certain times during the week, so call ahead and reserve your tour of the haunted establishment.

Address:	813 Congress Street (Congress at Travis), Houston, TX 77002
Phone:	713-229-9399
Contact:	Randall Davis and Carolyn Wengler
Business Information:	Hours: Weekdays: 12:00 P.M. to 2:00 A.M.; weekends: 1:00 P.M. to 2 A.M.

Happy hour:	Daily: 5:00 to 7:00 P.M.
Payment:	Cash only
References:	Personal communication, La Carafe

Virginia

Middletown
Manassas
Staunton
Charlottesville
Fredericksburg
Williamsburg
Hampton
Abingdon
Chatham
Virginia Beach

Camberley's Martha Washington Inn

*A*bingdon, with a population of roughly 4,500 inhabitants, was founded in 1778 at the junction of two Native American trails, in a location that Daniel Boone had camped years prior. Through the years the Martha Washington Inn became filled with priceless gifts and furnishings. The rare and elaborate Dutch-baroque grandfather clock measuring over nine feet tall and now residing in the East Parlor was shipped from England by one of the Preston daughters, Mrs. Floyd. It works yet today. Patricia Neal, Ernest Borgnine, and Ned Beatty stayed at the mansion before it was a hotel while they were appearing at the Barter Theater, the longest-running professional resident theater in America. Legendary guests have been Eleanor Roosevelt, President Harry Truman, Lady Bird Johnson, Jimmy Carter, and Elizabeth Taylor.

Camberley's Martha Washington Inn was built as a private residence for under $15,000 in 1832. The mansion's first family was General Francis Preston, his wife, Sarah Buchanan Preston, and their nine children. Born in Virginia, General Preston attended law school at William and Mary College, served in Congress, and was a member of the Virginia Assembly until 1797.

During the War of 1812 Preston was commissioned a colonel and marched with his regiment to Norfolk. In 1820 Preston was appointed a brigadier general. Ten years later construction began on the Preston Mansion. Once complete, many of Virginia's famous and powerful passed through her doors. Preston's son, William Campbell, while attending school in Europe with Washington Irving and Sir Walter Scott, transplanted a smoke tree from Napoleon's grave in France to the front lawn, and it survived until 1984.

After securing through marriages a foothold for his children in some of the South's best families, General Preston died in 1835. His wife survived until 1858. The Prestons' original brick residence still comprises the central structure of the famous inn. The original Preston family living room is now the main lobby, and the grand stairway and parlors are much as they were over one hundred fifty years earlier. The furnishings, which are now priceless antiques and carefully preserved by the Preston family and subsequent benefactors, are still an integral part of the inn.

After Mrs. Preston's death, their mansion served a number of purposes. In 1858 it was purchased for $21,000 and became an elite college for women. As Martha Washington College, the former residence soon became known as the "Martha." Benefactors of the Martha enhanced the mansion's furnishings, acquiring and showcasing the beautiful heirlooms and exquisite gifts. The school that bears Martha Washington's name owns a delicate teacup and saucer that belonged to the former First Lady, which was protected by a bell jar on the mantel of the front parlor.

During the Civil War the books were cast aside; the colonial costumes the girls donned annually to honor George and Martha Washington were exchanged for the uniforms of nurses, which many students became; and Virginia reels and minuets made way for marching soldiers. Then the mansion served as a makeshift hospital and the grounds became training barracks for the Washington Mounted Rifles. The college survived, but the Great Depression, typhoid fever, and a declining enrollment eventually took its toll. The Martha was closed in 1932, reopening in 1935 as a hotel. A half century later, in 1984, The United Company

purchased and applied an $8 million renovation to assure that period furnishings and room decor reflected the inn's extensive history.

According to L.B. Taylor (1995), the venerable old inn, steeped in southern custom and old-fashioned pamper-the-guest service, also is host to a variety of spectral activity. In fact, it may well be one of Virginia's most haunted edifices. If not, it certainly is one of the most discussed and written about. Most of the active psychic phenomena here swirls around incidents that occurred during the Civil War.

According to local legend and lore, the ghost of a riderless horse has been observed on moonless nights, searching for its owner on the south lawn of this inn. There is also the spirit of Beth, a student at Martha Washington College during the Civil War, who haunts the building. The story of Beth involves a tragedy that occurred during the Civil War, when Confederate soldiers ambushed Union forces passing through Abingdon. One Union officer, Captain John Stoves, was seriously wounded and brought back to the school where he was placed in a third floor room. A woman named Beth tended to the mortally wounded soldier and even played her violin to cheer him up. As he was about to die, he called out to her one more time to play him something. She obliged, played a tune, and he passed away in front of the weeping Beth.

From the legend that has been passed down for over one hundred years, Beth supposedly lasted only a few more days, developing a lethal illness, and died in the house. Some say it was typhoid, others, a broken heart. John Stoves, the Union soldier, was buried beside his Confederate sweetheart in Abingdon's Green Springs Cemetery. The battle between the North and the South did not separate true love. Not long after her passing, people began to hear the faint echoes of Beth's violin music filter through the corridors and rooms on the third floor of the Martha Washington Inn, especially when the moon was full. It was said that the mournful music soothed some of its listeners while making others melancholy.

Another spirit is said to belong to a young Confederate soldier who was in love with an Abingdon girl. The Martha Washington College was a frequent stopover point for the young soldier. Unfortunately, he stayed too long during one visit and was taken by surprise on the stairs by a Union reconnaissance party. The Union soldiers fired on the Confederate youth, and he died at his sweetheart's feet in a pool of blood. It is said his blood so deeply stained the floorboards that the marks are still there, and every effort to remove the stains is only temporarily successful. Today a carpet in the Governor's suite covers the recurring stains.

A third ghost belongs to a Union soldier who was shot while on horseback during a skirmish with Confederate soldiers along the alley east of the school. The mortally wounded soldier was carried over to the college, where he died just as the clocks of the town struck midnight. The Union soldier's horse followed its master to the college and waited outside. When the solider died, the horse must have sensed his passing, because legend has it that the horse walked away from the area and was never seen again. That is, not in the flesh. On some dark and moonless nights, a spectral horse is sometimes seen waiting on the south lawn without a rider—waiting and then vanishing. Although death cruelly separated the rider and horse, the horse still waits patiently, even in the afterlife, for its master to return.

Hotel management, staff, and guests who have visited the place since it became a world-famous hotel have experienced a number of strange phenomena including manifestations of a lonely Confederate soldier, who silently walks down one of the hallways, and wispy figures floating in and out of certain areas of the inn. Certain rooms have noticeable drops in temperature upon entering them. Doorknobs have been known to turn when no one is outside the door. A "smoky-like object" often appears in the lounge for a few minutes before vanishing. Apparitions have been spotted ascending and descending the main stairs. Spirits have greeted guests as they wake up, standing over their beds and then vanishing. The feeling of someone or something walking by and touching people is often reported, yet there is never anyone there.

The appearance of Beth, who returns to room 403 no doubt to repeat her routine in caring for the Union soldier who died there during the Civil War, is oftentimes reported. A security guard once passed a milky-like figure with long flowing hair on the stairway. Housekeepers have spotted a slim young girl sitting in a chair by the bed in room 403 and watched with astonishment as the figure faded into nothingness. The sounds of a violin playing are often heard late at night in the hallways near room 403. Guests and staff have tried to get into room 403 sometimes and find that they can't open the door no matter how hard they try; finally, upon entering, the person is softly slapped on the back, as if they have intruded on someone's privacy. A security guard was walking down the hallway about 4:00 A.M. when he passed a woman dressed in a bonnet, long apron dress, and high-button shoes. As she glided past him, he asked if she needed help. Within seconds the woman turned into a mist, walked toward the staircase, and vanished.

Other people have encountered the ghost of Beth or at least felt her too often to chronicle. Love, especially tragic love, seems to conquer time. A woman who tended a dying soldier, a soldier who died in his lover's arms, and a horse that lost its master. The Martha Washington Inn has it all: the history, tragedy, mystery, beauty, and plenty of good ole spirits!

Address:	150 West Main Street, Abingdon, Virginia 24210
Phone:	540-628-3161
Fax:	540-628-8885
Toll Free Number:	1-800-555-8000
Contact:	Ronald G. Lamers, general manager
Accommodations:	51 charming guestrooms, and 10 suites
Amenities:	Each guestroom and suite is different in decor, size, and configuration; dining room featuring regional specialties in an elegant setting; Sunday champagne brunch; complimentary afternoon tea; Grand Ballroom; conference room; gift shop; sundry shop
Payment:	All major credit cards are accepted
References:	Personal communication, Camberley's Martha Washington Inn; Dennis William Hauck, *The National Directory: Haunted Places: A Guidebook to Ghostly Abodes, Sacred Sites, UFO Landings, and other Supernatural Locations*; Robin Mead, *Haunted Hotels: A Guide to American and Canadian Inns and Their Ghosts*; L. B. Taylor, *Civil War Ghosts of Virginia*

Olde Towne Inn

The junction of the Manassas Gap and the Orange and Alexandria rail lines during the 1850s contributed to the formation of Manassas, now containing 28,000 hearty souls. During the Civil War, this small town was the way to the heart of Virginia and the site of the first and second battles of Manassas or Bull Run.

The Olde Towne Inn dates to the Civil War when it was used as a hospital. According to Dennis William Hauck, a ghost nicknamed Miss Lucy haunts room 52, in the old section of this building. Sometimes she wanders into room 50 or room 54, and she has been sighted strolling through the restaurant. Guests and employees have witnessed Lucy's playful antics on a number of occasions. She is blamed for strange scratching sounds, messing up the beds,

unplugging appliances, cold spots, doors opening and shutting by themselves, and unexplained footsteps.

During July 1991 a visiting couple was awakened in the middle of the night by a heavy presence on their bed. An hour later the husband levitated out of bed and was dropped on the floor. That morning the same couple encountered Miss Lucy in the restaurant.

The current manager said strange things continue to happen in many of the motor lodge rooms. Lights and televisions go on and off by themselves, and sometimes the barstools in the restaurant end up relocating themselves either in front of customers or at other locations within the restaurant.

A guest once reported spending the night with a friend in the Olde Towne Inn. The two men were aware of the rumors that it was haunted, so curiosity and bravado brought them to Manassas to challenge the spirits of the inn. To prove they weren't afraid, they checked into one of the most haunted rooms—number 34. Before retiring for the night, they joked about the rumors and even chided themselves for believing in such nonsense. After a few laughs, they clicked off the lights and bedded down.

Within seconds, however, both men noticed a drastic drop in the room's barometric pressure; one of them even began to feel a presence in the room. Their laughs and skepticism quickly changed to uncertainty. They couldn't see anything manifesting in the darkness, but they both felt a heaviness in the air—it became thick and all-encompassing. Within minutes, however, the feeling passed and they went to sleep.

About an hour later one of the guests felt a pulling or tugging sensation throughout his body, and once again the pressure and temperature in the room changed drastically. It didn't get colder as he expected, but warmer. The brief pulling sensation occurred two other times during the course of the night, accompanied by a pressure and temperature change. At 6:00 A.M. the same person was literally shaken awake. The pulling sensation was so strong that he thought he was being yanked right off the bed! This tugging feeling was accompanied by a humming sound that seemed to emanate from within his body, rather than coming from outside of it. He immediately woke up his friend, and they both began talking about feeling the same sensations during the night.

The next night one of the men noted that a pressure was being exerted on him, as if someone was stepping or sitting on top of his body. The experience lasted about a minute and a half before it passed. Both men experienced the atmospheric changes, as well as the humming and pressure. Although they never saw anything unusual the entire night, they were touched by "something" they couldn't explain. From that moment on both men gained a healthy respect for the unknown and the energy attributed to the Olde Towne Inn.

Miss Lucy, one of the resident spirits, seems to favor room 52. She continues to toy with staff and guests, playfully turning lights off and on, wandering down the hallways, and disappearing in front of startled guests; visiting the restaurant by walking in and then vanishing through walls; causing unexplained scratching and knocking sounds; disturbing the beds after they have been made; unplugging appliances such as vacuum cleaners while housekeeping is using them; and making her presence known as cold spots or as disembodied footsteps.

A visit to the Olde Towne Inn, in an area where so much remnant energy from the Civil War still remains, is sure to elicit something more than the usual "having a great time" response. It may be more like "toured a famous Civil War battlefield, had a delicious dinner, watched a movie, then was awakened by a female ghost who walked through our bedroom wall—wish you were here."

Address: 9403 Main Street, Manassas, Virginia 20110-5417
Phone: 703-368-9191
Fax: 703-361-7700
Reservations: 1-888-869-6446
Contact: Don Coleman, manager
Accommodations: Affordably priced accommodations
Amenities: Swimming pool; restaurant on the premises; cable television
Payment: All major credit cards accepted
References: Personal communication, Olde Towne Inn; Dennis William Hauck, *The National Directory: Haunted Places: A Guidebook to Ghostly Abodes, Sacred Sites, UFO Landings, and Other Supernatural Locations*; L.B. Taylor, *The Ghosts of Virginia*, Volume III

The Smythe's Cottage and Tavern

Fredericksburg, with a population of 19,000, was founded in 1728, even though a fort was built in the area as early as 1676. This strategic port city lies at the head of the Rappahannock River. The 1830s tavern restaurant is located on the corner of Fauquier and Princess Anne Streets. Sixty patrons can be seated in the two rooms downstairs, and another forty can dine outside in the summer. A tavern also caters to the needs of locals and tourists alike.

The original structure was built as a private residence during the 1850s and consisted of three rooms: The front dining room was the entryway/living room; the present taproom was the original kitchen; and a single bedroom was situated upstairs. Before the 1850s, the property upon which the building stands is believed to have belonged to the Kenmore Estates. After serving as a residence, the building became a blacksmith's shop, where it earned its name. During the 1860s there is an indication that the building may have served as a bordello. Over the years additions and conversions were made, and the building became an antique store. The antique store remained in operation until the late 1980s. At that time the building was converted into a restaurant.

Smythe's Cottage is positioned roughly halfway between the Rising Sun Tavern and the Mary Washington House. The spirit of a rather tall man with long, black hair, dressed in a full-length black coat, has been frequently sighted on the outdoor patio. Another spirit, that of Tootie Ninde, who died of cancer in the building, is occasionally spotted in the front of the house directly across the street. Her ghost has been seen crawling up the stairs or gazing out a front window. Additionally, according to owner Lonny Williams, faint ringing sounds, like iron being formed on an anvil, can sometimes be heard in the front dining room during the early evening hours.

A restaurant guest once asked a staff member why the elderly lady in that house was so rude. He then related how he had gone up to the front door, knocked, and an old woman peered at him through the pane of glass but wouldn't let him in. In fact, she turned away when he kept asking to be let in. He watched as the woman crawled up the stairs on her hands and knees, until she disappeared out of view. Of course the staff person just smiled and told the guest that he saw their resident ghost named Tootie, an eccentric town character. Tootie, because of her poor health and unable to afford assistance, would frequently have to crawl up the stairs to her room.

After Tootie's death, lights would go on and off in her room, and her apparition was occasionally sighted at the foot of the stairs before abruptly fading away. Tootie could also be heard late at night, climbing the stairs, although she was never sighted during these episodes. There have also been occasions late at night when guests would be rudely awakened by the sounds of music, voices, and the tinkling of glasses coming from the downstairs area. People thought a party was taking place, a party that lasted until

around 4:00 A.M. Unfortunately, no humans were ever allowed to join this ghostly party.

Some of the locals and management thought the phantom gatherings might be tied to the fact that at one time, while unearthing a cistern in the yard, one hundred champagne bottle-necks and various other remnants from the Civil War period were found. Perhaps there were celebrations before or after the war which continue to replay themselves. The source of the noises associated with the downstairs area, including conversations, meetings, and gatherings, has never been discovered—there is never anyone there.

Additionally, a tall, mysterious-looking man, wearing a long, black jacket, with long, black hair and a loose, western-style tie, has also been sighted on the outdoor patio. He appears and stands almost rigid for a few seconds and then slowly vanishes. The ghostly man has also been witnessed walking through the kitchen, where a worker was so frightened that he reached for a knife to defend himself. Within seconds, however, the phantom male just drifted away.

The cottage has also been the location for strange shadows, disembodied voices, and footsteps in an otherwise unoccupied room. Also, water faucets have been mysteriously turned on by themselves; a young female ghost has been seen walking around upstairs; doors will open and shut on their own; people report running into "something" that exerts enough pressure on them for a few seconds that they are unable to move, then the pressure just as quickly dissipates; and lights seem to have a mind of their own. A visit to this rustic retreat to celebrate and lift your spirits may also produce a memorable encounter with other spirits who are looking for the same pleasure in the afterlife.

Address:	303 Fauquier Street, Fredericksburg, Virginia 22401
Phone:	540-373-1645
Fax:	540-371-6551
Contact:	Jean Williams
Business Information:	Hours: Sunday noon to 9:00 P.M.; Monday, Wednesday & Thursday 11:00 A.M. to 9:00 P.M.; Tuesday closed; Friday & Saturday 11:00 A.M. to 10:00 P.M.
Payment:	Visa, MasterCard, Discover, American Express, Diners Club, Carte Blanche
References:	Personal communication, The Smythe's Cottage and Tavern; Dennis William Hauck, *The National Directory: Haunted Places: A Guidebook to Ghostly Abodes, Sacred Sites, UFO Landings, and Other Supernatural Locations*; L.B. Taylor Jr., *The Ghosts of Fredericksburg*; Jennifer Sycks, "Ghost Walk Tours Explore Haunted Fredericksburg," The *Mary Washington Bulletin*, October 19, 1993

Le Lafayette Restaurant

Located in Fredericksburg, the building features unusually elaborate woodwork in the southwest parlor section, complete with carved swags and garlands on the chimney piece and lattice-work friezes on the window and door frames. At the rear of the restaurant, there are remnants of a terraced garden leading toward the river.

The distinctive house, with two towering chimneys, was constructed around 1769-1771 as a Georgian-style townhome for Scottish merchant John Glassell. The structure is one of the most important colonial dwellings in Fredericksburg. Glassell didn't live in his new residence for very long. As a Royalist, he decided to return to his native Scotland when the Revolutionary War broke out. Over the years the house has been owned by a number of different families, including Nell Herndon, who later became President Chester Arthur's First Lady. Because it is dominated by its massive exterior chimneys, townspeople refer to it as The Chimneys.

The spirit of a young child has been frequently sighted at the mansion. Sometimes staff and guests hear a child's voice singing in unoccupied areas of the building. Other times distinct footsteps are heard throughout the house. There have been times when chairs will rock by themselves and windows and doors will fly open or slam shut—unassisted. On a few occasions pieces of china have been known to shoot across the room as if being tossed by unseen hands. Other times glasses have crashed to the floor, either after hours when no on else is around or in front of shocked witnesses.

No one is quite sure who haunts the restaurant, and the strange occurrences that take place have been noted for over one hundred years. Usually late at night staff and guests will report hearing a chair propel itself across the restaurant floor, see a rocking chair move back and forth, or hear someone walking upstairs along the wooden floors when there is no one in that area of the building. Additionally, workmen have reported glass crashing to the floor, but upon further inspection, nothing is ever found broken.

The owners have oftentimes heard the strange footsteps and watched the rocker swaying back and forth as if someone is actually sitting in the chair. It starts moving and then just as quickly stops. Some staff and guests also claim to have seen the playful spirit of a little boy roaming the restaurant. It may be that this youthful spirit is responsible for turning doorknobs, opening and closing doors, and leaving impressions on freshly made beds.

The ghostly boy was once sighted in the late 1800s by a prior owner, who saw the child sleeping in bed with her son in his upstairs bedroom. The woman assumed that the child belonged to a neighbor, that is, until there was no trace of the boy the next morning. She asked her son who his friend was that stayed over with him. Of course, the boy had no idea what his mother was talking about.

There are also the occasional sounds of someone singing in the old parlor. A mysterious voice has been heard giving a beautiful rendition of a melody from a long time ago. As quickly as the singing begins, it abruptly stops when someone goes to investigate. You can add to the litany of events a phantom piano player, who taps on the ivory keys when there is no one else in that part of the house, then abruptly stops.

There are as many strange phenomena to investigate in this beautiful restaurant as there are delicious meals and beverages to sample. Come see the unseen for yourself, and let Le Lafayette take you into a real world of sumptuous cuisine and the other world filled with spirited delights.

Address:	623 Caroline Street, Fredericksburg, Virginia 22401
Phone:	540-373-6895
Fax:	540-371-8841
Contact:	Edith and Pierre Muyard
Business Information:	Open for lunch, Tuesday through Sunday from 11:30 A.M. to 3:00 P.M.; dinner is served Tuesday through Sunday, from 5:30 to 10:30 P.M.; Sunday brunch is served from 11:30 A.M. to 3:00 P.M.
Payment:	Visa, MasterCard, Discover, American Express, Diners Club, Carte Blanche, and local checks
References:	Personal communication, Le Lafayette Restaurant; Dennis William Hauck, *The National Directory: Haunted Places: A Guidebook to Ghostly Abodes, Sacred Sites, UFO Landings, and other Supernatural Locations*; L.B. Taylor Jr., *The Ghosts of Fredericksburg*; Joan Bingham and Dolores Riccio, *Haunted Houses USA*

Tandom's Pine Tree Inn

Tandom's Pine Tree Inn is located in Virginia Beach, which is considered part of the Hampton Roads area of Virginia that includes Newport News, Norfolk, and Virginia City. The population of Virginia City is almost 400,000 inhabitants.

The restaurant has been operating since 1927 and was a roadside stopover prior to that. There are tales that during prohibition, poker games took place in a back room of the building. As one story goes, a well-to-do woman would frequent the poker games and, as it turned out, was a pretty good player. That is, until one of the macho players either caught her cheating or was tired of losing to a woman. One day the man got up from the table and shot the woman, killing her on the spot. A nifty story that lacks historic credibility—but it would help account for the ghost stories that have circulated over the years.

A feisty female ghost is said to haunt Tandom's. The spirit has been sighted in the ladies restroom, the kitchen area, the linen closet, and the main dining area. Although the female phantom usually confines her antics to impressing staff personnel, she has also been known to reach out and touch a few guests.

On one occasion a guest went into the powder room. After walking in she looked under the stalls to find an empty one before entering. While she was checking each stall, she noticed that a woman wearing very old-fashioned shoes occupied one of the toilets. The woman recalled that the shoes were the high leather type, with buttons all the way up. Entering an unused toilet a few stalls away, she began to hear a rustling sound, comparable to one made by someone wearing an old-fashioned skirt, coming from just outside her door.

After leaving the stall, she began looking around the room and under the stalls for the woman with the period shoes, because she remembered that no one ever came in or left while she was in the powder room. In addition, no one flushed the toilet or used the sink to wash up. To her amazement, there was no woman in the stall with old-fashion shoes or an old-fashioned skirt. There was no way, according to the woman, that anyone could have gotten up or left without her hearing them, yet she was, as plain as day, alone in the bathroom.

On another occasion, after closing, a staff person had to blow out twenty-five to thirty candles on the restaurant tables. After taking care of that chore, the person went to check on the kitchen area. After several minutes passed, a night manager asked the employee why the candles in the dining area hadn't been blown out yet. The stunned staff person ran back in the dining room, and sure enough, all the candles were lit once again. No one could

come up with a reasonable explanation as to how the candles relit themselves.

A presence has often been felt in the old linen closet, the kitchen, and the dining room. Other mysterious incidents attributed to the friendly ghost include cups of coffee vanishing into thin air; clean coffee cups, stacked right side up in the cupboard prior to closing, all found upside down the next morning; pots and pans rattling in the kitchen; and plastic flaps, hanging down from a doorway entrance, parted by unseen hands as if someone was pulling them back. Light bulbs that burn out before closing are found to work the next morning, as they are about to be changed; the dishwasher occasionally turns on and off by itself; drinks brought to awaiting guests vanish after the patrons look away; matches seem to be inexplicably tossed around by unseen hands; and an apparition of a young person with short hair likes to sort silverware.

The strange stories and weird events continue at Tandom's Pine Tree Inn, where the spirits like to join in the festivities from time to time. Perhaps your visit will produce a spirited welcome from some of the other-worldly occupants.

Address:	2932 Virginia Beach Boulevard, Virginia Beach, Virginia 23452
Phone:	757-340-3661
Fax:	757-340-0188

Contact:	Karen Thoms
Business Information:	Open Monday through Friday; lunch is served from 11:30 A.M. to 2:30 P.M.; dinner is served from 5:00 to 10:00 P.M.; Saturday dinner is served from 5:00 to 10:00 P.M.; Sunday brunch is served from 10:00 A.M. to 2:30 P.M., while dinner is served from noon to 9:00 P.M.; wheelchair accessible; pub menu available all day; piano music nightly
Payment:	Visa, MasterCard, Discover, American Express, Diners Club
References:	Personal communication, Tandom's Pine Tree Inn; Dennis William Hauck, *The National Directory: Haunted Places: A Guidebook to Ghostly Abodes, Sacred Sites, UFO Landings, and other Supernatural Locations*; L.B. Taylor, *The Ghosts of Virginia*, Volume I

The Chamberlin

Located in Hampton, across the Hampton Roads Beltway (Highways 664 or 64) north of Norfolk, the historic Chamberlin is listed on the National Register of Historic Places. In 1984 the Virginia Historic Landmark Commission recognized the architectural and historical significance of the hotel by granting the Chamberlin its own Historic Landmark designation independent of the Fort Monroe District designation.

The first hotel to occupy this magnificent spot was built in 1820 and called the Hygeia. This resort drew a number of important people including Edgar Allen Poe, who recited "The Raven" and "Annabel Lee" on the Hygeia's porch in 1849, a month before he died.

After serving as a hospital during the Civil War, the Hygeia was torn down. Another hotel sprang up in its place, followed shortly by the first Chamberlin establishment. When it burned down in 1920, the present edifice was erected.

The Chamberlin is imposing and quite haunted. According to management, there is more than one ghost walking the halls of this establishment. However, the most famous apparition belongs to a young woman who is frequently sighted by staff and guests. According to a mixture of history and legend, the girl's father, a fisherman, went to sea one day and never returned. The poor distraught girl still seems to be waiting for him.

She has been known to knock articles off of shelves every once in a while, and sometimes she plays the piano. Some say the young woman burned to death in 1920 on the eighth floor of the hotel while waiting for her father's return. The floor is now a storage area, but several staff and security personnel still report seeing Ezmerelda. She is described as beautiful, with long, dark-blonde hair and radiant face, who is sighted looking out an eighth floor window.

According to Denise Threlfall, in her article prepared for the hotel entitled "And They Call Her Ezmerelda," there are many legends that surround the history of the Hotel Chamberlin. By far the most believable legend is a sad one. It seems a young woman waited anxiously for her father to return from working the bay. As a guest of the hotel during its fateful fire in 1920, she became a permanent remembrance of what once was.

Threlfall and several friends decided to do a little ghost hunting one cold November evening. As her story continues, the intrepid ghost hunters, after stepping off the elevator onto the eighth floor of the hotel and turning towards the storage rooms which Ezmerelda reputedly inhabits, felt a presence was near. Fearful yet fascinated, they proceeded down the cold, dark hallway and gazed into the room where she supposedly waits for her father. It was obvious to the group that something was there, but no one could see a thing. Several minutes later, as everyone stood quietly between the corridor entrance and an exit sign at the end of the hallway, footsteps were distinctly heard. The gritty concrete floor echoed a step-tap-step pattern. Knowing they were the only ones in the dark hallway, they surmised that Ezmerelda was close by.

Suddenly, an elevator full of people arrived. The group made fun of the paranormal adventurers when they were told there was a search on for the spirit of Ezmerelda, the lady of the Chamberlin. After a few comments in jest about their quest, the original group of adventurers was left to their task at hand. Assuming Ezmerelda had been annoyed by the whole ordeal, the group started to leave. One member stopped by a moonlit room filled with old chairs. She felt drawn to the area. As the rest of the group gathered at the door entrance, Ezmerelda appeared. Standing in front of the window, looking longingly onto the Chesapeake Bay, she gradually became more definite in appearance. No one could believe their eyes. The ghost lingered for a few moments, then began fading.

Recapping the experience, Ezmerelda was described as having long, silky, straight, light brown hair, which fell softly across her shoulders and beyond. Her defined waist was easy to identify through the silhouette of her long, flowing, white robe. Her expression never seemed to change, and her determination to see her father was strong.

Threlfall concluded by saying, "After talking quietly for over five minutes about what we were envisioning, a feeling of uneasiness came over me. I mentioned to the others that she may not enjoy strangers watching her, and I suggested that we leave. Realizing I had become extremely hot, I touched my cheeks to confirm my status. Upon reaching the lighted area adjacent to the elevator, my friends told me my face was bright red. I was chilled initially during her visit, and now my temperature had risen dramatically.

Two members of the party went back upstairs after I left, only to see her once again. As she walked past them in the hallway, totally ignoring them, she touched her cheeks as I had earlier. She disappeared into the darkness."

The Chamberlain has an intriguing past and excellent accommodations. A visit to this delightful hotel would be warranted even without the spirit of Ezmerelda as a bonus to entice visitors.

Address:	2 Fenwick Road, Hampton, Virginia 23651
Phone:	757-723-6511
Fax:	757-722-3636
Toll Free Number:	1-800-582-8975
Contact:	Maggie Wilson
Accommodations:	185 guestrooms and suites
Amenities:	Restaurant; nine meeting rooms; hospitality suites; executive boardroom
Payment:	Visa, MasterCard, Discover, American Express, Diners Club, Carte Blanche
References:	Personal communication, The Chamberlin

Ħistoric Ɱichie Tavern

Charlottesville, with a population of some 40,000 people, lies in the foothills of the Blue Ridge Mountains, the home of Thomas Jefferson and James Monroe. Michie Tavern has a museum that is suitable for age groups from third grade through high school, and is open daily from 9:00 A.M. to 5:00 P.M. except on Christmas and New Year's. The tavern was the one-time haunt of such giants of history as Jefferson, Madison, Monroe, Andrew Jackson, and Lafayette.

The building was opened as a tavern in 1784 after Scotsman John Michie had purchased the land in 1746 from Patrick Henry's father. It was opened to accommodate travelers seeking food and shelter at his home. Its original location was on Old Buck Mountain Road in the Earlysville area, about seventeen miles from

Charlottesville. Historic Michie Tavern is near Jefferson's Monticello and is a tavern-museum that preserves the rural inn. It is also unique in that it depicts evidence of the preservation movement of the 1920s. In 1927 the inn was dismantled piece by piece and moved to its present location near the city, on Route 53, close to both Monticello and Ash Lawn.

Psychic experts, staff, and tourists swear that they have heard the sounds of parties taking place on the third floor of the tavern, where the ballroom exists. The only problem is, these gathering seem to be exclusively for ghosts. Staff persons will tell you there are at least two regular spirits who haunt the ballroom (not including the occasional ghostly party groups), the old general store, and the grist mill located down the hill from the tavern proper.

Events that have been noted over the years include cupboard doors that frequently open by themselves; footsteps heard walking around upstairs after all the tourists have departed; the sounds of laughter, music, and tinkling of glasses and the presence of a group of men and women thoroughly enjoying themselves in the ballroom, even though they are ghosts.

The spirits of Michie Tavern continue to enjoy themselves and only ask that when humans come to visit, they try not to disturb them when they are partying.

Address:	683 Thomas Jefferson Parkway, Charlottesville, Virginia 22902
Phone:	804-977-1234
Fax:	804-296-7203
E-mail:	info@michietavern.com
Business Information:	The Tavern's dining room, the Ordinary, features hearty fare offered by servers in period attire in a rustic tavern setting; the Ordinary is open year round from 11:15 A.M. to 3:30 P.M. April-October, and 11:30 A.M. to 3:00 P.M. November-March; handicapped access (dining room only); gift shop & general store; meeting area; special exhibits; special tours for kids; hands-on 18th century reproduction toys, clothing
Payment:	Most major credit cards accepted
References:	Personal communication, Historic Michie Tavern; L.B. Taylor, *The Ghosts of Charlottesville and Lynchburg, and Nearby Environs*; L.B. Taylor, *The Ghosts of Virginia*, Volume IV

Wayside Inn

Middletown, with a population of approximately 900 souls, is noted for the battle of Cedar Creek, which took place on October 19, 1864, between Jubal Early and Philip Sheridan. It is also known for the Wayside Theater and the Wayside Inn.

In coaching days, a servant boy would be sent to the nearby hill to sight an expected stagecoach. When he spotted the incoming carriage, he would race back to the inn to tell the proprietors. That way, when the passengers arrived, they could dine on a hot meal and drink in convenience while the team of horses was being changed.

The first travelers to the Wayside Inn began arriving in 1797, stopping for room and board as they journeyed across the Shenandoah Valley. During those early years, the Wayside Inn was known as Wilkerson's Tavern. When the early roadways were constructed out of the untamed wilderness during the early 1800s, the Shenandoah Valley Pike (Route 11) passed through Middletown, and the tavern became a stage stop and relay station.

During the Civil War, soldiers from both sides stayed at the inn, which was untouched during that time. Jacob Larrick bought the place and renamed the inn to Larrick's Hotel after the war. It was later sold to Samuel Rhodes, who added a third floor, expanded the inn on both sides, and renamed it the Wayside Inn. As automobiles replaced stagecoaches, the Wayside Inn became, or at least advertised that it was, America's First Motor Inn.

In the 1960s a Washington financier and antique collector bought the inn. He restored and refurbished it with antiques and decorated each room with its own unique charm. In the fall of 1985 a fire almost destroyed the structure, but the inn has been restored and has been able to retain its eighteenth-century atmosphere.

Staff and guests have reported a number of paranormal events at the Wayside Inn—and why not, with a history that dates back over two hundred years. Ghostly apparitions of Civil War soldiers standing around in the lobby have been frequently reported. On a number of occasions, guests have let the staff know that they appreciate the authenticity of the re-enactors they sighted as they entered the lobby. They are quite surprised when they find out there are no such re-enactors on the premises, and what they in fact witnessed were the ghosts of Civil War soldiers who made the inn a temporary haven during the war years. If guests and staff don't happen to see the soldiers, they have certainly felt their presence, often remarking about the numerous cold spots or the fact that they are sure someone was watching them while they were in various parts of the inn.

As if the apparitions of soldiers, cold spots, and feelings of being watched or followed are not enough, there have also been numerous stories about strange footsteps that cannot be easily

explained away. And eerie shadows pass in front of window areas during the day and nighttime hours. Many times people have commented that they felt someone breathing down their neck, only to turn and find no one anywhere near them. There are also ghosts in rooms 22 and 23 who like to share those quarters with the living. The spirits have been known to open and close doors, play with the water faucets, and awaken visitors with a gentle tug of their sheets or blankets.

When you are visiting the Wayside Inn area, try spending the night, having dinner, or relaxing in historic ambiance. As you pass through the building, keep your eyes peeled, because the spirits of the inn will most certainly be watching your every move.

Address:	7783 Main Street, Middletown, Virginia 22645
Phone:	540-869-1797
Fax:	540-869-6038
E-mail:	waysideinn@nvim.com
Accommodations:	29 guestrooms
Amenities:	Each room has its own unique period theme; all rooms have private baths; meals are served in seven dining rooms by servers in authentic colonial costumes

| Payment: | Visa, MasterCard, Discover, American Express, Diners Club, Carte Blanche |
| References: | Personal communication, Wayside Inn; L.B. Taylor, *The Ghosts of Virginia*, Volume II; L.B. Taylor, *Civil War Ghosts of Virginia*; L.B. Taylor, *Virginia's Ghosts: Haunted Historic House Tours* |

Eldon: The Inn at Chatham

The Eldon manor house is a half-mile from Chatham, north of Danville, on State Route 685. The inn has been graciously decorated with period antiques and is situated on a thirteen-acre estate with landscaped grounds, including a formal English garden, an orchard, and a fishpond.

Built in 1835 as a thirteen-room mansion for noted Virginia lawyer James Murray Whittle, the first buildings include the manor house, icehouse, smokehouse, and stable. The original estate encompassed 500 acres and was named after a British jurist that Whittle admired. In 1902 the governor of the commonwealth, Claude Swanson, bought the mansion and lived there until 1939 when he passed away. The building was restored and remodeled in 1991.

The legend of the ghost of Eldon has been retold by locals, who as children knew the house was haunted and avoided it on their way home from school. One of the two poems written about the ghost by a former occupant, Isabel Starbuck, "To the Eldon Ghost," follows:

O gentle ghost, I like you most, when I can only hear you;
The shutters creak, you do not speak, but yet I know I am near you.
I am not clever, and I would never attempt to exorcise you;
If I should do it I'm sure I'd rue it, and it would quite surprise you.
You are not frightful, but quite delightful while you remain unseen;
In fact, I'd truly say that you are the nicest ghost that's been.

The spirit of Eldon makes itself known to guests, staff, and management by manifesting as cold spots in the dining room, where reports of instant chills fill the room and pass right through startled guests. When the ghostly chill first strikes, individuals quickly look around to see if a window or door is opened, but this is never the case.

Other reports include the sighting of a misty apparition in an upstairs bedroom. On one occasion a guest happened to be reading in her room, when she looked up and noticed that an amorphous figure was standing at the foot of the bed. Not frightened, the guest just asked the spirit not to bother her while she was reading, and the ghost vanished.

The spirit of Eldon has also been known to call out people's names. Is there one ghost, or are there several spirits at this historic manor? Some individuals think the inn has several resident ghosts. The original owner James Murray Whittle was a strong Confederate sympathizer, and the house was used during the Civil War as a recuperation place for soldiers. In one case, an injured Confederate soldier lost his leg and then subsequently died in the house. Perhaps, as some surmise, his spirit also roams the house.

Whoever they are, the ghosts are considered extremely friendly. One likes to show itself occasionally as a misty form, while it may be several spirits who are responsible for the numerous cold spots, the doors that open and close unassisted, and the footsteps that can be heard in unoccupied parts of the manor.

Perhaps some lucky guest on their next visit to Eldon, when confronted by the friendly ghost or ghosts, can get their name or names or find out why it or they remain behind in this lovely, historic structure—as if they need a reason.

Address:	1037 Chalk Level Road, State Road 685, Chatham, Virginia 24531
Phone:	Bed & Breakfast: 804-432-0935
Phone:	Restaurant: 1-804-432-0934
Innkeepers:	Joy and Bob Lemm
Dining:	Joel and Peggy Wesley
Accommodations:	Three guest accommodations (The James Whittle Guest Room, The Governor Swanson Guest Room, and The Whitehead Guest Suite)
Amenities:	All guest rooms have private baths; a full breakfast is included; dinner is served in Eldon's own gourmet restaurant situated in the Manor Dining Room, on Wednesday through Saturday; Sunday brunch is served from 11:30 A.M. to 2:00 P.M.
Payment:	Visa, MasterCard, personal checks, travelers checks
References:	Personal communication, Eldon; L.B. Taylor, *The Ghosts of Virginia*, Volume IV

King's Arms Tavern

The King's Arms Tavern is located in Williamsburg, which began in 1633 as Middle Plantation, an outlying area affiliated with Jamestown. When Jamestown was no longer the capital of the colony, Middle Plantation was renamed Williamsburg and became the social, cultural, and political center of Virginia until the capital was relocated to Richmond in 1780.

The King's Arms was considered one of the most "genteel" of the eighteenth-century restaurants in Williamsburg. Featured on the menu are such old Virginia staples as peanut soup, country ham, Southern-style fried chicken, game pie, and Sally Lunn bread.

On February 6, 1772, an enterprising young woman opened the King's Arms Tavern. During the Revolutionary War, Mrs. Vobe supplied food and drink to American troops, and it is said that Baron von Steuben ran up a bill of nearly three hundred Spanish dollars for lodging, meals, and beverages. The tavern also served as a popular place where locals gathered to discuss business, politics, and to gossip. The spirit of the King's Arms remains as strong today as it did in the 1770s. This is due in part to the fact that the establishment is haunted.

The ghost of the King's Arms Tavern occasionally appears to staff, while choosing to rarely disturb the privacy of the clientele. Some people say that you don't have to go back to 1772 to discover who the spirit of the tavern is. They say the ghost is none other than a former manager named Irma who lived and died in an upstairs apartment. However, there are others, including a psychic, who believe that there are more spirits in the tavern than just

Irma. One of those "additional" spirits is referred to as George, another former manager.

Apparently Irma, or Irma and George, look out for her interests in the King's Arms—from the other side. Some of their well-known tricks include making trays fall off their stands when no one is around; extinguishing candles on the tables, even though they are protected by globes made of glass; making the menus fall off their wall stands; locking upstairs doors from the inside; causing cold spots to manifest; producing chills on the necks of staff persons; and manifesting as an apparition in the upstairs women's restroom while women wash their hands.

A staff person who went to freshen up in the ladies bathroom first heard the door open, then saw a woman staring at her in the mirror. When she turned around, the woman had vanished—the door did not reopen. A pantry worker and another employee saw a woman dressed in colonial costume, with long flowing gray hair, walk through a door. A hostess received a gentle shove to her back when she was at the top of the stairs. She turned around, and there was no one there.

George has been spotted upstairs in the Gallery Room, and many believe his footsteps are often heard in unoccupied rooms. He is also blamed for the lights that sometimes seem to have a mind of their own. The King's Arms Tavern is in good hands, even though those hands belong to ghosts. They are friendly spirits who seem to have the best interest of the place at heart. Although dining or imbibing there is a unique experience, imagine the experience when a friend from the other side decides to join you.

Address:	Duke of Gloucester Street, Williamsburg, Virginia 23187
Phone:	757-229-1000
Business Information:	11 separate dining rooms with seating for up to 250 people; all dining rooms have rustic wooden floors and period furniture; open daily for lunch from 11:00 A.M. to 2:30 P.M.; open daily for dinner from 5:00 to 9:30 P.M.; closed February 11-March 8
Payment:	Visa, MasterCard, Discover, American Express

References: Personal communication, King's Arms Tavern;
L.B. Taylor, *The Ghosts of Virginia*, Volume IV
(1998)

Frederick House

Frederick House is located across from Mary Baldwin College in the heart of Staunton, the oldest city in Virginia west of the Blue Ridge Mountains. The innkeepers rescued three stately old townhouses from demolition and transformed them into tastefully restored Greek Revival buildings. They completed the restoration process by furnishing the rooms with their personal collection of antiques and paintings by Virginia artists.

Frederick House landscaping incorporates the aesthetics of its hillside setting, with steps and terraces, small garden plots, and planters. Garden lovers will be intrigued with the herbs and flowering trees that add fragrance and color to the walkways. Made up of several connected buildings, the Frederick House was originally built between 1810 and 1910.

Management feels that the spirit of Frederick House may be that of a prior resident named Page, who lived in one of the six houses that now comprise this delightful retreat. Page was said to be a very headstrong woman in life and seems to remain that way in the afterlife. She occupied one of the rooms at the Frederick House during the 1920s, and although she died away from the house at the age of ninety-two, Page spent so much time there, people theorize she came back to the only home she ever knew.

Page was a dominant figure in life, and she has continued to be a very forceful presence in death. A number of individuals including management, staff, and guests have reported numerous encounters with Page. Some have reported that their hair stood on end when they entered "her" room. Others, while staying there, commented that items placed in a certain area before leaving their room would be moved to another location when they returned.

Some individuals have literally walked into the room and asked off-handedly if the place was haunted. Her presence, though benign, is definitely floating around the Frederick House. Page apparently still wants people to know that she was a force to be reckoned with in life and maintains that energy in the other world. A visit to this wonderful historic house may add another page to the story of one former resident who refused to leave.

Address:	28 North New Street, Staunton, Virginia 24401
Phone:	540-885-4220
Fax:	540-885-5180
Toll Free Number:	1-800-334-5575
E-mail:	ejharman@frederickhouse.com
Innkeepers:	Joe and Evy Harman
Accommodations:	14 guestrooms and suites; each room has a private bath, television, telephone, radio, and a private entrance; some have balconies
Amenities:	Smoking and pets are restricted; children are welcome; rates include a gourmet breakfast in Chumley's Tearoom on premise
Payment:	Visa, MasterCard, American Express, Diners Club, Novus
References:	Personal communication, Frederick House

General Lewis Inn

estled in the broad rolling Greenbrier Valley, surrounded by lush evergreen and maple covered mountains, Lewisburg blends a unique mixture of natural and manmade beauty. The Greenbrier River Trail is a seventy-five-mile-long former railroad line. Following the free-flowing scenic Greenbrier River, the trail's slope is never more than one degree. Now used for mountain biking and hiking, the trail begins four miles east of the inn. For a few miles or an all-day outing, arrangements can be made with local bike shops for rentals and shuttles.

The Greenbrier River is one of the outstanding "quietwater" and small-mouth bass fishing streams of the East. Canoe and fishing boat rentals and shuttles, complete with fishing tackle if you like, will pick you up at the inn's door. State forests and parks, lakes, and rivers in the surrounding area offer rafting, canoeing, hiking, and fishing. Nearby are public indoor and outdoor swimming pools, indoor and outdoor tennis, and a golf course within two miles. Greenbrier Valley Theater and their own Carnegie Hall present musical and cultural events. Self-guided walking tours of Historic Lewisburg and the Confederate Cemetery are within walking distance of the inn.

The dining room is on the first floor of the original 1834 home. The present doorways from the lobby were once windows, while the original front door now serves as the main inn entrance. The large, hand-hewn beams in the dining room and lobby were part of the quarters for slaves.

General Andrew Lewis, for whom this inn and the town of Lewisburg are named, was born in Ireland in 1720. He moved to Virginia with his parents in 1729. As a surveyor for the Greenbrier Land Company, he first came to the Greenbrier area in 1751, where he "discovered" Lewis Spring on the site of the present town of Lewisburg. In the years that followed, Lewis distinguished himself as a soldier in campaigns and expeditions against the French and their Indian allies. These endeavors earned him the respect and praise of many, including Colonel George Washington.

In 1774 the Royal Governor of Virginia, Lord Dunmore, ordered Andrew Lewis to assemble a militia force for an expedition against the united tribes of the Shawnees, Delawares, Mingoes, and Ottawa under Chief Cornstalk. Based on his prior experience in the western Virginia area, he assembled the army on the Big Levels, now Lewisburg, naming the assembly area Fort Union. After an arduous march of 161 miles, the Virginia militia met and defeated the Indians at the battle of Point Pleasant on the Ohio River. With the outbreak of the Revolutionary War, Lewis accepted a commission in the Continental army and campaigned against the British until 1781. On September 25, 1781, he died of a fever and was buried in Bedford County, Virginia. Subsequently his body was moved to Salem, Virginia, where a monument was erected in his honor.

The General Lewis has been operated by the Hock family since 1928. The eastern end of the building, including the dining room, the kitchen, and a suite of rooms on the first floor, plus two bedrooms and a suite on the second floor, was a brick residence built in the early 1800s by John H. Withrow. It was purchased from Withrow's daughter by Mr. and Mrs. Randolph Hock.

The main section and the west wing were designed according to their plans by Walter Martens, a well-known West Virginia architect, who also designed the Governor's Mansion in Charleston. The Hock family spent years gathering antiques from Greenbrier and adjoining counties to complete the inn, including spool and canopy beds, chests of drawers, china, glass, old prints, and other memorabilia.

The hand-hewn beam in the dining room was added when the wall separating two front rooms was removed to enlarge the dining room. This beam, as well as ones in the living room and lobby, were taken from old slave quarters behind the residence. The original front entrance was near the stairs in the dining room. The handsome door was moved to the present main entrance, and the mantle from the original dining room was moved to the living room.

The following information regarding the spirits of the General Lewis Inn was prepared by Tina White and provided by Nan Morgan of the inn for use in our book. What strange incidents have occurred behind the doors of this historic building? These questions can best be answered by those who have experienced the dark side. According to Elizabeth Keys, dining room manager, and Phyllis Johnson, who has cooked at the inn for over twenty-five years, the building is haunted.

Both Keys and Johnson have heard the loud, distinct moaning of the ghost in the kitchen and dining areas. Employees have seen lights turn out, heavy items fall off shelves, and silverware flip over in its container. Keys claimed she saw the ghost one day. She saw a figure in black enter the dining area, and when she went to serve the "person," no one was there. The employee who was working the front desk, which is in clear view of the dining area, saw no one enter or leave.

Jeanne Christie, a former employee and local resident, said that since working at the inn she now believes in the ghosts. Christie was working upstairs in an L-shaped room with a limited view of the hallway when she heard someone at the door. Catching a brief glimpse of the figure, she heard the person ask if anyone was there. Anderson went to investigate and found no one there. Anyone leaving through the back would have been spotted by one of the housekeepers who were in the hallway. One housekeeper heard the voice, too, but thought Anderson was speaking to someone. The front entrance, according to the desk clerk, was not used by anyone.

Another employee explained that the ghost could be a slave who was hanged behind the inn for the murder of his master. The sad story goes that a slave owner said, "you'll never be free while I'm alive" to his slave. The huge beams located in the dining room were taken from the slave quarters where he died. Guest have stayed at the inn with no prior knowledge of the stories and complained of moaning from a room when it was unoccupied. Guests have also told of shaking beds and unusual noises. One lady felt the presence of someone leaning over her while she was in bed. She said she could even feel the breath on her face, but no one was there. A small child ghost seems to sit on the bed with many guests.

A front desk clerk said she'd been frightened by the ghost a number of times. She and another clerk have both heard footsteps behind them as they walk through the dining area late at night. One night she was walking through and suddenly turned to go the other way. She walked directly into someone, but not anyone she could see. "I could feel someone there, but I couldn't see them," she said. One night she tape-recorded the moaning sounds, which lasted for three hours. The tape was blank the next morning. Guests have reported that their attempts to record the sounds have failed also.

Jim Morgan Jr., the owner's son, lived in the inn for a winter. One night, when no one else was there except for the desk clerk, he heard deep moaning that seemed to be coming from the room next door. He said the sound was a type of moan like someone trying to say something. Another time when a friend was staying with him, they both heard it. This time Morgan said the sound was very illusive. Whenever his friend tried to discover the area it was coming from, it would appear to be coming from someplace else. Morgan said the noises could not have been coming from the pipes because it was completely different noise.

Many more stories have circulated about the ghost of the General Lewis Inn, but the spirits are friendly. So when you visit the inn, management wants you to be assured that they cater to the visible clients, as well as the invisible ones, and everyone seems to get along extremely well. However, sometimes they're not always quite sure if they're servicing a new guest or an old ghost.

Address:	301 East Washington Street, Lewisburg, West Virginia 24901
Phone:	304-645-2600
Fax:	304-645-2601
E-mail:	info@generallewisinn.com
Innkeepers:	Mary Noel and Jim Morgan and Nan Morgan
Accommodations:	24 guestrooms
Amenities:	All rooms have private baths; wheelchair accessible in dining area, and one room; serving breakfast, lunch, and dinner; breakfast from 7:00 to 11:00 A.M.; lunch from 11:30 A.M. to 2:00 P.M.; dinner from 6:00 to 9:00 P.M.; Sunday hours: breakfast from 7:30 to 11:00 A.M.; dinner from noon to 9:00 P.M.
Payment:	Visa, MasterCard, Discover, American Express
References:	Personal communication, General Lewis Inn

Richard's Olde Country Inn

The inn is located approximately twenty miles south of Elkins on U.S. 219 South, and twenty miles north of Snow Shoe on Highway 219 North in Huttonsville, West Virginia. Richard's Olde Country Inn is a Pre-Civil War mansion, built in 1835 and lovingly restored to its original splendor. Colonel Crouch had six slaves in the house. This was one of the few houses in West Virginia to own slaves.

Guests and staff alike have grown accustomed to the friendly spirits who wander through the inn. Several guests have reported waking up to shadows dancing on the walls of their room. Other individuals have occasionally sighted strange, moving shapes on the walls in some of the second-story hallways. A few of the manifestations have been described as having crude, human-like shapes, but they are all transparent when encountered.

There have also been a number of reports by guests and staff personnel of hearing women laughing in unoccupied areas of the building. In every case, a thorough search produces nothing. Doors are also known to open and close by themselves in front of startled onlookers. Many times guests have reported hearing loud footsteps pacing outside their rooms or walking past their doors, and after a quick look, no one is ever sighted. There have been numerous events involving cold spots that, when passed through, leave the person chilled to the bone.

Perhaps Colonel Crouch or his slaves are still wandering around the building, still reprising their roles in life. Guests visiting this historic West Virginia treasure never leave without favorable comments and lasting memories. When you come and visit, take note that the spirits are provided at no extra charge.

Address:	Rt. 1, Box 11-A1, U.S. Route 219, Huttonsville, West Virginia 26273
Phone:	304-335-6659
Fax:	304-335-0823

Toll Free Number:	1-800-636-7434
E-mail:	lvargas@neumedia. net
Innkeepers:	Richard S. Brown
Accommodations:	10 guestrooms, eight with private baths and two with shared baths, some with fireplaces
Amenities:	Air-conditioning; television; telephone; pets with permission; children welcome; wheelchair accessible; meeting facilities; restored restaurant open daily for light lunches and fine dining; robust West Virginia breakfast included in rates
Payment:	Visa, MasterCard, American Express
References:	Personal communication, Richard's Olde Country Inn

The Iron Rail Inn/Quinn's Cellar Pub

Charles Town, with a population of roughly 3,100 people, was named after Charles Washington, the brother of George Washington, who laid out the town in 1786. Adding to its historic reputation, the town was also the site of John Brown's trial and subsequent hanging after his raid on Harper's Ferry. From Charles Town, it is six miles to the Virginia border. The original one-room courthouse, built in 1803, and where John Brown was tried, still stands. The original portion has been incorporated into the current building and is open to the public.

The Iron Rail is situated on a plot of land on the corner of Washington and Samuel Streets. It was conveyed to Mahlon Anderson in 1795 by Charles Washington, brother of the nation's first president. Anderson then constructed the original house, which consisted of about two-thirds of the present structure, and a shop, which is located behind the house facing Samuel Street. The style of the east wing is typical of the late eighteenth century, while the west wing reflects the Victorian era.

In July of 1806 Mahlon Anderson sold the house and shop to Curtis Grubb. From that time the property changed hands several times until it was purchased by Andrew Hunter in 1830. Andrew Hunter was probably best known as the prosecuting attorney at the trial of John Brown. In 1840 he served as a Whig president elector and was nominated to Congress in 1846. During the Civil War, Hunter served as an advisor to Robert E. Lee. The property was sold again in 1858, this time to Sidney Rooker. Since the ownership by Sidney Rooker, a number of individuals have lived and conducted business in the building, and some of their descendants still reside in Jefferson County.

According to those who have managed or owned the building, including the current owners, George and Ruth Quinn, a couple of its previous owners still reside in the house as ghosts. However no rent is charged.

A number of odd and unexplainable events have taken place in this building over the years. Most of the present-day staff and management are used to the occasional things that go bump in the night. Even customers who frequent the restaurant and cellar pub have had their run-ins with the paranormal. Late one night, the bartender and an Irish customer were the last ones in the bar. As they were talking, the door to the cellar pub opened. The men, expecting someone to walk in, waited, but no one was there. The customer, thinking it was the wind that forced the door open, leisurely got up and closed the door. As the customer was heading back to his favorite chair at a table near the bar, a chair next to the bar suddenly slid out and then back in place, as if someone had entered the room and sat down. Neither of the men saw who was responsible for the event, and they didn't wait around to find out.

According to the Quinns, most of the staff have had paranormal events take place while they worked at the Iron Rail. The strange events have ranged from doors opening and shutting on their own and unexplained footsteps, to voices calling out their names. The voices are occasionally heard calling out to various staff members from the concourse between the pub, which is subterranean, and the first floor dining room. No one is quite sure how the spirits learn the names of the individual staff members. Perhaps the ghosts are just standing around when work is in full swing and hear names called out and then repeat them. Who knows.

The Quinns think that one spirit in particular used to live in the building when it was a boardinghouse. According to legend, there was a man living in the basement, which now contains the pub, who rented the rest of the building out to tenants. He was an intelligent man who attended an Ivy-league school. Apparently, his fiancee jilted him and left him a "dear John" note before walking out of his life for good. From that point on, the man became a recluse, keeping to himself in the basement area, only surfacing to take in the rent checks. He supposedly died in the basement and, according to those who work down there, never left. On a number of occasions, his apparition has been sighted, particularly in the downstairs men's bathroom. Strangely, no one has ever seen a full apparition, only a partial sighting, perhaps because of the man's reclusive nature in life. Presently, there is no name for this spirit who manages to hang out in the Cellar Pub.

On other occasions, several staff-persons were relaxing in the pub area after a hard day of work. As they were kicking back, they kept hearing what sounded like a man's footsteps heading downstairs toward the pub. No one ever showed up as the footsteps neared the door. Finally, the courageous group grabbed some flashlights and began a thorough search of the building. They searched every nook and cranny but could find no person of substance responsible for the strange footsteps.

Another favorite trick played by the ghost or ghosts of the Iron Rail occurs in the dining room. Staff always set the tables in the same manner in preparation for serving meals. Sometimes, after they finish the place settings, they will return to find the dinner fork and salad fork rearranged in the shape of a cross. When the utensils are put back in their proper place, they will manage, within a short time, to be rearranged like a cross. This frustrates the staff who have other chores to attend to, but it apparently pleases the playful spirits. There are other times when the cabinets will not open until an exasperated staff person literally has to ask them to open—and they usually do.

There is also a phantom woman diner who is often spotted sitting at one of the tables. As stunned staff and guests look on, the woman vanishes. Her presence is also felt by waitresses who are walking near the tables and feel the presence of a woman, as if they have walked right through her. They have remarked how they felt chilled to the bone, and their hair stood on end after passing through what seemed like a wall of energy. They all sense that the energy belonged to a woman, not a man. The building, noted for fine local cuisine, is also notorious for at least two unnamed spirits who seem to think the structure is theirs. The Iron Rail and Cellar Pub are worth a visit, even if the spirits are not restless the night you choose to enter.

Address: 124 East Washington Street, Charles Town, West
                              Virginia 25414
Phone/Fax: 304-725-0052
Contacts: George and Ruth Quinn
Business Information: Inn/Restaurant: lunch: Tuesday-Saturday: 11:30
                              A.M.-2:00 P.M.; dinner: 5:00 P.M.-9:00 P.M.; Sunday:
                              12:00 noon-7:00 P.M.; closed Monday
Business Information: Pub: Tuesday-Saturday: 11:30 A.M.-until late eve-
                              ning; Sunday: 1:00 P.M.-7:00 P.M.; closed Monday
Payment: Visa, MasterCard, American Express, Discover
References: Personal communication, The Iron Rail

Bibliography

Anderson, Jean. *The Haunting of America*. Boston: Houghton Mifflin Company, 1973.

De Bolt, Margaret Wayt. *Savannah Spectres and Other Strange Tales*. Norfolk, Virginia Beach: The Donning Company, Publishers, 1984.

Duffey, Barbara. *Angels and Apparitions: True Ghost Stories from the South*. Eatonton, Georgia: Elysian Publishing Company, 1996.

Franklin, Dixie. *Haunts of the Upper Great Lakes*. Michigan: Thunder Bay Press, 1997.

Great Food and Friendly Spirits: A Collection of Private Recipes and Spirited Tales from Marcia Baer Larsen's Alamo Street Restaurant. San Antonio, Texas: Talkin' Texas Productions.

Guiley, Rosemary. *The Encyclopedia of Ghosts and Spirits*. New York: Facts on File, 1992.

Hauck, Dennis William. *The National Directory: Haunted Places: A Guidebook to Ghostly Abodes, Sacred Sites, UFO Landings, and Other Supernatural Locations*. New York: Penguin Books, 1996.

Hensley, Douglas. *Hell's Gate: Terror at Bobby Mackey's Music World*. 1994.

Hoffman, Elizabeth. *Here a Ghost, There a Ghost*. New York, New York: Simon & Schuster, 1978.

Holzer, Hans. *Great American Ghost Stories*. New York: Dorset Press, 1990.

_____. *The Phantoms of Dixie*. Indianapolis: Bobbs-Merrill Company, 1972.

Hubbard, Sylvia Booth. *Ghosts! Personal Accounts of Modern Mississippi Hauntings*. Brandon, Mississippi: QRP Books, 1992.

Huntsinger, Elizabeth Robertson. *Ghosts of Georgetown*. Winston-Salem, North Carolina: John F. Blair, Publisher, 1995.

Kaczmarek, Dale. *National Register of Haunted Places*. P.O. Box 205, Oak Lawn, Illinois: Ghost Research Society.

Mead, Robin. *Haunted Hotels: A Guide to American and Canadian Inns and their Ghosts*. Nashville: Rutledge Hill Press, 1995.

Michaels, Susan. *Sightings: Beyond Imagination Lies the Truth*. New York: Simon & Schuster, 1996.

Moore, Joyce Elson. *Haunt Hunter's Guide to Florida*. Sarasota: Pineapple Press, Inc., 1998.

Myers, Arthur. *The Ghostly Gazetter: America's Most Fascinating Haunted Landmarks*. Chicago: Contemporary Books, 1990.

_____. *The Ghostly Register: Haunted Dwellings, Active Spirits, A Journey to America's Strangest Landmarks*. Chicago: Contemporary Books, 1986.

Rhyne, Nancy. *Coastal Ghosts: Haunted Places From Wilmington, North Carolina to Savannah, Georgia*. Orangeburg, South Carolina: Sandlapper Publishing, Inc., 1985.

Riccio, Dolores and Bingham, Joan. *Haunted Houses USA*, New York: Pocket Books, 1989.

Roberts, Nancy. *Georgia Ghosts*. Winston-Salem, North Carolina: John F. Blair, Publisher, 1997.

_____. *Ghosts and Specters of the Old South*. Orangeburg, South Carolina: Sandlapper Publishing Company, 1984.

_____. *Ghosts of the Carolinas*. Columbia: University of South Carolina Press, 1992.

_____. *Haunted Houses: Tales from 30 American Homes*. Chester, Connecticut: Globe Pequot Press, 1988.

Sanders, Tom. *A Brief History of the Island Hotel*. Island Hotel, Cedar Key, Florida.

Scott, Beth and Norman, Michael. *Haunted America*. New York: Tom Doherty Associates, 1994.

Taylor, L.B. *The Ghosts of Fredericksburg, and Nearby Environs*. Williamsburg, Virginia: L.B. Taylor, 1991.

_____. *Civil War Ghosts of Virginia*. Williamsburg, Virginia: L.B. Taylor, 1995.

Taylor, L.B. Jr. *The Ghosts of Charlottesville and Lynchburg, and Nearby Environs*. 1992.

_____. *The Ghosts of Virginia*, Williamsburg, Virginia: L.B. Taylor, 1993 Volume I-IV.

_____. *The Ghosts of Virginia*, Volume II. 1994.

_____. *The Ghosts of Virginia*, Volume III. 1996.

_____. *The Ghosts of Virginia*, Volume IV. 1998.

_____. *Virginia's Ghosts: Haunted Historic House Tours*. Alexandria, Virginia: Virginia Heritage Publications, 1995.

Taylor, Troy. *Ghosts of the Prairie*. Alton, Illinois: Whitechapel Productions.

Warren, Joshua P. *Haunted Asheville*. Asheville, North Carolina: Shadowbox Publications, 1996.

Williams, Docia Schultz and Byrne, Reneta. *Spirits of San Antonio and South Texas*. Plano, Texas: Republic of Texas Press, 1993.

Williams, Docia Schultz. *Best Tales of Texas Ghosts*. Plano, Texas: Republic of Texas Press, 1998.

_____. *Ghosts Along the Texas Coasts*. Plano, Texas: Republic of Texas Press, 1995.

_____. *When Darkness Falls: Tales of San Antonio Ghosts and Hauntings*. Plano, Texas: Republic of Texas Press, 1997.

Wlodarski, Robert and Wlodarski, Anne Powell. *Spirits of the Alamo*. Plano, Texas: Republic of Texas Press, 1999.

_____. *The Haunted Alamo: A History of the Mission and Guide to Paranormal Activity*. West Hills, California: G-HOST Publishing, 1996.

Newspapers and television broadcasts:

Press Argus-Courier, "Landmark building noted for ghostly past," by Dennis MaCaslin, February 18, 1998.

Reader's Digest, "Quest for the Unknown," Pleasantville, New York, 1992.

FATE Magazine, "Psychic Frontiers," by Loyd Auerbach, July 1994.

Cocoa Tribune, "Brutally Murdered Body of Cocoa Girl Is Found Yesterday," November 22, 1934.

Florida Today, "Lingering Guests," by Billy Cox, July 4-8, 1982.

St. Petersburg Times, "Spirits in the Night," by Jeff Klinkenberg, September 10, 1986.

Newcomer's Guide, "Spirits Linger in Legend and Sighting," Marietta, Georgia, July 22, 1990.

Ghost Trackers Newsletter, Ghost Research Society, P.O. Box 205, Oaklawn, Illinois 60454, February 1992.

FATE Magazine, "The Haunted Honky-Tonk," by Patricia Bowskill, April 1997.

International Society for Paranormal Research (ISPR), P.O. Box 291159, Los Angeles, California 90027.

National Trust for Historic Preservation, Historic Hotels of America, Washington, D.C., 1996.

The History Channel, *Haunted History, New Orleans*, 1998.

Daena Smoller, "The Official ISPR Self-Guided Ghost Expedition of New Orleans," 1988.

The Natchez Democrat, "Ghost Stories From the Tavern," by Maria Giordano.

The Enquirer, "Face-to-Face With a Ghost," by Sylvia Hubbard.

Paramount Studios, Ann Daniel Productions, *Sightings*, 1996.

"Welcome to the Historic Menger Hotel: Historic Hotels of America, a Self-Guided Tour." The Menger Hotel, San Antonio.

Jen Scoville Ghost City Texas, http://www.texasmonthly.com/travel/virtual/ghostcity/hunt.html.

The Antique Traveler Newspaper, "Three Ghosts Haunt Catfish Plantation," by Lissa Proctor, February 1990.

The Dallas Morning News, "Spirited: Restaurant Offers Remarkable Fare," by Judy Williamson, Sunday, December 6, 1987.

Texas Highways, "Haunted Places in Texas," by Randy Mallory, October 1997.

San Antonio Express News, "Supernatural Guests Welcome at Boerne Restaurant," by Roy Bragg, Metro Section, Wednesday, January 7, 1998.

The Marshall News Messenger, "Hallowed Chambers," by Glenn Evans, October 25, 1998.

Star-Telegram, "Have a Ghost of a Good Time at the Jefferson Hotel," by Cindy Brown, May 17, 1998.

The Wall Street Journal, "In One Room, All the Towels Mysteriously Disappeared," by Jonathan Weil, October 29, 1997.

The Mary Washington Bulletin, "Ghost Walk Tours Explore Haunted Fredericksburg," Jennifer Sycks, October 19, 1993.

Other Reference Books

Barnes, Rik. *Complete Guide to American Bed & Breakfast*. Gretna, Louisiana: Pelican Publishing Company, 1997.

Fenster, Julie. *America's Grand Hotels*. Cold Spring Harbor, New York: Open Road Publishing, 1998.

Menger, Tracey. *The Annual Directory of Southern Bed & Breakfasts*. Nashville, Tennessee: Rutledge Hill Press, 1998.

Sakach, Deborah. *The Official Guide to American Historic Inns: Bed and Breakfasts and Country Inns*. Dana Point, California: American Historic Inns, Inc., 1989.

Ḥelpful Information on Ghosts

This information does not represent a complete or final listing of all organizations that deal in the paranormal, ghost hunting, tour providers, or paranormal investigation. The list is intended as a reference service, to provide our readers with additional information about ghosts, and the paranormal, and as time goes on, will be updated and modified. Additionally, the authors take no responsibility for the quality of information provided by each presenter, nor are these listings to be construed as being endorsed by the authors. Just like the subject of ghosts, we provide the information, and you be the judge. Good luck!

Adi-Kent Thomas Jeffrey Ghost Tours, New Hope, Pennsylvania, Adele Gamble, PO Box 3354, Warminster, PA 18974, 215-957-9988

African Image Tours, PO Box 947, Howick, 3290, South Africa, 0332-302972, E-mail: Tambuku@netactive.co.za

American Society for Psychical Research, 5 W. 73rd St, New York, NY 10023, 212-799-5050

Antonio Garcez [Adobe Angels Series]: redrabbit@zianet.com

Apparition Expedition: www.apparitionexp.com, or call toll free, 877-273-3694

Art Bell - Ghosts Page 2: www.artbell.com/ghosts2.html

Lloyd Auerbach, Director of the Office of Paranormal Investigations, PO Box 875, Orinda, CA 94563-0875, 415-553-2588

The Berkeley Psychic Institute is: www.berkeleypsychic.com/index.html

The Civil War Ghost Tour, Martinsburg, West Virginia, 304-267-0540

Columbus Landmarks Foundation Ghost Tour, Columbus, OH, 614-221-0227

Dennis W. Hauck: P.O. Box 22201, Sacramento, CA 95822-0201 or DWHauck@poetic.com or http://www.haunted-places.com

Excursions into the Unknown: Haunted Chicagoland Tours, PO Box 205, Oak Lawn, Illinois, 60454-0205, 708-425-5163 www.ghostresearch.org

FATE Magazine: fate@llewellyn.com

Fort Delaware Ghost Tours: 302-834-7941

Garrison Ghost Walk, Fort Meigs State Memorial Park, 29100 West River Road, Perrysburg, OH 43551, 419-874-4121

G.H.O.S.T.: http:///theghosthunters.com or ghost@theghost-hunters.com

Ghost Bus Tours of Chicago: Howard E. Heim, PO Box 479463, Chicago, Illinois 60647, 773-252-8114

Ghost Club of San Antonio [Adam Flippo]: 210-433-6839 or CEDADFL@aol.com

Ghost Guide Tours, PO Box 471039, Brookline, Massachusetts 02147, 617-232-5539

Ghost Stories: www.sitemart.com/ghost/stories.html

The Ghost Hunter's Society, 825 Pinehurst Lane, Schaumburg, Illinois 60193, 847-352-7359

The Ghost Hunters of Baltimore: www.angelfire.com/biz/ GhostInvestigation or GhstHntr@aol.com

Ghost Research Society [Dale Kaczmarek], PO Box 205, Oak Lawn, Illinois 60454-0205, 708-425-5163 Fax: 708-425-3969

Ghost Tours of Key West Florida: 416 Fleming Street, Key West, Florida, David Sloan, 305-293-8009

Ghost Tours of San Antonio: Alamo City Paranormal [Martin Leal], 210-436-5417 or jleal@stic.net

Ghosts, Ghostly Encounters, Ghost Happenings: http://members.aol.com/Inside463/ghost.html

Ghosts of Gettysburg Candlelight Walking Tours [Mark Nesbitt], 717-337-0445

Ghosts of Gettysburg - Ghost Hunter Society Gallery of the Ghosts of Gettsyburg: www.ghostweb.com, or www.ghostweb.com/ghost_gb.html

Ghosts of Key West - The Ghost Tours & The Ghosts Book: www.hauntedtours.com/

Ghosts of the Prairie, and Haunted Decatur Tours: Troy Taylor & the American Ghost Society: www.prairieghosts.com/ or 217-875-2366 or 1-888-GHOSTLY

Ghosts: The Page that Goes Bump in the Night: www.cama-lott.com/~brianbet/ghosts.html

Global Psychics: http://www.globalpsychics.com/lp/Animalstalk/Artbio.htm

Grave Line Tours: 800-797-3323 or 213-469-4149

Gulf Coast Paranormal Research Team: jeevs@swbell.net

Haunted History Tours: Ghost, Vampire, and Voodoo/Cemetery Tours of New Orleans, 504-861-2727 or toll-free 888-6GHOSTS

Haunted Martinsburg [West Virginia], Boarman Center, Martinsburg, WV, 304-267-0540

Haunted Parkersburg [WV], 917 26th Street, Parkersburg, WV 26104 - 304-428-7978

Haunted Places of Gettysburg, 717-337-0445

The Haunting of Ellicott Mills [MD] Ghost Tours, 410-313-1900 or 1-800-288-TRIP

Hauntings: True Tales of the Unexplained: www.ednet.co.uk/~spirit_insights/frames.html

Honolulu Time Walks, 2634 S. King St. Suite 3, Honolulu, HI 96826, 808-943-0371

IGHS [Dave Oester and Sharon Gill]: ghostweb@ghostweb.com

International Fortean Organization, PO Box 367, Arlington, Virginia 22210

International Ghost Hunters Society: http://www.ghostweb.com

Institute of Paranormal Investigation: http://members.aol.com/CHILLRPG/index

The International Society for Paranormal Research [Dr. Larry Montz and Daena Smoller]: P.O. Box 291159 Los Angeles, California 90027, 323-644-8866, E-mail: Ghost@hauntings.com

Kansas Ghost Hunters [Shawn Barger]: http://home.swbell.net//shawnb/

Lantern Ghost Tours of Fort Delaware, Pea Patch Island, Delaware City, DE, 302-384-7941

Leesburg Ghost Tours Leesburg, Virginia, 703-913-2060

National Ghost Hunter's Society: Jim Snell, 10 Old New Liberty Rd., Owenton, Kentucky 40359

New Bern Historical Society Ghost Walk, New Bern, NC, New Bern Historical Society, 919-638-8558

New England Society of Psychic Research [Ed & Lorraine Warren]: http://www.warrens.net/

New England Supernatural Ghost Tours, Jim McCabe, PO Box 812128, Wellesley, MA 02181-0014, 617-235-7149

Newport Ghost Stories and Graveyard Tour - Newport on Foot, 401-846-5391

North Jersey Society of Paranormal Research: www.prognetsys.com/paranormal or www.prognetsys.com/ep or gary@prognetsys.com

Not So Dearly Departed Tour, Waynesville, OH, Historically Speaking, PO Box 419, Waynesville, OH 45068, or Waynesville Chamber of Commerce 513-897-8855

The Ghost Stalkers' Guide: www.ghoststalkers.com/

Paranormal Investigations: http://www.SwiftSite.com/ PARANORMAL INVESTIGATION or ghosthunter@aol.com

The Paranormal Network: www.mindreader.com

PARAseek.com - The Paranormal Search Engine: www.paraseek.com

Paranormal Research Center of Rhode Island: http://www3.edgenet.net/prcri/main.htm or prcri@pop.edgenet.net

Paranormal Spiritual Investigations: www.angelfire.com/nj/
    PSInvestigations/index.html or psinvestigations@hot-
    mail.com

Philadelphia Ghost Hunters Alliance [Lewis and Sharon
    Gerew]: http://members.aol.com/Rayd8em/index.html

The Psychology Department of Franklin Pierce College
    (Rindge, New Hampshire): www.fpc.edu/academic/
    behave/psych/para.htm

Real Ghosts: members.tripod.com/~GSOLTESZ/Dframe4.html

Richard Senate: www.phantoms.com/ghost.htm or www.ghost-
    stalkers.com.

Shadowlands Haunted Places Index: www.serve.com/shadows/
    places/places.htm

S.I.M. Supernatural Investigators of Maryland@hotmail.com or
    www.geocities.com/~hitchcockc/ghost.htm

S.P.I.R.I.T.: http://www.ghosthunter.org/

Spirit Quest: P.O. Box 230, Stratford, CT 06497, 203-384-22491

Spirit Walk: Charlottesville, Virgina, Albemarle County
    Historical Society, 804-296-1492

Strange Reports [Mark Chorvinsky]: strange1@strangemag.com

Supernatural Investigators of Maryland:
    http:www.geocities.com/~hitchcocke/ghost.htm or
    anotherwriter@hotmail.com

Vapor Trails: www.vaportrails.com/USA/USAFeatures/Ghost/
    Ghost.html

Ventura [California] Ghosts and Ghouls Tour, 805-658-4726.

The WWW Virtual Library: Archive X, Paranormal Phenomena
    Archive X. Ghost Stories and Folklore: www.crown.net/X/
    GhostStories.html

Index

Other ghost books from Republic of Texas Press

Best Tales of Texas Ghosts

Docia Schultz Williams

A spirited medley of spine-tingling tales and a collection of the most haunting stories from the Texas Ghost Series. From the *Ghosts Along the Texas Coast* to the *Phantoms of the Plains* and throughout San Antonio, the most haunted city in the state *When Darkness Falls*, this guide also includes new stories, actual accountings, sightings, and recent documentation of mysterious happenings from the Piney Woods of East Texas to Dallas. *Best Tales of Texas Ghosts* is a seductive resource for those seeking evidence of ghosts and a "must read" for the most intense ghost hunters in the state.

408 pages   1-55622-569-5 $18.95

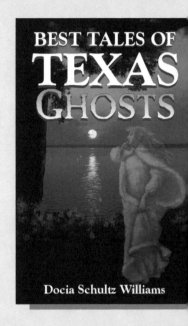

Ghosts Along the Texas Coast

Docia Schultz Williams

Take a thrilling journey with author Docia Williams as she introduces you to the ghosts that roam the warm beaches of Port Aransas and South Padre Island. You may want to keep the night light on as she investigates the mysterious hauntings of La Bahia at Goliad, the Golden Triangle, and the presidios of far South Texas. Using tangible evidence and first-hand testimony, Williams attempts validate some of the bizarre and disturbing accounts of ghosts along the Texas coast.

248 pages   1-55622-377-3 $16.95

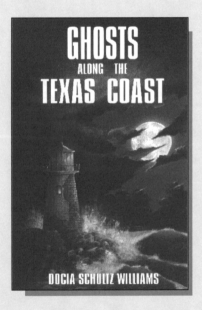

Other ghost books from Republic of Texas Press

Phontoms of the Plains
Tales of West Texas Ghosts

Docia Schultz Williams

There are some departed souls gripped with a purpose not realized in life. Whether they linger to protect, seek revenge, or to complete a task, these "spirits" appear doomed to an elusive world between the living and the dead. The third in a series about Texas' ghosts, this book introduces the reader to far West Texas, where the ghosts of former residents also have found good reason to remain "home on the range," haunting the mystical, magical land of the high mesas and rolling plains.

208 pages   1-55622-397-8 $16.95

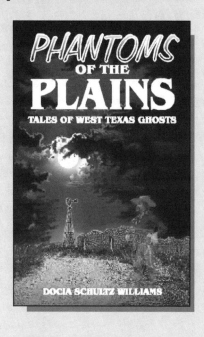

Spirits of the Alamo

Robert Wlodarski and Anne Powell Wlodarski

Spirits have frequently been sighted within the battlefield area and throughout the Alamo over the past 160 years. The intense moments of the final siege have been etched in time, repeating themselves over and over to unsuspecting visitors and employees of this monument to Texas courage. Along with the spine-chilling stories of tragic spirits who still occupy the Alamo are maps of haunted locations.

216 pages   1-55622-681-0 $16.95

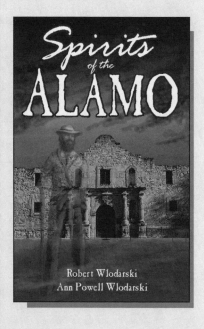

Other ghost books from Republic of Texas Pres

Spirits of San Antonio and South Texas

Docia Schultz Williams and Reneta Byrne

The number one tourist destination in Texas may also be one of the most haunted cities in the entire state. Steeped in history and tradition, San Antonio has many locations that are claimed as home for some interesting and intriguing spirits. Docia Williams has spent years tracking down the spirits of San Antonio and has found them in such interesting places as the Alamo, the Institute of Texan Cultures, numerous hotels and restaurants, the city library, the choir loft of a Methodist church, the Midget Mansion, and the haunted Sea Captain's house.

224 pages   1-55622-319-6 $16.95

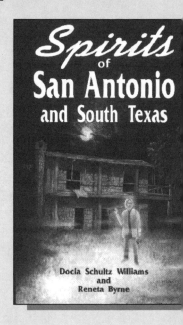

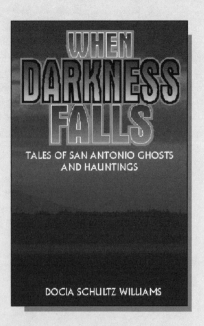

When Darkness Falls
Tales of San Antonio Ghosts and Hauntings

Docia Schultz Williams

San Antonio is such an interesting and fascinating place to live, it seems a lot folks just don't want to leave when it's their time to go: So, those "Spirits of S Antonio" just keep on returning—mos often *When Darkness Falls*.

Once again, well-known ghost story writer Docia Williams brings us an exciting book about ghost sightings an mysterious happenings in the Alamo C A chilling book for those wanting a gui to places where spirits are known to rendezvous or for those who just like good "ghost story."

360 pages   1-55622-536-9 $16.95